Detroit 1967

DETROIT
1967

ORIGINS   IMPACTS   LEGACIES

Edited by Joel Stone

with a foreword by Thomas J. Sugrue

A Painted Turtle book
Detroit, Michigan

ISBN 978-0-8143-4303-6 (jacketed cloth); ISBN 978-0-8143-4304-3 (ebook)

Library of Congress Cataloging Number: 2017933721

∞

Designed and typeset by Andrew Katz

Wayne State University Press
Leonard N. Simons Building
4809 Woodward Avenue
Detroit, Michigan 48201-1309

Visit us online at wsupress.wayne.edu

Contents

Contents

Contents

Foreword

Thomas J. Sugrue

No day figures more prominently in the history of modern Detroit than July 23, 1967. Early that morning, the Detroit Police Department decided to bust a "blind pig," an illegal after-hours bar on 12th Street, then one of black Detroit's most prominent business districts. Rather than making a handful of arrests and dispersing the revelers, the police officer who directed the raid decided to arrest all eighty-five people present. By four in the morning, an hour after the bust, nearly two hundred had gathered to watch the proceedings. As the arrestees shouted allegations of police brutality, tempers rose. The crowd began to jeer and to throw bottles, beer cans, and rocks at the police. William Scott III, a son of one of the blind pig's owners, threw a bottle at a police officer and shouted, "Get your goddamn sticks and bottles and start hurtin' baby." By 8:00 a.m., a crowd of over three thousand had gathered on 12th Street.

Over the next several days, looting and burning spread over nearly one hundred square miles of the city. Aerial photographs showed the Motor City's sky shrouded in smoke. Property damage, still visible in vacant lots and abandoned buildings in Detroit, was extensive. Rioters damaged 2,509 buildings; $36 million in insured property was lost.

By the end of the week, more than seventeen thousand law enforcement officers and troops, including five thousand members of the US Army's elite 101st Airborne, had deployed in the city; 7,231 men and women were arrested on riot-related charges; forty-three people died, most at the hands of the city's police force and the Michigan National Guard. The police were especially brutal, beating arrestees and in one case vandalizing and firebombing a black-owned shop. Three police officers, responding to rumors of sniping, raided the city's Algiers Motel and executed three young black men on the premises, none of them participants in the uprising.

To many observers in 1967, Detroit seemed a most unlikely location for a mass uprising. Detroit had established a reputation in the 1960s as a "model city" in mitigating racial antagonism. Jerome Cavanagh, Detroit's mayor since 1962, was lauded as an effective urban leader who had a future in national politics. The Cavanagh administration was especially effective in tapping into the largesse of Johnson's Great Society. Detroit's urban planners delivered grant proposals to Washington, DC, sometimes only hours after new programs were announced. Detroit was indeed on the front line of the War on Poverty, receiving more federal funds than every city but New York and Chicago between 1964 and 1967.

But those who were surprised by Detroit's uprising were blind to the city's long and troubled history of racial and economic inequality. In the preceding quarter century, whites had vandalized the homes of more than two hundred African American families who were the first or second to move into formerly all-white neighborhoods. In a massive grassroots movement, white homeowners formed hundreds of neighborhood organizations with the sole purpose of keeping their neighborhoods racially "pure." Detroit ranked near the top of the nation's most racially segregated cities.

The gap between black and white incomes in Detroit remained substantial throughout the 1960s. About 19 percent of Detroit's African American population lived beneath the poverty line. As was the case in other large American cities, Detroit's neighborhoods and schools were highly segregated. Police-community relations in the Motor City were poisonous, the result of decades of systematic harassment of African American civilians and countless incidents of police violence against blacks suspected of committing a crime. Hundreds of files tucked away in the papers of the Detroit branch of the National Association for the Advancement of Colored People from the middle of the twentieth century document the indignities and dangers of walking and driving while black in the city, from police officers shouting racial epithets to stopping, frisking, and beating young black men who were in the "wrong neighborhood" at night.

Detroit experienced the most violent uprising of the 1960s, but what happened in the Motor City had counterparts all over the United States. The same summer that Detroit exploded, 163 other towns and cities burned, ranging from Newark, New Jersey, where thirty-four were killed, to little Wadesboro, North Carolina, with a population of a little more than a thousand. Riots erupted in suburban Plainfield, New Jersey, in inner-city Buffalo, New York, and in troubled Cairo, Illinois.

What happened in Detroit and other cities can be understood only in the broadest historical context. The clashes on the city's streets reflected a long, unresolved history of racial conflict, much of it submerged beneath historical consciousness. Many people perceived the North—the region where most of the 1960s black uprisings occurred—as somehow immune from the nation's troubled racial past, overlooking the fact that the region had its own history of slavery, systematic racial exclusion, and white-on-black violence over housing and education. Through the middle of the twentieth century—until civil rights protestors raised their voices in opposition—metropolitan Detroit had Jim Crow restaurants, hotels, bowling alleys, swimming pools, and amusement parks. Despite the valiant efforts of trade unionists to open up Detroit's factories to black workers, racial discrimination persisted on the city's assembly lines through the 1960s. Detroit's skilled trades—in the auto and construction industries—were nearly all-white. Some black activists considered Detroit to be the nation's "northernmost southern city," a bitter description of a place where the promise of racial equality was still a distant dream despite the rhetoric of color blindness and racial inclusion.

Detroit's 1967 riot is conventionally portrayed as a moment of collective lawlessness and disorder or as an irrational outpouring of rage. Those descriptions are woefully inadequate. The events in late July were an outgrowth of years of protest. To use the contested language of the 1960s, black Detroiters engaged in an uprising against a racially unequal status quo, a rebellion against brutal police and exploitative shopkeepers. There is no evidence that the burning, looting, and vandalism that happened on the city's streets in July 1967 was organized, despite pervasive conspiracy theories that outside agitators, whether communists or advocates of black power, had orchestrated the riot. But there is abundant evidence that many of those who took to the streets saw their actions as a challenge to the legitimacy of white authorities. Many of the participants in the 1967 riot took the opportunity to exact revenge for economic hardship. Looters singled out merchants, especially owners of food stores who routinely overcharged their inner-city customers. Some saw looting as redistributive justice.

Like all rebellions, Detroit's had unanticipated consequences. Few who took to the streets had a vision for what the postriot city would look like. In the aftermath of July events, Detroit's civic leadership—for a time—channeled money into community economic-development projects. Foundations sponsored job training and creation programs. City officials haltingly implemented programs to diversify the public employee workforce, even though they faced fierce resistance, especially among the city's overwhelmingly white police force. But the long, hot summer also fueled an already intense, bipartisan demand for tough "law and order" politics, including militarizing police departments and expanding the prison system. The fallout from the urban uprisings also gave whites who had long fiercely opposed housing and educational integration a new justification for keeping blacks out of their neighborhoods and schools. Half a century after 1967, Detroit remains near the top of the list of America's most racially divided metropolitan areas. Many whites continue to rally around calls for tough policing and continue to discount African American grievances as special-interest pleading.

Fifty years after Detroit's uprising, the events of 1967 are sadly relevant. The protests in Ferguson, Missouri, after the 2014 police shooting of Michael Brown; the burning and looting in Baltimore in the spring of 2015 after the death of Freddie Gray while in police custody; the anti-police-brutality marches in violent Chicago in 2016; and the uprisings in Milwaukee and Charlotte in August and September 2016 are all reminders of the fact that many of the underlying causes of the long, hot summers of the 1960s remain unaddressed. The essays in this volume, spanning nearly three centuries of Detroit's history, are a reminder that the line between past and present is a blurry one. They demand that we remember rather than whitewash Detroit's—and America's—troubled past. They challenge our complacency in the face of America's ongoing racial crises. They remind us that until we confront and overcome our troubled history of discrimination, exploitation, and violence, our cities will continue to burn.

Acknowledgments

Detroit '67: Looking Back to Move Forward may be the most significant project ever undertaken by the Detroit Historical Society. This book is an important part of that effort.

The Board of Trustees, staff, and supporters of the Society recognized the opportunity that 2017—the fifty-year commemoration of the tumultuous summer of 1967—held for Detroit, the region, and beyond. We embraced the opportunity, bringing together diverse voices and communities around the effects of this historic crisis to find their place in the present and inspire the future.

We have collected the important stories of the past one hundred years in our digital oral history archive, as part of our exhibition at the Detroit Historical Museum, and on the pages of this book. Detroiters who were alive in 1967—residents, business owners, police officers, national guardsmen, judges, government officials, journalists, waitresses, and cab drivers—have all helped tell the story, sharing their feelings, recollections, insights, and often-varying interpretations of what occurred and why. It is our hope that understanding the origins, impacts, and legacy of these events can help in understanding where we are today and the challenges and opportunities that lie ahead.

The inclusion of diverse voices is at the heart of the Society's *Detroit '67: Looking Back to Move Forward* project. We have partnered with hundreds of individuals, community organizations, businesses, governmental agencies, museums, and cultural institutions to tell this story in a comprehensive and balanced way.

Wayne State University Press has been an enthusiastic partner in this project. Kathryn Wildfong, Emily Nowak, Kristin Harpster, and Andrew Katz helped shepherd the process. Joel Stone, the Detroit Historical Society's senior curator, accomplished author, and remarkable Detroit historian, guided the effort from inception to completion, including the recruitment of the outstanding authors who accepted our invitation to be part of it, embraced the challenge and contributed their time, expertise, and voice.

In addition, *Detroit '67* project director Marlowe Stoudamire and Kalisha Davis, director of community outreach, along with Society staff members Kate Baker, Tobi Voigt, Tracy Irwin, Alease Johnson, and Sarah Murphy also provided invaluable input that has resulted in this extraordinary work.

Douglas Fisher and Mark Kwicinski served as wordsmiths and style advisers, and so many other friends and colleagues, too numerous to mention, stepped up to support Joel with direction, feedback, and advice. Our sincere thanks and gratitude for everyone's commitment to this important endeavor.

This book is like few others. It is a comprehensive look at over three hundred years of interaction between blacks and whites in a major American city. It is told by the people who were in Detroit in the past, who live here now, and who are looking to what the future holds for Detroit, the region, and America in the years to come.

We hope the dialogue in this book brings to light new insights and perspectives, generates discussion, and perhaps encourages sometimes difficult communication. With the past as our compass, we can look back to move forward.

Robert A. Bury
Executive Director and CEO
Detroit Historical Society

Introduction

Joel Stone

1967: A Pivotal Year

On Sunday, January 1, 1967, the New Year's Day edition of the *Detroit Free Press* carried an auspicious theme, branded through each section with a special logo: "1967—Pivotal Year." Nationally, it would be a "year of decision" regarding the war in Vietnam and for President Lyndon Johnson's Great Society. This included the likely prospect of higher taxes to accompany an expansion in Medicaid coverage. Dominating the front page was a large photograph of Michigan Governor George Romney being sworn in for a second term. This was unusual, not because the picture showed him surrounded by his wife, Lenore, and grandchildren at his Bloomfield Hills home but because the ceremony had taken place on December 31, a day prior to the state's constitutionally defined swearing-in date. As a devout Mormon, Romney never conducted official business on Sunday. Special arrangements were made, setting the tone for a most unusual, pivotal year.

Nineteen hundred sixty-seven would be pivotal for many reasons. Romney was expected to throw his hat into the ring for the Republican nomination for the upcoming presidential election. In Detroit, a *Free Press* editorial suggested that the legacy of Mayor Jerome Cavanagh and his Model City "both hang in the balance." The paper noted that the makeup of the Common Council was shifting as the liberal majority was stepping away to take positions in the private sector. Reflective of the previous administration, former mayor Louis Miriani had been indicted on corruption charges. The sheriff of Wayne County—Detroit's county—and his undersheriff were being tried for willful neglect of duty.

Most pointedly, the *Free Press* noted that the crisis in the Detroit Public Schools (DPS) had reached a pivotal point, citing the Northern High School walkout and the striking shift in demographics. In the spring of 1966, two thousand students at Northern, most of them black, staged a well-orchestrated strike against what they perceived as racist attitudes within the school's administration. They created an alternative learning environment at a nearby church, got a university professor and hundreds of volunteer teachers to create and support a curriculum, and forged ahead outside the strictures of the DPS. Within a few weeks, the Detroit Board of Education reassigned the principal and his assistant, and the students returned to Northern, vindicated and encouraged but understanding that their educational futures was at a critical juncture.

Learning the Hard Way

Today, half a century later, the *Free Press* editors' predictions for 1967 appear eerily prophetic. To most native Detroiters alive at the time, 1967 *was* a hugely pivotal year—the "year that everything changed"—the year of "the riots." The events of July 1967 are called different things by different people, but most will agree that July 23 was a turning point for the fate and future of Detroit. The concept has become ingrained in the psyche of the city.

Certainly, many things changed. Demographic shifts already in progress accelerated. Political trends already under way accelerated. The uprising prompted a reappraisal of the region in every sphere and sparked active involvement by the business community in local social institutions.

While many things changed, many others did not. In fact, writers toward the end of this book paint a picture of a vibrant city in 2016, which could also describe Detroit in 1967. They also depict a city that still finds a majority of its poor lacking access to the basics—employment, health care, education, transportation, and healthy food options—much like 1967. City services are beginning to recover from decades of dwindling budgets and a management structure hobbled by corruption and nepotism. Crime has not gone away and is again fueled by a nationwide opioid and heroin epidemic. Police kill unarmed looters. Citizens snipe at police. Vietnam ended, but a series of military actions has—seemingly without pause—spanned fifty years. Today, 1967 does not seem so far away.

Which begs the question: Was that year and the events in July entirely pivotal? One of the goals of this book is to add new perspectives to the many narratives surrounding 1967 and Detroit's long—and often contentious—relationship with class inequity and racism. It should be noted that for the purpose of this volume, the racial issues discussed generally involve whites and blacks. Of course, early French settlers did not treat Native Americans as equals, nor did the British or Americans after them. With the growth of ethnic neighborhoods following the Civil War, factional battles were not uncommon, particularly if an immigrant's job, pride, or heritage was threatened. Until the late twentieth century, Asian, Latino, and Arabic populations in southeastern Michigan were numerically small, accounting for less than 1 percent each of the total, and mostly in specific enclaves in Detroit. The murder of Vincent Chin in 1982 shows that any cultural group, no matter how small, can experience racially motivated tragedy.

— —

The text in this volume has been developed in five chronological parts. The chapters in the first part offer perspective, following Detroit's maturation from prehistory through the end of World War II. The second part sets the scene in the city where America's worst civil disturbance would take place, followed by a third part that details the weeklong uprising. A fourth part delves into the immediate reactions and repercussions for the region and the people living here, and selections in the fifth part examine the state of the city today and how Detroiters address the legacy of 1967 as we stand together, moving forward.

It is out of scope for historians and historical organizations to attempt to define the future. As professionals, it is not what we do. However, it is our responsibility to offer the public an enlightened examination of the past and put it in context with the present. We can discern patterns, identify logical opportunities and proven pitfalls, and ultimately—we hope—learn something that will help direct informed initiatives for our community in years to come. As the following narratives reveal, too often we have learned the hard way, at great expense.

A Checkered History

The earliest evidence of consistent habitation in this region dates to roughly a thousand years ago and has been related to the Cahokian tradition based near present-day St. Louis, Missouri. Other artifacts suggest that people had been traveling the area for several thousand years prior to that. When Europeans settled permanently on the strait—*le detroit* to the French *habitants*—in 1701, they established a farm community that thrived on the Native American fur trade. The stockaded village grew slowly, suffered through Indian and European wars, and then became the preeminent trading center in the Old Northwest. Bill McGraw's chapter, which opens the first part of the book, discusses the critical role that unfree people—slaves and servants who were black, white, and Native American—played in establishing Detroit.

Waves of immigrants followed initial settlers. Generally speaking, Germans and Irish led the antebellum rush, raising the town's population from fourteen hundred following the War of 1812 to forty-six thousand by 1860. This tremendous leap was not without pain. Roy E. Finkenbine describes Detroit's place as a primary egress point on the Underground Railroad and the racial implications of that activity for the citizenry. Included here are the personal memories of William Lambert, a leader in the local black community and an Underground Railroad organizer.

During the last three decades of the nineteenth century and into the early years of the twentieth century, Detroit's racial problems were low profile but not insignificant. De Witt S. Dykes Jr. illustrates how African Americans interacted with a second and a third wave of European immigrants, laying the foundations for businesses and social structures that later supported blacks coming north in the Great Migration.

The early twentieth century was tumultuous in Detroit, for better or worse. Much of the old city disappeared as new skyscrapers and neighborhoods were built to reflect the prosperity generated by automobile businesses. Kevin Boyle examines a newly evolved middle class, which included both blacks and whites, forced by tradition and law into two different worlds. Efforts to break down those barriers were seldom successful and occasionally fatal.

World War II accelerated the region out of the devastating depths of the Great Depression, as local manufacturing created America's "Arsenal of Democracy." With dynamic changes came consequences, as detailed by Charles K. Hyde. Bringing blacks into traditionally white automotive plants—even to speed up production and assist the war effort—was met with overt animosity, strikes, and violence.

The violence came to a head during Detroit's only real race riot, described by Gregory Sumner. Fomented by housing protests in 1942, a deadly conflict erupted in the summer of 1943, which found whites and blacks locked in vicious personal clashes that left thirty-four people dead and hundreds wounded.

In the last offering of this part, Tommie M. Johnson offers personal memories of the 1943 race riot, including a very close brush with racial-motivated disaster.

A Deteriorating Situation

Following the war, Detroit began to create some of its most iconic automobiles, entering what many people consider the golden age of "Detroit metal." Behind the scenes, though, factors were at play that would set the stage for a likely human confrontation. Thomas A. Klug maps the path that manufacturers within the city were taking to the suburbs and eventually to other states. Essential workers, suppliers, and services followed the jobs, leaving behind an increasingly poor population to occupy the once-dynamic city.

Offering firsthand perspective, Marsha Music relates memories of her father's business on Hastings Street and the toll that urban renewal had on the once-vibrant district. That toll became more personal when relocation again turned to destruction in 1967.

This departure of entrepreneurial resources and capital fostered growing inequity between the city and its suburbs. Additionally, urban-renewal projects removed large sections of traditional black neighborhoods like Black Bottom and Paradise Valley, further disrupting demographic patterns. Jeffrey Horner explains how the black community increasingly faced declines in quality housing, education, entertainment, and employment options.

In an effort to defend "separate but equal" segregation, activists in white communities formed homeowners' associations and block clubs. These organizations were ostensibly designed to promote neighborliness and increase property values, but William Winkel leverages their rhetoric to show that these groups aggressively and overtly used peer pressure and political clout to keep unwelcome residents from moving in, with mixed results.

Relations between blacks and city government were further exacerbated by national trends in police policy. Alex Elkins draws parallels between "get tough" enforcement theory shared and practiced among American law enforcement groups and the reality of that approach on Detroit streets. Dragnet arrests and stop-and-frisk techniques targeting the poorest neighborhoods meant that blacks constantly faced unprovoked harassment, while white areas of the city operated under a different set of rules.

A Riot by Any Other Name

Workers in the blast furnaces and foundries of Detroit know that water and molten metals do not mix. Liquid steel or iron poured into an improperly dried crucible or ladle can instantly cause a catastrophic explosion that blows the roofs off buildings and creates shockwaves felt miles away.

In emotional terms, Detroit's black community was at its boiling point. On a hot July Sunday morning, a little after 3:00 a.m., a team of Detroit police officers working vice squad along 12th Street unsuspectingly threw cold water in the crucible. When busting a popular illegal beer joint, they ignited years of pent-up emotion and anger. The explosion was felt across the country, and the shockwaves still resonate.

This part examines several aspects of the events between July 23 and August 1, 1967. It opens with a timeline gleaned from primary sources that explores the progression of activity from the time the police crew went on duty Saturday night until a week later, when the state of emergency was lifted and troops went home.

Two credible firsthand testimonies exist regarding the minutes— perhaps twenty or so—during which anger toward police and the establishment changed from grudging toleration to aggressive protest. One side is told by one of the four officers involved in the blind-pig bust ("blind pig" was a slang term for an illegal after-hours drinking establishment). The other is related by the club owner's son. Blended, they provide a unique perspective on events. There are expected contradictions, and this narrative is speculative, based on available records.

What is not speculation is the reaction of the Detroit Police Department to the new crisis. Hubert G. Locke, assistant to the police commissioner, offers perspective from the middle of that maelstrom.

When things heated up on 12th Street following the bust, there was a rebellious atmosphere that expressed itself in property destruction. Gradually thrill seekers, opportunists, and bored residents joined in the mayhem. Ever after, there has been a debate about what term best describes the event. Ken Coleman explores the various names that "the riots" have borne over the years and the ongoing debate regarding the terms employed.

No matter the uprising's descriptors, most observers understood its main cause to be poor police relations. Melba Joyce Boyd taps into memories from Detroit's literary community to give that particular dynamic depth.

When chaos erupts, the progression of events often gets beyond the control of the participants and officials. Mistakes get made. Judgment gets fogged. However, Danielle L. McGuire makes it clear that the carnage created by Detroit police officers in the annex of the Algiers Motel was not a mistake or bad judgment; it was cold-blooded murder.

As the chaos unfolded, City Hall attempted to control its spread by stifling local media stories. Timothy Kiska explores how television, radio, and newspaper outlets kept a lid on it for several hours—a scenario impossible to imagine today. When they finally unleashed their reporters, the manner in which various outlets approached the uprising changed Detroit's corporate media landscape for years.

As chief of the *Detroit News* City Hall desk, Berl Felbaum offers a glimpse inside the mayor's office and the halls of power.

The union leader Walter Reuther referred to these as the "days of madness," but amid lunacy were stories of interracial compassion and cooperation. Kathleen Kurta told her tale to the oral history team at the *Detroit '67* project. It adds a tender and poignant humanity to the sad events.

Out of the Ashes

In the immediate aftermath of the devastation, a state of shock cloaked the region. Residents reacted with fear, anger, disgust, blame, and resignation. It prompted retrenchment and lethargy in some realms and energetic—even creative—action in others. Some people looked to recover what they had lost, while others sought new directions.

When school started in the autumn of 1967, a substitute teacher in the Detroit Public Schools, Steven Balkin, engaged his charges in a creative-writing exercise. He asked them to share honest, anonymous memories of what happened in their neighborhoods in July. Out of many, we have chosen a representative sampling, adding more perspectives to the story. One wonders if there was not also a therapeutic aspect to this emotive project.

In the years that followed, the relationship that civil rights activists, black activists, and the black community had with the Detroit Police Department remained contentious. A number of events illustrate the proactive nature of officials toward any activity that threatened to revive the anger exposed on 12th Street. Other events involved aggressive behavior from the community where police were concerned. Too often billy clubs and firearms were part of the equation.

An example of nonviolent counterprotest was the people's tribunal, organized to seek justice for victims of the Algiers Motel slayings. As a primary instigator and logistical leader, Daniel W. Aldridge recounts that event with satisfaction.

Activists in the black community, in play before 1967, became increasingly outspoken after the uprising. Responding to a perceived call to action, radicals took control of the dialogue related to empowerment and self-sufficiency within the black community, gaining a wider audience than before. Leaders of the movement were even included in the New Detroit Committee, adding stark contrast to the voices of more moderate and traditional African American organizations.

Young journalist Betty DeRamus, writing in 1967, examined the importance of this political shift to the city and encouraged her audience to respect its power. Equally important, activist Mike Hamlin recalls the prevailing social consciousness of the 1960s that encouraged active—if fleeting—militancy.

Contrary to a widely held belief, not all white people wanted to abandon Detroit for the suburbs after 1967. Many of those who remained fought valiantly to improve the city. As William Winkel points out, they had various opinions on what "improved" looked like. Some chose the quiet path of community service and leadership. Others chose more aggressive approaches to divergent agendas.

The More Things Change . . .

Fifty years later, the city has not yet fully healed from the violent unrest. With the distance and perspective afforded by time, it can be argued that Detroit was not entirely healthy to begin with, and there is some solace in that. Time also permits a turning away from assessments of cause and effect and allows us to ask, "So where are we today? What has really changed? What does it portend for the future?"

Peter J. Hammer details some of the many problems still facing Detroit and southeastern Michigan. The development of spatial racism has left the city more segregated than it was in 1967, with opportunities for quality housing, employment, and education within Detroit's borders statistically marginal—almost nonexistent. Without changing this fundamental issue in the communities, the region will remain constrained and unable to reach its potential.

While openly discussing the events of July 1967 remains difficult and uncomfortable for many people, there is evidence that healing is not only possible but in process. By examining how shifts in media framing have altered public perception of the uprising, as exemplified in reporting done for the fortieth anniversary ten years ago, Casandra E. Ulbrich concludes that some progress toward reconciliation has been made. The words used by a new generation suggest an increased compassion and understanding, opening the door to greater dialogue.

On a final note, Desiree Cooper offers observations of hope and caution. She is hopeful about the revitalization that Detroit is currently enjoying and is encouraged that enough of the factors that triggered the uprising have changed—at least in Detroit, if not the rest of the nation—that the likelihood of a 1967 repeat is slim. But she cautions against ignoring the clear deficiencies in our institutional structures, particularly those designed to help the poorest classes, both white and black. Detroit's rising tide needs to lift all boats. People left to drown can be justifiably angry.

A Basis for Continued Discussion

Throughout the narratives that follow, a few things become evident. First, when compared to other large cities in the United States, Detroit tends to be somewhere in the middle on most issues—neither the most enlightened nor the most atavistic. At various times, it has been named "fastest growing," "deadliest," and "most segregated," but these are transient labels that merely reflect an unhealthy competition with fellow cities.

Second, while issues of race and class discrimination are not limited to African Americans, this population has been ill treated to a greater degree and for a longer time than other non-European groups in the region. Such treatment resulted in the events of July 1967, and after fifty years, it deserves reflection, clarification, discussion, and perhaps some closure. If we are fortunate, there is also hope.

Third, you will find that there is some crossover between writers; redundant material was not edited out. The thinking in this regard was twofold: individual chapters should be able to stand alone, requiring all pertinent information to be present; and individual presentation styles can lend a variety of perspectives to the same detail or event.

Finally, stylistically it was decided to create a more accessible work, not a scholarly tome, with the intent of engaging a broad spectrum of readers. Indeed, the writers are all scholars chosen for their command of topics and time periods, but their writings are straightforward and easy to digest. There are no footnotes or endnotes. Instead, there is an in-depth bibliography that will point interested readers to a wealth of source material.

This book is a success if it corrects misconceptions, broadens perspectives, and prompts informed discussion. We hope you enjoy reading it.

Part I

A Checkered History

This part covers 244 years, from early European habitation to the end of World War II in 1945. During this period, Detroit transformed from a frontier village built on trade with American Indians into one of the premier manufacturing cities in the world.

Like all cities in the United States, Detroit is a city of migrants. There are over seventy nationalities and ethnic groups represented in today's regional population, many of whom came from around the world for manufacturing jobs. From the beginning, all of them—including the Indians—came to this area from somewhere else. The vast majority came of their own free will, but some came in bondage. Most people settled in neighborhoods near others who shared their language and traditions.

Not all were welcomed with open arms. As in any migrant population, newcomers posed a threat to established residents by creating competition for jobs and housing, introducing new and unfamiliar customs and religions, and altering the familiar face of the status quo.

In time, most migrants were accepted, sometimes grudgingly. They settled into their new home, intermarried, and became the new faces of a kaleidoscopic American melting pot. One group, however, was not allowed to share this new world on an equal footing. Because of the color of their skin, they were easily shunned and singled out for discrimination by laws that prevented upward mobility. These were people of African origin. Negroes. Coloreds. Blacks.

In 1827, the legislature of Michigan Territory passed the "Act to Regulate Blacks and Mulattoes." People of color were supposed to post a $500 bond (about $12,000 in 2016 dollars) with the county court to assure the citizenry that they had the means to be good neighbors. The law was only loosely enforced, but no other race or nationality was similarly singled out by burdensome legislation.

Only women shared a similar legal discrimination. Concurrently, the suffragette movement, labor union activism, and the civil rights movement created strategies that gradually found success in the form of legislation, public relations, and societal change.

Until the 1920s, Detroit's black population was a small percentage of the total. White residents of the city and nascent suburbs had only occasional interaction with blacks, if at all. Separate but equal was accepted as the rule—if anyone even thought about it. Most whites had little appreciation for the situation of the Negro; in this scrappy, working-class town, everyone was just trying to survive.

But the field was not level. Through the 1940s, there were many Detroit businesses that openly excluded people on the basis of race. Insurance and real-estate rules enforced de facto segregation. Opportunities for advancement in education and employment were highly restricted. Detroit was not the Jim Crow South, but if you were black, it could sometimes be difficult to tell.

Detroit's Forgotten History of Slavery

Bill McGraw

Sitting in storage in the Detroit Public Library's Burton Historical Collection is a powerful relic of Detroit's long history: a ledger book that is more than two hundred years old. Its cover is cracked, and its pages are yellowed and brittle. The book holds the will and inventory of the estate of William Macomb, a wealthy farmer and land baron who died in 1796.

Written in ornate penmanship, the book contains hundreds of entries for such possessions as goats, cows, shovels, furniture, saddle bags, and books that Macomb kept on his spread along the Detroit River, plus his vast real-estate holdings, which included Grosse Ile and Belle Isle.

The book also lists twenty-six names. Along with livestock, orchards, and china, Macomb owned people. They were his slaves, and the ledger notes that they were worth a total of 1,655 pounds in New York currency.

"I give and bequeath to my loving wife, Mrs. Sarah Macomb, for her own use, all my moveable estate wheresoever," Macomb wrote. "My slaves, cattle, household furniture, books, plates, linen, carriages and my utensils of husbandry."

The people Macomb enslaved had only first names, except for one man, Jim Girty. Among the others were Scipio, Guy, Charlie, Tom, and Lizette, Scipio's wife. There was also seven-year-old Phillis. She was valued at forty pounds.

Macomb had a large number of possessions because he was one of the wealthiest residents of the Detroit River region at the time of his death. But he was not the only slave owner. There were three hundred slaves on the American side of the river in 1796. Macomb simply owned more slaves than anyone else.

The Macomb family, whose name lives on in a Detroit street and a suburban county, is one of numerous southeastern Michigan pioneer families who owned slaves during the French, British, and early American periods of the region's history. Many roads, schools, and communities across metro Detroit carry the names of slave-owning clans: Campau, Beaubien, McDougall, Abbott, Brush, Cass, Gouin, Meldrum, Dequindre, Beaufait, Groesbeck, Livernois, and Rivard, among many others.

Antoine Laumet de la Mothe Cadillac, Detroit's founder, owned one slave and was godfather to another. The city of Detroit's first mayor, John R. Williams, the namesake of two streets in Detroit—John R and Williams—owned slaves. So did his uncle, Joseph Campau, whose namesake street is the main drag in Hamtramck, which happens to be the name of another slaveholder, Jean-Francois Hamtramck, a commandant of the Detroit fort, who died in 1803.

Detroit's Original Sin

The Catholic Church in Detroit was heavily involved in slavery: priests owned slaves and told the French residents to have their slaves baptized or suffer eternal damnation. The so-called "Father of Grosse Pointe," a British naval commander named Alexander Grant, owned several slaves. Lewis Cass, the Detroiter who served in the cabinet of President Andrew Jackson and ran for president during the national slavery debate of 1848, always denied he had been a slave owner. But his biographer Willard Carl Klunder discovered an 1818 letter that appears to show Cass, then governor of Michigan Territory, negotiating the sale of a servant named Sally with a member of the Macomb family.

Slaves in the area labored on farms, served as servants and domestics, and even worked as store clerks, blacksmiths, and assistants to fur trappers. One slave became a wedding present, given by her owner to the bride and groom on their big day. Another owner traded his slave for a horse.

Slavery was woven tightly into the fabric of early Detroit society. Toward the end of the French period, 25 percent of the residents of Detroit owned slaves. Most residents who could afford slaves owned them, and the slaveholding era lasted from the city's founding in 1701 until at least the 1820s. Slavery, which has been called "America's original sin," is equally Detroit's sin. Slavery is as much a part of our history as Vernor's ginger ale, the automobile industry, and the Red Wings.

Enslaved people walked on ground that two centuries later became

In 1837, Detroit commerce was supported by over 150 registered Great Lakes vessels, powered by sail, steam, and oar. This illustration, engraved by William Bennett, shows the busy waterfront as viewed from Sandwich (today Windsor, Ontario). Both towns had growing black populations, represented here by the fishermen and boatmen in the foreground. From the Detroit Historical Society Collection.

the streets of the blackest big city in America, where in 1963 Rev. Martin Luther King Jr. led 125,000 people in one of the largest civil rights demonstrations in the nation's history and where such giants of local African American life as Coleman Young, Rev. C. L. Franklin, and Rosa Parks lived and died.

Yet for occupying such a significant place in Detroit history, slavery is largely forgotten in the early twenty-first century. Few individuals know anything about it. It is not commemorated with statues or plaques.

What is well-known, and constantly recounted, is the much more uplifting history of the Underground Railroad and the city's role in helping many escaped slaves from the South find freedom across the Detroit River in Canada from the 1830s through the Civil War.

Why do we know so much about how some of our forebears helped escaped slaves and not the fact that others owned slaves?

One of the reasons for the imbalance is that local students learn about the Underground Railroad in school, but Detroit's slave history is rarely taught. When metro Detroiters talk about slavery, they talk about black men and women picking cotton in the sunbaked fields of Georgia and Mississippi, because that is what students study in southeastern Michigan.

"A Society with Slaves"

Since the early 1970s, a small number of scholars have researched and written about slavery in Detroit in academic articles that are read mostly by other academics and advanced students.

One graduate student, Arthur Kooker, wrote his doctoral dissertation in 1941 at the University of Michigan on abolitionists in Michigan fighting slavery in the South before the Civil War. In his preface, Kooker related a familiar feeling for serious students of local history: surprise and bewilderment at the moment when they realize that slavery existed in Michigan.

"As the work progressed one fact that seemed to require an exploration kept bobbing up," Kooker wrote. "Rooted deep in Michigan's past was the very institution which had called the antislavery movement into being."

Detroit, though, was not South Carolina. The early settlement was busy with swashbuckling traders, soldiers, trappers, and Native Americans of many tribes. But the farms were small, hardly the sprawling plantations of the antebellum South, and Macomb, with his twenty-six slaves, was probably the leading slaveholder in Detroit history, at least on the American side. By comparison, Thomas Jefferson owned more than six hundred slaves in his lifetime.

Despite the significant number of Detroiters who were slave owners, slaves never exceeded 10 percent of the population; in the South before the Civil War, slaves made up 33 percent of all the residents. Jorge Castellanos, a former professor at Marygrove College, wrote that Detroit was not a "slave society" but a "society with slaves."

The work of slaves helped build Detroit, just as the toil of slaves helped build America. And as in the South, slavery in Detroit was reinforced by violence. Slaves worked without any pay for their entire lives, under threat of the lash and death. And, just as in the South, slaves sometimes rebelled and attempted to flee when the chance arose.

In 1807, Nobbin, a black slave belonging to James May, chief judge of the Common Pleas Court in Detroit, fled the May household and wound up on the British side of the Detroit River. Nobbin refused to return to Detroit for fear of being whipped.

Detroit's history of slavery is complicated by the fact that African Americans were not the only people held in captivity. Native Americans were also enslaved here, especially during the early decades of the eighteenth century, when the French ran Detroit.

Slavery Was "Central to Detroit's Expansion"

Marcel Trudel, a Quebec historian who studied slavery in New France—which included Detroit—calculated that of 650 slaves he recorded in Detroit, 523 were natives and 127 were black. Trudel cautioned, though, that his sample did not include the entire 120-year period of slavery in Detroit and that many slaves were not listed in the records on which he based his research.

Indian slavery predated the arrival of Europeans in the Great Lakes and was a very different system from the form of black slavery that Europeans brought to North America. Indians enslaved other Indians, and they did not consider slaves property but believed that slaves possessed symbolic value. They used them as gifts during trade and negotiations and to take the place of dead warriors. Unlike black slaves, Indian slaves could sometimes gain their freedom, and their children were not automatically classified as slaves.

Eventually, though, Indian slavery mixed with European slavery and produced a hybrid form of bondage that played a major role in relations among Indians and Europeans in Detroit throughout the eighteenth century.

Indian slavery was "central to Detroit's expansion," writes Brett Rushforth, a historian at the College of William & Mary in Virginia who also has done extensive research on slavery in New France. "Per household, slave owners cultivated almost three times as much land and produced more than twice as much wheat and oats as non-slaveholding families," Rushforth writes. "Although slaveholders constituted only one-fourth of Detroit's population, they produced about half of the town's wheat, oats, and beef, the three most important provisions for the military garrison."

Indian slaves often arrived in Detroit after harrowing journeys that began on the distant Great Plains or in the South. They were often captured by fellow natives and passed from tribe to tribe to, eventually, French traders, often in exchange for goods. The slaves were frequently disfigured with a gouged-out eye or hacked-off ear from the ritual torture to which natives often subjected their captives. Slaves did not live long: of those slaves whose ages at death were known, Trudel calculated the average life for Indian slaves was 17.7 years; for black slaves, it was 25.2 years.

Indian female slaves played a particularly critical role in the economy of the Great Lakes. They became key facilitators in the alliances between the French and native villages around Detroit, Rushforth posits, especially in business relationships.

Traders in Detroit's early days used female Indian slaves as backcountry wives, for companionship, sex, and labor and as a way to ingratiate themselves with the women's relatives. That enhanced the traders' ability to do business with natives, who put great value on kinship ties.

"Sexual violence permeated the slave experience" in the Great Lakes, Rushforth writes. Yet because Indian slavery was much more fluid than African American slavery, native female slaves sometimes could rise to social acceptance and freedom, but not before a "prolonged submission to what could be defined as serial rape."

"I Bring You My Flesh"

From the remove of 250 years, "serial rape" might seem to have defined the relationship between a female slave and John Askin, a wealthy businessman who was known for his aggressive trading practices and use of alcohol to seal deals. But Askin's story also illustrates the complexities inherent in how Indian slavery became intertwined with white society.

In the early 1760s, Askin purchased an Ottawa woman named Monette (also known as Manette) for fifty pounds at Michilimackinac, on the Straits of Mackinac, another center for slave trading in early Michigan. Through Monette, Askin gained access to her fellow tribal members, further expanding his growing trading network.

"Rum and sex paved the way for Askin's success," writes the historian E. A. S. Demers.

Askin had three children with Monette, two girls and a boy. They were known as métis, the offspring of European men and Indian women.

In an indication of the elasticity of the boundaries between slavery and freedom among native and European peoples, Askin treated the children as his own, according to the researcher Nicole Satrun in "British Métis in Eighteenth-Century Detroit," from *Revolutionary Detroit*. They grew up free, enjoying education and "honorable marriage contracts." Had the children been black, those normal lives would have been unlikely.

Askin freed Monette in Detroit in 1762 and then married into the Barthe family, a well-off French clan that also owned slaves, once again spreading his business alliances. Askin had nine children with Marie Archange Barthe. Askin also took advantage of another form of unfreedom of that era in employing indentured servants, who entered into voluntary bondage for a contracted period of time. In exchange for transportation costs or the forgiveness of debt, indentured servants committed to three to seven years of unpaid servitude to a master. In 1778, almost 10 percent of Detroit's 2,164 residents were under indenture contracts, which could be sold or traded by the owners.

— —

Slaves and slavery played central roles in a number of important moments of Detroit's early years in the ongoing tug-of-war for dominance between natives and Europeans.

In 1712, amid vicious fighting between the Fox tribe and the French and their native allies, a famous Fox chief named Pemoussa attempted to negotiate with the Detroit commander. Painted with green earth and decorated with wampum belts tied together like shackles, Pemoussa marched into the fort in a dramatic bit of stagecraft with three other chiefs, who chanted to the manitous—spirits—and beat drums. Seven female slaves, also painted, accompanied the chiefs.

"I bring you my flesh in the seven slaves," Pemoussa told the commander, offering the slaves to signify his friendly intentions, according to Rushforth, and defining himself as a kinsman, rather than an enemy, to the French and their native allies. The French commander rejected the offer, setting the stage for a massacre of the Fox by the French and years of French-Fox warfare.

Half a century later, an Anglo-American businessman in Detroit bought two Indian slaves, a man and a woman, and took them on a business trip in a canoe. Upon the return to Detroit, the slaves cut off the businessman's head and threw his body overboard.

The male slave escaped, but British officials, hoping to send a tough message to the Indians about the dangers of harming English people, hanged the enslaved woman in April 1763—after she gave birth to a baby girl in prison—and displayed her body in public. That enraged already-restive native tribes around Detroit, including Pontiac, the famous Ottawa chief, who believed the British wanted to enslave all natives in the region. Pontiac led an attack on the fort weeks later that was the first volley in the natives' year-long war against the British.

Performing Acrobatics from the Steeple of Ste. Anne's

Black slaves became more numerous in Detroit after the mid-eighteenth century. During the American Revolution—Detroit was still in British hands at the time—Indians sold to Detroiters black slaves whom they had captured during raids on American settlements to the south and east, and some Detroit families bought black slaves from New York and Montreal businessmen.

Askin, for example, by the 1780s and beyond, owned both Indian and black slaves. Grant, the Great Lakes naval commander, had four black slaves and four native slaves between 1783 and 1798, according to Trudel's research.

Campau, who was considered Detroit's wealthiest person when he died in 1863, owned several African American slaves toward the end of the region's slaveholding era. One, named Crow, whom Campau purchased in Montreal, was known for performing acrobatics from the steeple on Ste. Anne's Church. To enhance the show, Campau dressed Crow in scarlet. Another slave, Mulet, served as a clerk in one of Campau's businesses. One of John R. Williams's slaves, Hector, ran the office of a newspaper that evolved into the *Detroit Free Press*.

In 1774, a French Detroiter, Jean-Baptiste Coutencineau, and a black female slave, Ann Wiley, were convicted of teaming up to commit burglaries. Their sentence was death by hanging, but Justice of the Peace Philip Dejean was unable to find an executioner. In the end, Wiley was offered the job, in exchange for her freedom. As much as the residents of Detroit despised the burglar, they were outraged that a black slave had been allowed to execute a white man, and they rebelled against Dejean, whose previous actions already had stirred up resentment.

The Northwest Ordinance of 1787 outlawed slavery in territory claimed by the new United States. That included Michigan, though the British did not leave Detroit until 1796. The ordinance did not free people who were already slaves, and neither did the Treaty of Paris that ended the American Revolution in 1783.

In 1807, Judge Augustus Woodward of the Michigan Territorial Supreme Court handed down two important decisions in cases involving slaves that helped create a legal climate in which slaves on each side of the Detroit River could cross the border to freedom.

In one, *Denison v. Tucker*, Woodward ruled that children born after the American takeover of July 11, 1796, were to be free, but other children, with earlier birthdates, were to remain slaves, at least for twenty-five years. That ruling prompted two of the Denison children involved in the case to flee across the river, where they were free. In 1793, John Graves Simcoe, the lieutenant governor of Upper Canada (today Ontario), had led an effort to pass a measure that banned the importation of new slaves and freed the future children of enslaved women when the children turned twenty-five. In 1833, the British Parliament passed a law banning slavery throughout the empire, including Canada.

In the case titled *In re Richard Pattinson*, Woodward ruled that an enslaved couple named Jane and Joseph Quinn, who had escaped from their Canadian owner and fled to Detroit, were free to remain in Michigan Territory. citing in his decision the principle that "a right of property cannot exist in the human species."

Woodward, an eccentric New Yorker who was appointed to his post by President Thomas Jefferson, personified the confusion about slavery in Detroit during the early nineteenth century. While Woodward made clear his opposition to slavery, he owned an elderly Indian slave who worked as his servant.

Gradually, slaveholding died out in Detroit. By 1810, the town had only seventeen slaves, and in 1835, the first state constitution outlawed slavery. Michigan entered the Union as a "free state" in 1837 amid the national debate about slavery in the South.

Remembering Slavery

The prominence of slavery in the history of Detroit is belied by its almost complete absence in the collective memory of Detroiters. One reason was that after slavery ended in the South with the Civil War, there was embarrassment in those parts of the North with slaveholding histories and a tendency to minimize those chapters of their pasts.

In an 1872 speech about slavery in Detroit to the Detroit Pioneer Society, recorded in the first volume of the *Report of the Pioneer Society of the State of Michigan*, the historian J. A. Girardin said, "As a class the negroes were esteemed by our ancient population," and "little cruelty was practiced by their owners. . . . Everyone lived in Arcadian simplicity and contentment. The negro was satisfied with his position, and rendered valuable services to his master, and was ever ready to help him against the treacherous Indians."

Slowly the curtain has begun to rise across the country on slavery and other forms of historical racism, such as Girardin's flawed assumption. Most notably, the communal amnesia that allowed the North to absolve itself of involvement in slavery while castigating the South is disappearing. People are realizing that understanding slavery is central to understanding the origins of America itself.

Prodded by activists and historians, a number of institutions, organizations, and individuals have acknowledged their historical ties to slavery and other extreme racist behavior and in many cases have asked for forgiveness. In 2004, the historian Ira Berlin wrote in the *Journal of American History* that "slavery has a greater presence now than at any time since the end of the Civil War."

A partial list of those institutions that have performed a self-examination of the past, and often issued an apology or moved for reconciliation, includes the US government (by President Bill Clinton); Brown University; Yale University; Harvard University; Wilmington, North Carolina; New York City; Philadelphia, Mississippi; Duluth, Minnesota; Birmingham, Alabama; London, England; various insurance companies; the Southern Baptist Convention; the US Senate; the *Hartford Courant*; the *Raleigh News and Observer*; the *Lexington (KY) Herald-Leader*; and J. P. Morgan Chase and several other banks.

Detroit's selective memory remains intact. Almost nothing has been done to seek out the truth about the role of slavery in the city's past, even in a region where racism, the theoretical underpinning of slavery, remains a paramount issue.

Does racism in the twenty-first century have a lineage? Is there a connection between James May suggesting he would whip his slave in 1807 and two Detroit police officers using their flashlights to beat to death a Detroit black man, Malice Green, in 1992? Is there a link between black slavery in Michigan Territory in the nineteenth century and the mass incarceration of black men in the twenty-first century?

Detroit's slaveholding era seems so distant. But is it significant that two former slaveholders, Joseph Campau and John R. Williams, led the group of investors that launched the *Free Press* in 1831? As the national debate over slavery became more heated, the paper grew in influence. It vehemently opposed the freeing of the slaves, assailed Lincoln, and published racist invective on virtually a daily basis until late in the nineteenth century. Is there a connection between its message and the racial turmoil of Detroit in the early twentieth century, the Ku Klux Klan and Black Legion attacks on African Americans, the creation of the ghetto, and the vicious race riot of 1943?

Slavery is not a happy story. For a nation and a city built on the notion of freedom to consider the idea that slavery was also a major part of the foundation is difficult and disillusioning. But telling the truth about our history can be a start on telling the truth about today.

"Slavery is the ground zero of race relations," Berlin wrote. "There is a general, if inchoate, understanding that any attempt to address the question of race in the present must also address slavery in the past."

The Underground Railroad and Early Racial Violence

Roy E. Finkenbine

The half century between the end of the War of 1812 and the close of the Civil War proved to be an important formative period for race relations in Detroit. Hundreds of southern slaves, as well as free blacks from the upper South and the Northeast, made their way to the city, settling into a few neighborhoods on the near east side. Their presence provoked occasional incidents of violence, which assumed at least two different forms. In the pre–Civil War decades, members of the African American community (sometimes with the aid of white allies) used force or the threat of force to protect runaways in their midst who were faced with a return to bondage. During the Civil War, a growing competition for resources between African Americans and working-class (often immigrant) whites led to a bloody pogrom against black districts in the city.

Freedom seekers from the South began heading toward Detroit in small numbers beginning in the 1790s. The Fugitive Slave Act of 1793 permitted slave owners to track their runaway slaves anywhere in the United States. That same year, Upper Canada (today Ontario) passed legislation placing the district on the road to emancipation. Because of Detroit's emerging position as an international border crossing after the British withdrew from the city in 1796, it soon became a principal destination for freedom seekers from the upper South—particularly Virginia, Kentucky, Tennessee, and Missouri. The volume of runaways reaching Detroit grew dramatically after the War of 1812. This also attracted slave catchers, who regularly made their way to the city by the 1820s. Runaway-slave advertisements also appeared occasionally in the *Detroit Gazette,* the city's leading newspaper, during the decade. By 1830, approximately three hundred blacks lived in Detroit and vicinity on both sides of the river. This number continued to grow in the decades that followed.

The presence of so many freedom seekers in the midst of a growing African American community and the constant threat of slave catchers led to the establishment of a substantial Underground Railroad network in the city. This consisted of many members of the city's African American community, as well as dozens of white allies. Their willingness to protect fugitives in their midst led to occasional acts of racial violence. In pre–Civil War Detroit, most incidents took the form of what David Grimsted labels in *American Mobbing, 1828–1861* as fugitive-slave riots. These were a product of the growing number of freedom seekers reaching the city via the Underground Railroad, coupled with the city's proximity to Canada and the willingness of its black and white citizens to protect fugitive slaves who were threatened with capture and a return to slavery. At least six fugitive-slave riots occurred in Detroit before the Civil War.

Detroit's first fugitive-slave riot took place in December 1828. Ezekiel Hudnell of Kentucky tracked two of his runaway slaves, Daniel and Ben, to the city and had them detained under the Fugitive Slave Act of 1793. According to Wayne County Sheriff Thomas C. Sheldon, quoted in Karolyn Smardz Frost's *I've Got a Home in Glory Land*, this action prompted "great excitement in Detroit . . . which excitement extended itself to the Canadian shore opposite, where great numbers of runaway slaves had collected and armed themselves." While Hudnell awaited a certificate allowing him to return the two runaway slaves southward, he took them to a waiting vessel in the lower Detroit River, but they were attacked by a mob of black men from both sides. Daniel and Ben escaped to Canada in the excitement.

The city's most notorious fugitive-slave riot was the so-called Blackburn Riot of June 17, 1833. It involved the runaway slaves Thornton and Lucie Blackburn, who had posed as free blacks to escape from Louisville, Kentucky, to Detroit two years earlier. Eventually claimed by slave catchers acting on behalf of their owners, their return to slavery was ordered by the Wayne County Court, acting under the Fugitive Slave Act of 1793.

The local African American community was incensed and threatened to burn the city. Dozens encircled the courthouse. Blacks on the Canadian side of the Detroit River took the ferry across to join the protest. Others in nearby rural Michigan Territory filtered into the city and attached themselves to the growing mob. Hundreds milled about in the streets for three days with guns, clubs, knives, and swords, while others occupied the docks where the Blackburns were to be loaded on a steamer for the return to Kentucky. Local black leaders, working with a few prominent white allies, planned an elaborate rescue. On June 16, two free black women visited Lucie Blackburn in jail following Sunday services. After changing clothes with one of the women, Lucie left the jail under cover of darkness. Her escape was not discovered until the next morning. By that time, she was across the river in Canada.

Determined to return Thornton to slavery, Sheriff John Wilson, the jailer, and one of the slave catchers started to accompany Thornton to the waiting vessel when they were confronted by an armed mob—mostly black. When the jailer and slave catcher saw what awaited them, they retreated into the jail and locked the door, leaving Wilson and Thornton outside. Someone in the mob tossed Thornton a pistol, and he fired it into the air. The crowd surged forward. In the ensuing melee, one protester was shot, and Wilson was severely beaten and mortally wounded. Thornton was helped into a waiting cart and rushed to the river, where members of the mob helped him break his shackles and paid a boatman to take him across.

Both Thornton and Lucie were arrested on the Canadian side and thrown into a Sandwich (today Windsor) jail. The acting territorial governor of Michigan, Stevens T. Mason, sought the Blackburns' extradition for inciting the riot. Canadian officials refused, eventually crafting what became the basis of Canadian extradition policy to this day. The Blackburns settled in Toronto, where they became people of prominence. Thornton established and operated the city's first horse-drawn taxi service.

Back in Detroit, tensions reached a fever pitch. Officials declared martial law, and soldiers from Fort Gratiot patrolled the streets. Blacks suspected of involvement in the riot were detained, and a few did prison time. Several black homes were burned to the ground. As a result, many Detroit blacks fled across the river and settled in Sandwich, Amherstburg, and other Canadian communities. It took several years for Detroit's black population to reach preriot numbers.

In spite of the backlash resulting from the Blackburn riot, other fugitive-slave riots followed. In October 1839, a ruling by Judge Ross Wilkins of the US district court that Henry, a runaway slave from Missouri, should be returned to his master prompted Detroit blacks and a few white allies to congregate at City Hall to protest the decision. The mob attacked the Brady Guards, who had been called out to escort Henry back to the city jail. The protesters were eventually repelled, and four were arrested; but local citizens later purchased the slave's freedom. Eight years later, members of the Colored Vigilant Committee, the city's dominant Underground Railroad network from 1842 to 1862, aggressively freed the Missouri fugitive Robert Cromwell from the clutches of his master, David Dunn. With the complicity of a county clerk, the mob forced its way into the county courthouse, rescued Cromwell, and whisked him away to Canada.

Such actions prompted slave owners in the South and their political allies in Congress to push for a more rigorous fugitive-slave law. The third case under the resulting Fugitive Slave Act of 1850 came that October when the federal marshal C. H. Knox, collaborating with two slave catchers and local authorities, arrested the Tennessee runaway Giles Rose. The Colored Vigilant Committee mobilized local blacks, and another three hundred streamed over from Canada West (today Ontario) to attempt Rose's rescue. Hundreds of protesters filled the streets. Some followed the slave catchers to their hotel and threatened them with violence. Three companies of federal troops were called out to prevent civil disturbance. The threat of mob action prompted the federal commissioner to adjourn the hearing and allow the defense additional time to gather evidence of Rose's alleged free status. In the meantime, the city's leading citizens took up a collection and bought his freedom.

In June 1859, twenty to thirty local blacks rushed onto a boat named the *North Star* when it docked in Detroit, in a partially successful attempt to free two slave girls who were accompanying their slave mistress on the return trip home to Winchester, Kentucky, after "summering" on Lake Superior. One of the girls, frightened by the excitement, locked herself in a stateroom; the other departed with the mob, which conveyed her to freedom in Windsor. No charges were brought. Mentions in the local press suggest that there were many other lesser-known acts of racial violence aimed at aiding and protecting fugitive slaves in Detroit.

Detroit generally avoided more traditional forms of racial violence until the Civil War. This differed from the experience of other cities in the Northeast and Midwest during this time. Dozens of bloody racial pogroms took place against African Americans in cities such as Cincinnati, Providence, New York, and Washington, DC, between the 1820s and the 1850s. No city, however, experienced the number or severity of the race riots that troubled antebellum Philadelphia—the City of Brotherly Love. Antiblack rioting broke out there in 1820, 1829, 1834, 1838, 1842, and 1849, with periodic waves of looting and burning in the city's black neighborhoods that often targeted the symbols of free black success: churches, businesses, and the homes and persons of the black elite. Sometimes these episodes of "hunting the nigs" were generated by mobs of working-class immigrants; at other times, however, they were led by "gentleman of property and standing."

The coming of the Civil War altered the dynamics of racial violence in Detroit, making it more like Philadelphia and other northern cities. As Union forces advanced into the Confederacy, slaves no longer needed to flee north to find freedom. The local Underground Railroad soon ended its work, ferrying the last freedom seeker across the Detroit River in April 1862. A growing and changing population, however, combined with the social tensions produced by the war itself, meant that the potential for racial violence remained high. These tensions exploded in a pogrom against the city's African American neighborhoods on March 6, 1863. It was, the *Free Press* observed the following day, "the bloodiest day that ever dawned upon Detroit" to that time.

Precipitating the riot was the February 26 arrest and subsequent trial of William Faulkner, a forty-two-year-old tavern keeper. Authorities charged him with the rape of two nine-year-old girls, Mary Brown (white) and Ellen Hoover (black), at his Michigan Avenue tavern ten days earlier. Immediately after his arrest, the *Free Press* alleged that he was a black man, even though his neighbors and city officials had always assumed him to be white. Faulkner himself claimed "mixed Spanish-Indian blood." As rumors circulated through the city, public anger grew.

Faulkner was brought to trial on March 5. As sheriff's deputies escorted him back to the city jail at the corner of Beaubien and Clinton Streets at the end of the day, he was accosted by a mob numbering in the hundreds. The deputies were forced to point their revolvers at the crowd to maintain order. Even so, Faulkner was hit in the head with a paving stone before reaching the jail. The following day, authorities escorted Faulkner to the court before sunup to elude another mob attack. Nevertheless, the *Free Press* reported that a crowd of close to one thousand gathered outside the courthouse "intent on bringing mob justice to Faulkner." Blacks who passed were subjected to "kicks, cuffs, and blows." Although Faulkner pled not guilty, the jury convicted him on all counts after deliberating less than ten minutes, and the judge sentenced him to life in prison at the state penitentiary at Jackson. He languished there for six and a half years, until Mary Brown came forward and admitted that she had perjured herself, fabricating the charge of rape and persuading Ellen Hoover to go along.

As Detroit had no professional police force in 1863, city officials requested that the recently mustered-in federal Provost Guard in the city accompany Faulkner to his cell. They marched with bayonets fixed as the crowd hurled both rocks and insults at the prisoner. According to one black eyewitness quoted by the *Free Press*, "They were yelling like demons, and crying 'kill all the damned niggers.'" When some of the stones and brickbats began to be hurled at the Provost Guard, the officer in charge ordered his men to load a round of blanks and fire a warning at the crowd. When the crowd refused to disperse, a few soldiers—acting on their own—fired live rounds. A twenty-four-year-old German immigrant shopkeeper named Charles Langer, apparently an innocent bystander, was killed instantly. When Langer fell, a riot began in earnest. The Provost Guard marched hastily (and curiously) back to its barracks, leaving a local militia company to provide a protective cordon around the jail and leaving the infuriated mob in control of the streets.

The mob then turned its fury against the black neighborhoods on the city's near east side, screaming, "Kill the negroes, kill the negroes." Hundreds, armed with axes and beer, streamed southward from the jail through Brush, Beaubien, St. Antoine, Lafayette, and Fort Streets. One of the first attacks was on a cooper shop on Beaubien, where Joshua Boyd and other black men were at work. A member of the mob knocked Boyd in the head with an axe, producing a gaping, bleeding wound. Boyd died some thirty hours later, a "mangled child of sorrow," in the words of one observer, recorded in the 1863 monograph *A Thrilling Narrative from the Lips of the Sufferers of the Late Detroit Riot*. Many black residents of the city's Third Ward were severely beaten, while their homes were looted and set ablaze. Those who fled were pelted with brickbats and stones. One black eyewitness reported that he saw a burning man flee his blazing home only to be attacked by twenty Irish immigrants wielding clubs and screaming, "Kill the nager." Some victims fled to the city's docks, hoping to make their way across the Detroit River to Canada West. Ferrymen, sensing an opportunity, tripled and quadrupled their usual charges. Others fled into the countryside. Detroit's Third Ward burned throughout the late afternoon and early evening of March 6, from Croghan Street (now Monroe), down Brush and Beaubien, as far south as Congress. Houses on Lafayette, between Beaubien and St. Antoine, were nearly stripped of all their furniture and possessions, which then provided fuel for the bonfires that were set in the middle of the street.

The riot was quelled late in the evening by the arrival of more local militia, a detachment of the 19th US Regular Infantry, stationed at Detroit's Fort Wayne, and five companies of the new 27th Michigan Volunteer Infantry, which had been rushed by special train from Ypsilanti. The mob, faced with armed soldiers and having satiated much of its anger, melted away. By the next morning, all was quiet except the smoldering remains of burning houses and businesses in Detroit's black neighborhoods. When the smoke cleared, officials tallied the damages. Two Detroiters lay dead: one black, one white. Scores of other African American residents had been badly beaten. Hundreds had fled across the river to Windsor or into the countryside. Some thirty to thirty-five black homes and businesses were burned to the ground. Many more were severely damaged.

The tensions that produced the riot had been building for some time. The Civil War itself played a role. The conflict brought dramatic growth in population, crime, inflation, and labor conflict. The people of Detroit were anxious and unsettled. Furthermore, the ethnic makeup of the city had been changing for more than a decade. Growing numbers of immigrants from Europe—primarily Irish and German—had been arriving in Detroit since the late 1840s. At the same time, the local black population had grown tenfold from 1840 to 1860. Though it was still small (about 1,402 lived in the city in the latter census), it was now a visible presence living in a few defined neighborhoods. Moreover, it continued to increase rapidly, about 60 percent during the 1860s. Blacks and immigrants, especially the Irish, often competed for the same jobs, housing, and recreation space. There had been a growing number of minor racial incidents between immigrants and blacks in the six-month period preceding the riot.

Furthermore, the riot occurred the same day that the federal Enrollment Act became law. For the first time, all able-bodied male citizens and immigrants intending to become citizens (age twenty to forty-five if unmarried and twenty to thirty-five if married) were subject to a military draft. This, coupled with the Emancipation Proclamation two months earlier, which turned the Union war effort into a struggle for black freedom, troubled many white working-class Detroiters, especially immigrants. The law extended federal power into local communities as never before, adding to its unpopularity. As Paul Taylor observed in *"Old Slow Town": Detroit during the Civil War* (2013), "The new enrollment act and its perceived intent of forcing poor white men into the army to fight for the black slaves' freedom became the powder keg's short fuse." One of the rioters swore in less eloquent fashion, "If we are got to be killed up for niggers then we will kill every nigger in this town."

Adding fuel to the fire, the *Democratic Free Press* had been encouraging racial hysteria among its working-class and immigrant readers for months. The paper frequently ran antiblack news stories and editorials in which

African Americans were blamed for threatening whites' jobs, demeaning white citizenship, being the cause and continuance of the deadly war, and seeking interracial relationships with white women. When Faulkner was arrested, the *Free Press* immediately identified him as "a black fiend" and urged its readers to take action. Five days before the riot, it announced of Faulkner, "It is thought that an excited and indignant mob would have intended to wreak summary vengeance upon him." The day after the riot, the city's Republican paper, the *Advertiser and Tribune*, characterized the rioters as "a *Free Press* mob." African American leaders said much the same.

The riot represented a new form of racial disorder in the city. Gone were the fugitive-slave riots that Detroit had experienced before the Civil War. These had been replaced by a targeted, ferocious attack on the city's growing African American population. The 1863 riot in Detroit, the worst that occurred in the Midwest during the Civil War, was a dress rehearsal for the more famous New York Draft Riots of July 13–16, 1863. Many people feared that it was also a sign of things to come locally. In response, Detroit's city fathers established the first professional police force as a way to preserve public order in the city.

Between 1815 and 1865, the streets of Detroit exploded in occasional outbursts of racial violence. At first, these incidents took the form of fugitive-slave riots aimed at protecting runaway slaves in the city. In 1863, as economic competition and social tensions fostered tensions between working-class whites (mainly immigrants) and blacks in the midst of a civil war, a racial pogrom gutted sections of the city's African American neighborhoods. It was a portent of things to come.

Freedom's Railway

REMINISCENCES OF THE BRAVE OLD DAYS OF THE FAMOUS UNDERGROUND LINE

William Lambert

From the *Detroit Tribune*, January 17, 1886, p. 2. This is an excerpt of an interview with William Lambert, aged seventy, an enterprising Detroit businessman and an active leader of the African American community. He came to the city in 1840 and managed local operations of the Underground Railroad. Here he describes a typical evening.

"I was expecting a train from the south and we were waiting for it at the lodge on Jefferson Avenue [between Bates and Randolph Streets]. This was our custom. The fugitives were brought in from the country from Wayne and Ann Arbor so as to arrive at night. They would be brought to the vicinity of the lodge, when we would go and test them, and all those with them.

"When we had received the people at the lodge we then took them to the rendezvous, which was the house of J. C. Reynolds, an employe[e] of the company then constructing the Michigan Central railway. He had been sent by Levi Coffin of Cincinnati, who was the head of the underground railway in the west. His residence was at the foot of Eighth Street, just opposite the place where the first elevator was subsequently built. The house has long since been torn down. We would fetch the fugitives there, shipping them into the house by dark one by one. There they found food and warmth, and when, as frequently happened, they were ragged and thinly clad, we gave them clothing.

"Our boats were concealed under the docks, and before daylight we would have everyone over. We never lost a man by capture at this point, so careful were we, and we took over as high as 1,600 in one year. Sometimes we were closely watched and other rendezvous were used. Ald. Finney, Luther Beecher, McChubb and Farmer Underwood could tell you lots about these details. Finney's Barn used to be filled with them some times. It stood opposite the hotel property which bears Finney's name."

Race Relations in Detroit, 1860–1915

De Witt S. Dykes Jr.

African Americans in Detroit after 1860 experienced a mixture of opportunities and restrictions. First they inherited a legacy of strong antislavery activity and assistance to fugitive slaves throughout the state. Also Michigan enacted Personal Liberty laws to make it harder for authorities to return runaways to slavery. Still antislavery attitudes were not the same as support for racial equality. African Americans had limited economic and educational opportunities, faced great restrictions on the use of public facilities, and found a limited choice of housing available to them.

The Civil War involved large numbers of northern whites and African Americans volunteering to fight to restore the southern states to the Union. In addition to the thousands of whites who volunteered, 1,673 African Americans served in the 1st Michigan Colored Infantry Regiment, later renamed the 102nd Regiment, US Colored Troops.

African Americans were occasionally the objects of unjust accusations and violence. In March 1863, for example, a black store owner, William Faulkner, was accused by two nine-year-old girls, one white, one black, of molestation. In response to the accusation, many whites rioted, killing two blacks, injuring many others, and destroying property in the black section of Detroit. Faulkner spent seven years in jail before being released after the girls admitted that they had lied.

African Americans across the country faced extensive and ingrained racial prejudice from whites who assumed all blacks not only were inferior to whites but also were less capable of intellectual or occupational achievement. Blacks were often the objects of stereotyped caricatures and public ridicule as members of an inferior race. Such attitudes limited opportunities

In 1878, the *Detroit Free Press* columnist Charles Bertrand Lewis created a fictional organization called the Lime Kiln Club. Written in an exaggerated southern dialect, the club's "debates" disparaged both African Americans and politicians. Lewis's brand of humor was popular with the newspaper's Democrat-leaning readers. The articles were syndicated nationally and eventually published as a book, adapted to vaudeville, developed as a cigar brand, and used as the basis for a Bert Williams movie. This image was produced by Detroit's Calvert Lithographing Company in 1882. From the Detroit Historical Society Collection.

for jobs, occupational training, adequate housing, and education. Due to slave owners' frequent sexual exploitation of slave women, many whites blamed the women and their descendants, assuming all postslavery black women had loose morals.

Michigan passed an 1867 law stating that "all residents of any [school] district shall have an equal right to attend any school therein," intending to prohibit racial segregation in public schools. Yet it was necessary to file a lawsuit to desegregate public schools in Detroit. The Michigan Supreme Court overturned Detroit schools' segregation practices in *Workman v. Board of Education of Detroit* in 1869. Fannie Richards, who taught in Detroit's "colored school" from 1865 to 1869, became Detroit's first African American teacher in a racially integrated school. She taught racially integrated classes until her retirement in 1915. Despite her success, Detroit limited the number of African American teachers working in public school facilities—only two to four at a time—until the 1930s, when it changed policies and hired more African American teachers.

The state legislature continued approving laws to give African Americans equal legal status with other citizens. In 1883, the legislature overturned a ban on interracial marriage and enacted the Michigan Civil Rights Act in 1885. Despite this law, efforts to achieve equal treatment in public accommodations continued to be a constant struggle in theaters, restaurants, and hotels until the 1950s.

Though the legal standing for African Americans continued to improve, economic opportunities were weak and unstable. Unlike other northern industrial cities, Detroit's African American population grew very slowly. Immediately following the Civil War, an influx of blacks from Canada boosted the segment from 1,403 to 2,235 by 1870, or about 2.8 percent of Detroit's total. Thereafter, immigration from Europe in the 1880s and 1890s more than offset minor growth in the black community, and the percentage fell to 1.6 percent by 1890 and to 1.2 percent two decades later.

Most working-class African American men were either general laborers or service workers, establishing a tradition as hotel porters, waiters, and cooks. Others were proprietors of barbershops catering to white men. Most African American working women were domestic employees. Many families achieved some level of economic stability and social status in a variety of jobs by the 1870s, but significant changes occurred by the 1890s. The heavy immigration from Europe resulted in the loss of most of these positions, as immigrants replaced African American men. Similarly, African Americans in the service sector, such as gardeners, butlers, and coachmen, were released.

An organized committee sought new positions for black men to compensate for job losses, resulting in the first hiring of blacks in positions as conductors and motormen on the street railways and a few workers in one of the stove companies. Another opportunity developed for African American musicians—almost exclusively men—who entertained white audiences in hotel ballrooms, in dance halls, and on steamships. Theodore Finney's Orchestra was a fixture in the city, launching the careers of such influential band leaders and composers as Fred S. Stone, Harry P. Guy, and Ben Shook.

A few individual blacks and several black families were able to make political or social connections and gained advancement and status as a result. Political connections led to three African Americans—William W. Ferguson, Joseph H. Dickinson, and Dr. James W. Ames—serving a combined five terms in the Michigan state legislature between 1893 and 1901. Others were elected or appointed to local city positions in Detroit. These political positions were achieved due to the "flexibility" of the convention system, in which party officials named the candidates, used a principle of "ethnic balancing" of the slate of candidates in order to appeal to many ethnic groups, and could depend on most party loyalists to vote a straight party ticket regardless of who the candidates were. The direct primary, a political reform that enabled party supporters to choose the party nominees, ended blacks' opportunity for elective office until a substantial increase in black voters occurred later in the twentieth century.

Black political support of the Republican Party led to the hiring of several black men as Detroit police officers. The first, Joseph Stowers in 1890, was terminated after two months. Four others were appointed in the 1890s, with three serving between two and four years and one, George Carmichael, having a long career of twenty-nine years. Other long-serving officers were Warren Richardson, appointed in 1900, who served twenty-six years, and Daniel O. Smith, appointed in 1901, who served thirty-one years. In 1919, thirteen black officers were hired, including the first black female, Gracie W. Murphy, and the first blacks were promoted to the positions of sergeant and detective. Still, black police worked only in the black community and had limited authority to deal with white suspects, having to turn them over to white officers. White Detroit firefighters prevented racial integration of the Detroit Fire Department until 1937.

Significant advances were made in the realm of education, employment, and business development. Having experienced modest gains, some successful blacks took advantage of the favorable legislative climate to push back at racial discrimination. On August 15, 1889, William Ferguson—at that time the owner of a printing business—entered the restaurant of Gies's European Hotel for supper and sat down at a dinner table. The waiter, and subsequently the owner, Edward Gies, told Ferguson and his companion that they could not be served at the tables with linens and silverware. Instead, Gies informed them, they could be served on the other side of the room—the barroom side—where the tables were uncovered and had ordinary flatware. Ferguson declined to move, and Gies refused to serve them. Ferguson hired the prominent Detroit attorney D. Augustus Straker, who took the case to the Michigan Supreme Court, which in 1890 found in favor of Ferguson. It was an important victory but had little effect on discrimination in Detroit's public places.

In an era when a relatively small percentage of the US population attended high school, the Robert Pelham family had five of its seven children graduate from the Detroit High School and go on to make valuable

The only major riot to take place in Detroit between the Civil War and 1930 became known as the Great Trolley Strike of 1891. It came in response to union organizing activity by drivers and conductors on the city's twenty-two hundred horse-drawn streetcars. The privately owned Detroit City Railways Company paid very low wages and forced employees to work at least twelve hours a day with one day off every other week. When union organizers were fired by the company, remaining employees went on strike. Strikers were supported by the general public, which decried high fares and poor service. Independent of the union, citizens disrupted traffic by blocking tracks, wrecking cars, and prompting demonstrations whose crowds numbered in the thousands. This photograph shows hired "strike breakers" attacking prounion activists during the two-day riot. When Mayor Hazen Pingree sided with the strikers, the street-car company quickly capitulated. From the Detroit Historical Society Collection.

personal and social achievements. Joseph Pelham served as principal of a high school in Missouri for forty years. Meta Pelham was a teacher in Missouri before returning to teach in the Detroit Public Schools. In the 1880s, the Pelhams became newspaper publishers, starting a widely circulated weekly paper, the *Plaindealer*, that was published for ten years until 1894. In an age of male supremacy, four men—Robert H. Pelham Jr., Benjamin B. Pelham, W. A. Anderson, and W. H. Stowers—were listed as editors, but it is well documented that Meta Pelham not only was a general writer on the editorial staff but also did other tasks including helping to print the paper. This endeavor was facilitated because the Pelham brothers worked for the *Detroit Tribune* newspaper and were allowed to use the *Tribune's* presses and equipment when available.

Later, Robert Pelham Jr., a talented man, used social and political connections to get government jobs, ending as an employee of the US Census Department in Washington, DC, and publishing a newspaper, the *Washington Tribune*. Benjamin B. Pelham became an employee of Wayne County, Michigan, government, rising from an initial appointment as a clerk to become effectively the chief executive administrator of Wayne County, serving in appointed office for forty-seven years. He was able to have his son Alfred M. Pelham Sr. hired as a clerk in the office, enabling him to rise to the position of director of budget and finance for Wayne County.

Other notable achievements were Henry Fitzbutler's graduation from the Detroit Medical College in 1869 and his continuation of medical study at the University of Michigan, graduating in 1871. He had a distinguished career in Louisville, Kentucky, starting a medical college for African Americans that operated from the late 1880s until its closure in 1912.

Ida Gray (later Ida Gray Nelson Rollins) received a degree in dentistry from the University of Michigan in 1890, practicing first in Cincinnati before moving to Chicago. Frederick B. Pelham received a bachelor's degree in civil engineering from the University of Michigan in 1887, the first African American graduate of the Michigan College of Engineering. The second African American graduate in engineering was Cornelius L. Henderson in 1912. Though African Americans were accepted as students in Michigan's universities, they were not allowed to stay in residence halls or participate in study groups with white classmates. They lived off campus in private housing. Integration of the residence halls at the University of Michigan began in the late 1930s after the threat of a lawsuit.

Also, job possibilities for black graduates varied. Frederick Pelham graduated from engineering school at the head of his class, and when officials of the Michigan Central Railroad asked the faculty of the College of Engineering to recommend two graduating students for employment, Pelham was one of the two recommended. He was hired in 1887. By 1912, Cornelius Henderson was not so fortunate, being turned down by Detroit companies and finding work only in Canada for most of his career.

African American churches played a key role not only in meeting the spiritual needs of blacks but by serving as organizations that addressed the social needs of a growing black community. In the mid-1910s, many blacks were among the thousands attracted to Detroit seeking high-paying jobs. Additional services to the black community were provided in 1912, when the National Association for the Advancement of Colored People (NAACP) established a Detroit chapter to pursue civil rights issues, and in 1916, when the National Urban League started the Detroit Urban League to assist migrants seeking jobs, housing, and wholesome recreation.

By the early decades of the twentieth century, African Americans in Detroit had made modest but important inroads within the community. They established businesses that became the foundation for the vibrant Black Bottom neighborhood that grew tremendously during the Jazz Age of the 1920s. They also experienced the growth of an upper middle class that was able to lead health, education, and social initiatives into the new century.

The Rages of Whiteness

RACISM, SEGREGATION, AND THE MAKING OF MODERN DETROIT

Kevin Boyle

McClellan Dixon was breaking the law when the two cops came in. It wasn't much of a crime, though, drinking with his buddies in a blind pig at half past two in the morning. And when the officers told everyone to clear out, he joined the line going down the stairs; having spent a lifetime following white men's orders, he had no reason to defy this one. Maybe he should not have changed his mind, turned around, and headed up again, but he wanted to see why his friend was still in the bar. And if he said something to one of the patrolmen as he tried to squeeze by—alcohol having a way of talking—that did not give the cop the right to shove him so hard that he tumbled down the steps to the pavement. Later the officers said Dixon came up swinging. Everyone else said the cop was over him before he got to his feet, pummeling him with his nightstick, blow after blow to the head, until he wasn't moving anymore. They would have left him there, sprawled in the doorway, witnesses claimed, except that the crowd started shouting at them, demanding that they do something to help. The two cops seemed to think it safer to call for an ambulance than to walk away—better to let Dixon die in a hospital bed than on the streets of Detroit on a suddenly brutal night in December 1924.

It was not supposed to be this way. In the decades after the Civil War, African Americans and their white allies had shattered Michigan's blatantly discriminatory legal regime. Down came the laws that denied African

Americans the vote; required the segregation of schools; sanctioned discrimination in restaurants, theaters, and other public places; and prohibited interracial marriage. Deep injustices remained, of course, none worse than the discriminatory practices that kept most of Detroit's tiny African American population in the lowest-paying jobs and therefore in its poorest neighborhoods. Still, by the turn of the twentieth century, Detroit's long-standing color line had been weakened, and the possibility of equality haltingly, imperfectly advanced.

Then the boom began. It started in the autumn of 1908, when Henry Ford unveiled the Model T, his bone-jarring car for the common man, then spread with the extraordinary power of imitation and innovation. Fordism, social critics called it: the perfection of mass production, carried out in the cutting-edge factories the automakers would build over the next twenty years, from Ford's fabled Highland Park plant, which opened in 1910; through Packard, Hudson, Studebaker, Cadillac, Briggs, and Dodge; to the River Rouge complex, completed in fits and starts from 1917 to 1928. By then, Detroit had become one of world's greatest manufacturing centers, a machine of a city oiled by some 270,000 industrial workers, enough to support a population of 1.5 million people, five times the number who had lived there in 1900. "Detroit is Eldorado," wrote the reporter Howard Willard for the *Woman's Home Companion* at the height of the boom. Quoted by Peter Gavrilovich and Bill McGraw in the *Detroit Almanac*, Willard continued, "It is staccato American. It is shockingly dynamic." Many of the migrants who poured into the city agreed. Barry Gordy Sr. recalled in Richard Thomas's *Life for Us Is What We Make It*, "I was reading in the paper, and it say where the plumbers were making twelve dollars a day and the brick layers and plasterers, too. . . . Well, that's more than I ever made in a regular job . . . down in Georgia. Down there when the crop was in and it was wintertime pay [was not] over two dollars a day. So, I just know I could make big money in Detroit."

Dynamism had its dark side. As the city grew, it seethed with tensions: at the hiring gates, where newcomers scrambled to grab the wages they had come to Detroit to earn; on the factory floor, where the job a worker managed to claim determined not only his pay but also his safety and dignity; in the neighborhoods, where the relentless demand that the boom's massive migration created put enormous strain on the city's housing stock; on the ragged end of the commercial strips, where the young men who dominated the migration packed into the staggering number of bars and brothels that made Detroit a notoriously open town; in the city government, where equity, authority, and social control collided; and all along the color line, where the city's conflicts came together.

The convergence was rooted in demographics. The vast majority of the migrants who poured into Detroit were white, many from abroad, many others from rural America, north and south. But a substantial minority was black. There were only 4,100 African Americans in Detroit in 1900, a minuscule 1.4 percent of the population. Thirty years later, there were 120,000, a 3,000 percent increase. That dramatic change triggered a fierce backlash; from the mid-1910s onward, whites increasingly demanded that Detroit be segregated, its black population cordoned off. The dynamic was painfully clear. Whites had been willing to support integration as long as there were not many African Americans to integrate. As blacks established a substantial presence in Detroit, though, the promise of equality was swamped by a rising tide of racism.

But racism alone cannot segregate a city. Someone has to take the ideas on which racism rests and turn them into a system of enforceable rules and regulations that give racial injustice its form and force. In Detroit, as in most of the urban North, there were not any serious campaigns to repeal the legal advances African Americans had made in the late nineteenth century: to strip them of the vote, to require that they ride in the back of city buses, or to restrict their children to schools that had been segregated by law. Instead, in the 1910s and 1920s, segregation raced through Detroit's workplaces, neighborhoods, and social spaces—that is to say, through its flashpoints—the process driven by a toxic mix of hatred, fear, and power.

The precise combination differed from sector to sector. Only in the skilled trades did workers have any control over hiring. As much as whites wanted to segregate their workplaces then, most of them had no ability to do so. But their bosses did. During the boom years, major employers continued the pattern that had been set before the economy took off. The few who hired African American women placed them in the lowest levels of service work. At Hudson's elegant department store, for instance, black women could work as maids or, if they were light-skinned enough, as elevator operators, but they were never put behind the sales counters. African American men did more than their share of service work too, as janitors, bellhops, chauffeurs, and porters. Far more went into the auto plants. There too employers established a strict racial hierarchy. Blacks were almost never allowed into skilled work or placed along assembly lines. That left them a narrow band of jobs so miserable or so dangerous that only the most desperate of whites would take them. African Americans could work at Dodge

Main in the poisonous cloud of paint that filled the spray room, at Briggs Manufacturing in the wet-sanding department, at Packard on the janitorial crews, and in the foundry of every major factory because no one spent nine hours a day in a foundry unless he had no other choice.

Auto work was segregated from the executive suites down, rather than up from the factory floor. Once the rules were in place, though, white autoworkers embraced their bosses' handiwork; a number even came to believe that African Americans had worked the full range of factory jobs until whites had driven them off, a fiction that made whites' work seem more valuable simply because they had prevented blacks from doing it and therefore made workplace segregation a right worth defending. Housing segregation followed a different trajectory, bubbling up from the streets to the real-estate industry's central institutions, its value tied not to an abstract psychological wage but to the very real price of homes in a rapidly escalating market.

There had always been African American neighborhoods in Detroit, the largest a strip of streets on the eastern edge of downtown, an area known as Black Bottom. But in the early twentieth century, those neighborhoods were not completely African American any more than Poletown was completely Polish or Corktown completely Irish; even in Black Bottom, poor blacks and whites lived side by side, while a substantial number of more well-to-do African Americans lived in otherwise white areas. In the late 1910s, however, whites began to insist that African Americans degraded neighborhoods—making them less clean, less safe, less desirable, and less valuable—a problem that could be solved only by confining blacks to areas they had already dominated. The whites could not use the law to do it: in 1917, the US Supreme Court prohibited city governments from segregating neighborhoods. But they could use violence. Threatening letters stuffed into mailboxes, bricks tossed through windows, garages mysteriously torched, gangs of whites storming into houses to drag blacks' belongings onto the street—the incidents began during World War I when the African American migration grew so intense that Black Bottom's dilapidated housing threatened to collapse under the pressure. The incidents continued with mounting ferocity through the fevered summer of 1925, when white mobs tried to drive five different African American families out of white neighborhoods, the last time with fatal consequences.

In that time, the demand for segregation had risen from the streets to the marketplace. No longer would landlords and realtors show African

Americans properties in white neighborhoods for fear of offending white sensibilities, nor would the downtown banks extend to African Americans the credit they needed to buy anywhere outside of Black Bottom or one of the smaller black enclaves scattered across the city. And more and more large developers were placing restrictions on the deeds of the new houses they were building on Detroit's outskirts, prohibiting them from ever being sold to an African American or, in most cases, a Jewish American. Those practices had two intertwined effects. They systematized neighborhood segregation, putting in place barriers African Americans could not overcome unless they had enormous personal resources at their disposal. In the process, they dramatically reinforced whites' connection of race and property values. Now an African American who moved into a white neighborhood did in fact drive down the price of homes, not by anything he did but because his presence made realtors less likely to show whites other houses in the area and banks less likely to lend there. Instead of dampening violence, the new real-estate practices intensified it, since whites decided that they had to beat back any African American incursion into their neighborhoods, no matter how small. They did just that. By 1930, the vast majority of African Americans were locked into Black Bottom, which had become almost completely black, mostly poor, and dangerously overcrowded; most of the rest were locked into neighborhoods that were as strictly bounded.

From the segregation of neighborhoods flowed other forms of racial injustice. Detroit's schools became sharply segregated too, in defiance of state law. The city government starved Black Bottom of basic services: as late as 1920, a quarter of its houses did not have indoor toilets, thanks to an inadequate sewer system that officials refused to upgrade, even as they ran new lines out to the housing developments that barred black buyers. Inadequate sanitation bred horrifyingly high levels of disease. In 1919, 595 African American babies were born in Detroit; 89 of them were dead by the end of 1920, an infant mortality rate far in excess of white Detroit's. Dividing neighborhoods also divided the city's roiling social spaces. The process was never complete. But African Americans were not allowed into many bars and restaurants in white areas, from the high end—Hudson's tasteful thirteenth-floor dining room, for instance—to the shot-and-a-beer dives that inevitably surrounded the auto plants. The overwhelmingly white Detroit Police Department, meanwhile, did its best to restrict the city's thriving vice trade to Black Bottom, so as to save whites the indignity of having pimps and hopheads, drunks and johns fill their streets on a Saturday night. To add injury to insult, the cops then patrolled the neighborhood with the swagger of an occupying army, letting whites indulge in the temptations the department quietly sanctioned while brutally suppressing the locals' smallest transgressions, even something as small as a fifty-two-year-old black man's decision to go the wrong way on a stairway.

African Americans fought back, of course. There were organizational efforts against the segregationist surge in the 1910s and 1920s, run through chapters of the Universal Negro Improvement Association, the National Association for the Advancement of Colored People (NAACP), the National Urban League, and the more militant black churches. And there were personal acts of resistance, most so small that they barely left a trace and a few with enormous repercussions, such as Ossian and Gladys Sweet's decision to take possession of their new home on Garland Avenue in September 1925, despite their new neighbors' threats. The Great Depression widened the possibilities, even as it brought Detroit's two-decade boom to a catastrophic conclusion that ended the first Great Migration. In the early 1930s, the Communist Party established itself on the left wing of African American political life. Shortly thereafter, Franklin Roosevelt and his more liberal New Dealers—among them Detroit's Frank Murphy, late of Recorder's Court and the mayor's office—opened the Democratic Party to black activism. Late in the decade, the United Automobile Workers (UAW) and its parent organization, the Congress of Industrial Organizations, swept through the city's auto plants with the promise of interracial unionism, supported by a radicalized NAACP. And in the heart of Black Bottom, two African American migrants, W. D. Fard and his disciple Elijah Muhammad, launched a religious movement that in time would shake the nation.

But not yet. For all the promise of the 1930s, it did not break the patterns set in the previous decades. While the New Deal welcomed African American voters, it also launched sweeping reforms of the housing market that explicitly embraced the connection between race and property values through its infamous redlining program and by so doing reinforced neighborhood segregation. UAW leaders committed themselves to racial equality. Yet when workers organized at Dodge Main, Chrysler Assembly, Ford Rouge, and most of Detroit's other major plants, they created seniority systems that prevented African Americans from moving out of the jobs to which they had been relegated. And in 1935, the police drove Elijah Muhammad from Detroit; when the Nation of Islam's moment came a quarter century later, the shockwaves rumbled out of Harlem and South Side Chicago, not Black Bottom.

The Rages of Whiteness

ON MAY FIRST

Monday at 4 p. m., Grand Circus Park

LOCAL MAY DAY MARCHES TO GRAND CIRCUS PARK WILL START AS FOLLOWS:

FERRY HALL, 1343 East Ferry Ave, 2 p. m. GRANDY HALL, Grandy and Hendrie, 1:30 p. m. ALGER HALL, Oakland and Alger, 1:00 p. m. BRADY AND LIVINGSTONE, 2:30 p. m. LODGE PARK, 8935 Center-line, 1:00 p. m.

TO ALL WORKERS AND WORKERS ORGANIZATIONS!
TO ALL THE NEGRO PEOPLE OF DETROIT!
TO THE FOREIGN BORN WORKERS OF DETROIT!
TO ALL THE NATIVE BORN PEOPLE OF DETROIT!
TO ALL MASS ORGANIZATIONS—CLUBS—CHURCHES!

A Call to come out on the streets May First in solidarity to struggle for Unemployment Insurance, Freedom of Tom Mooney, and the Scottsboro Boys, and All Class War Prisoners.

On May First, 1933 we must continue the struggles which begun in Chicago in 1886 in the struggle for the 8 hour day, beginning with the Heroic struggle of the American movement May Day has become a day of struggle where the working class demonstrates its strength, throughout the world, in every land, workers and oppressed peoples of all colors and creed demonstrate their determination to end exploitation forever.

The Capitalist world is going thru the deepest and most devasting crisis mankind has ever known. Tens of millions of workers have been thrown out of the factories. Millions are starving and are being daily evicted from their homes. Workers protest against cutting off your water, gas and electricity. Stop the increase of deportation of the Foreign Born and legal lynching of the Negro workers.

UNITED FRONT MAY DAY CONFERENCE,
1343 E. Ferry Ave.

ALL OUT—Demand Unemployment Insurance. Freedom of Tom Mooney, Scottsboro Boys and All Class War Prisoners!

During the Great Depression, labor unions made significant progress at uniting Detroit's industrial workers. This flyer for a 1933 May Day rally illustrates efforts to include African Americans and immigrants in the fight to end discrimination and exploitation. From the Detroit Historical Society Collection.

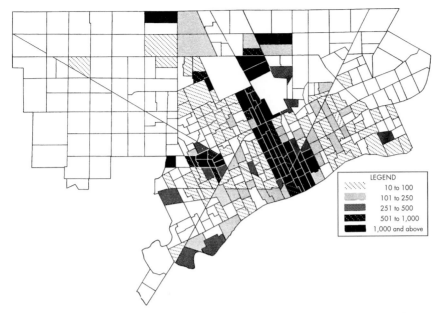

LEGEND
10 to 100
101 to 250
251 to 500
501 to 1,000
1,000 and above

Black population, 1940. Based on US Bureau of Census Statistics, prepared by Richard V. Marks, Mayor's Interracial Committee.

By then, McClellan Dixon had been dead for forty years, and the two patrolmen who had tried to dump his battered body in a doorway were at the end of their long careers, one having risen to inspector, the other to head of the department's vice squad. Maybe no one remembered what they had done when they were still beat cops, staging a pointless raid on a blind pig, forcing everyone into the street, wielding a power meant to humiliate, one of them swinging a nightstick again and again, wood against breaking bone. But it is hard to forget the sight of a man being beaten to death. So maybe the memory lingered somewhere in the city, one more entry into the long list of injustices created by the racial system that came to define Detroit during its boom years, one more step toward a steaming summer night at another blind pig in one of America's most segregated cities.

The Arsenal of Democracy-for-Some

Charles K. Hyde

The coming of World War II and the explosive growth of defense production by the Detroit automobile industry brought enormous changes to Detroit's African American community as well as to its relationship with majority-white institutions. The massive growth of defense-industry jobs was accompanied by a sharp decline in the numbers of traditional autoworkers, who either joined the armed forces by way of the draft or enlisted on their own. The defense industry recruited labor it had not previously employed in large numbers, namely, women, white southerners, and African Americans. The traditional autoworkers who remained behind did not always welcome these new workers, particularly African American workers, and often engaged in bitter battles to keep them out of the plants. Blacks who migrated to Detroit in search of job opportunities and a better future also faced severe housing shortages and severe discrimination in most areas of public life.

Well before World War II, substantial numbers of African Americans migrated to Detroit to work in the burgeoning automobile industry and elsewhere. They were part of the much-larger "Great Migration" of African Americans from the South to cities in the Northeast and Midwest between the start of World War I and the early 1930s. Detroit's black population, a mere 5,700 in 1910 (1 percent of the total) exploded to 120,000 in 1930 (8 percent of the total). Detroit's overall population jumped from 466,000 to 1,596,000 over those two decades. Worsening economic and social conditions in the South "pushed" these migrants north, while industrial jobs "pulled" them to cities like Detroit.

There were limited job opportunities in Detroit for African American men before the automobile industry began hiring them in the late 1910s. They mainly held unskilled, menial positions in the service and construction industries. Ford Motor Company, reflecting Henry Ford's paternalistic views on race, began hiring black workers in the late 1910s. Ford employed 2,500 black workers in 1920, only 4 percent of its enormous workforce. By 1926, Ford Motor Company had 10,000 black workers, roughly 10 percent of its employees, and it maintained that ratio through the 1930s. As late as 1941, only a handful of auto companies other than Ford had substantial numbers of black workers: Chrysler had nearly 2,000 African American employees, roughly 2.4 percent of its workforce, and Briggs Manufacturing (automobile bodies) had 1,300 black employees, or 10 percent of its labor force. The automakers, including Ford, gave African Americans the most unpleasant, difficult, and dangerous jobs in the plants, in part to minimize white workers' opposition to their presence. Black workers typically worked in foundries or performed spray-painting, heat-treating, and sanding operations. Only Ford gradually promoted black employees to assembly work and to more skilled trades.

In 1940, when preparations for war were already beginning, African Americans made up only 4 percent of autoworkers nationally, with the vast majority working for Ford, Chrysler, or Briggs. Once full mobilization for war got under way, enormous numbers of men and women entered military service. Combined US military forces, fewer than 500,000 in 1940, peaked at roughly twelve million in 1944 and 1945. The auto industry was hard-pressed to staff its plants for defense production and began hiring black workers to fill its needs. A second "Great Migration" from the South increased the black population in Wayne, Oakland, Macomb, and Washtenaw Counties from more than 170,000 in March 1940 (7 percent of the total population) to 259,000 in June 1944 (10 percent of the total).

As more black workers came into the defense plants and employers placed them in previously all-white departments, white workers in those departments and throughout the plants typically went on strike and refused to return to work until the black workers were removed. These were "wildcat" strikes, not authorized by the United Automobile Workers (UAW) International but often supported by the local unions and the rank-and-file union members. This form of resistance to black workers, more commonly called "hate strikes," began in earnest in 1941 and peaked in 1943, before practically disappearing in 1944 as a result of efforts by the UAW, the military services, and employers to squelch them.

Employees at the Murray Body Plant in Detroit work on B-17 wingtips on the framing line. Image courtesy of the National Automotive History Collection, Detroit Public Library.

Hate strikes were simply a reflection of the widespread and deep-seated racism that permeated American society, including northern cities. Many Detroit automobile plants had disproportionate numbers of white workers from Appalachia, Kentucky, and Tennessee, and their racism was part of the cultural baggage they brought when they moved north. Established European ethnic groups found in large numbers in the auto plants, including Poles, Italians, and Germans, also felt threatened by African Americans. Frequently, white workers refused to share bathrooms with black workers and would not even work on the same machines as blacks. In May 1943, when Packard Motor Car Company workers had a confrontational meeting with the UAW International president, R. J. Thomas, over an ongoing hate strike, one union member shouted, "I'd rather see Hitler and Hirohito win the war than to work beside a nigger on the assembly line!"

Midsized plants such as Packard, the Hudson Motor Car Company, and Timken Axle had the most hate strikes. Chrysler had multiple incidents in its numerous Detroit plants, while General Motors had fewer and Ford none. The Packard plant in Detroit had by far the most, the largest, and the longest-running hate strikes of the war, starting in October 1941 and extending through November 1944. The circumstances at Packard almost guaranteed racial unrest: the vast majority of the workers were southern whites and Polish Americans, both hostile to African Americans; the UAW local union was allegedly controlled by members of the Ku Klux Klan; and the personnel manager at Packard was openly racist. Following dozens of earlier hate strikes, Packard workers walked off the job in May and June 1943 to protest the promotion of three black foundry workers to aircraft-engine assembly work. Colonel George Strong, the Army Air Force representative at the plant, threatened to fire all strikers, thus making them eligible for the draft. Strong, the UAW, and Packard agreed to fire thirty ringleaders behind the strike, thus ending the dispute.

Among all workers seeking jobs in the defense plants, black females faced the most serious and persistent discrimination, mainly from white women workers who believed that most black women had venereal diseases that they could contract by sharing the same bathrooms. Citing this issue, more than two thousand white women workers at the US Rubber Company plant in Detroit went on strike in March 1943 after the company hired black women. The introduction of black females into the workforce also set off multiple hate strikes at Packard, at the Hudson Naval Arsenal in Center Line, Michigan, and in several General Motors plants. When African American women managed to get hired, they were often assigned extremely difficult and dangerous jobs. Companies that eventually hired black women allayed the fears of their white women workers by creating segregated departments with segregated bathrooms and lunchrooms.

By any numerical measure, war production provided African Americans with increased job opportunities, especially in the Detroit auto industry. In 1940, African Americans accounted for only 4 percent of automobile-industry employment nationally. By October 1941, African Americans made up 9 percent of the workforce in Detroit-area auto plants, then 13 percent in April 1943 and 15 percent in April 1945. Black workers held an even higher share of jobs (21 percent) in all defense work in the Detroit area in 1945. African American women made much slower progress. A December 1942 UAW survey of Detroit-area auto plants showed 63,630 women workers, but only 1,033 of these, less than 2 percent of the total, were black women. Less than a year later, in September 1943, black women accounted for 15 percent of all women employees.

Some automakers, such as General Motors, were slow in hiring black women, while others, including Ford, staunchly resisted hiring black women until later in the war. The employment history at the Chrysler Corporation during the war reflected that of most of the Detroit auto companies. Chrysler's workforce increased from 82,243 in 1940 to 125,481 in March 1945, the peak of wartime employment, a jump of more than 50 percent. The number of African American workers employed at Chrysler skyrocketed during the same time span, from 1,978 (2.4 percent of the workforce) to 18,148 (14 percent of the total). Chrysler had no black female employees in 1940, but by March 1945, it employed 5,060 (roughly 4 percent of its workforce).

African Americans in Detroit during the war years faced many challenges beyond discrimination and hostility in the workplace. For blacks, housing was rigidly segregated, substandard, overcrowded, overpriced, and hard to find. Public housing built by the Detroit Housing Commission in the late 1930s and the early war years was rigidly segregated and woefully inadequate for the needs of the black community. A few efforts by the federal government to build housing for blacks in Detroit and suburbs such as Dearborn were abandoned when widespread, vehement, local opposition appeared.

One exception was the Sojourner Truth Homes, a housing project built by the Detroit Housing Commission and earmarked to house two hundred African American families. Located near Ryan Road between McNichols and Seven Mile Road on Detroit's northeast side, the homes were ready to be occupied in mid-February 1943, but growing opposition from white residents in this area and threats of violence delayed the moving day until February 28. Then, more than twelve hundred white protesters blocked blacks from moving in, and there was scattered violence all day. The move-in was postponed until April 29, when a thousand Michigan National Guard troops and twelve hundred Detroit police and Michigan State Police officers maintained order.

The boiling cauldron of racial conflict in Detroit finally blew its lid on June 20, when a bloody race riot began on Belle Isle Park and then spread to large areas of Detroit. This outbreak was not particularly shocking to anyone closely observing Detroit's racial terrain. There had been scattered racial incidents, including the Sojourner Truth riots, over the previous year. Ten months before the Detroit riot, *Life* magazine published an article, "Detroit Is Dynamite," that examined the city's problems but focused on race relations. The article concluded that "Detroit can either blow up Hitler or it can blow up the U.S." During the days of the riots, black workers stayed away from their factory jobs, and there were minor demonstrations at some of the factories; but none of Detroit's defense plants closed. This upheaval is covered in detail in the next chapter.

The overall experience of African Americans living and working in Detroit during World War II was at best mixed. Along with the rest of the general workforce, blacks enjoyed lower unemployment rates and higher pay as the result of war production. Within the automobile plants, African Americans moved into more skilled and better-paid jobs than the ones they had before the war. At the same time, they faced significant discrimination from management and hostility from white coworkers, particularly in the case of black women workers. Most African Americans who found jobs in the defense industry worked in factories that remained tightly segregated by race. Outside of work, African Americans had to cope with an environment as rigidly segregated as any part of the South, most notably with regard to housing. They also had to face ongoing hostility and violence from whites, especially from the police. African Americans did achieve economic advances during the war but made little progress with regard to segregation, discrimination, and civil rights.

Following the war, returning GIs were welcomed back to their old jobs, displacing many of the new workers who had taken their place. Many—but not all—of the women workers were willing to return to their traditional roles in the home, as reflected by the postwar baby boom. However, black employees, both men and women, lost positions in large numbers. Despite having proven themselves capable workers, racial tensions on factory and shop floors remained strong. The resultant high unemployment foreshadowed a persistent and festering issue facing the black community moving into Detroit's auto-boom years.

Detroit 1943

"A REAL RACE RIOT"

Gregory Sumner

When Detroit residents talk about the sudden, widespread eruption of looting and violence that so changed the direction of their city—often with very different narratives, depending on the race of the speaker—they are usually referring to the events of July 1967. The historian who is asked about "The Riot," however, can be forgiven for asking the question, "Which one?"

Close observers were not surprised when the Motor City experienced the worst race riot in the country during the Second World War, in 1943. The bustling capital of America's Arsenal of Democracy faced all the opportunities and challenges that came with becoming a boomtown after a decade of depression. Civic leaders were unprepared to deal with the waves of newcomers who poured in for the employment now available with the conversion of the auto industry to munitions production. At the time, Mayor Edward Jeffries likened his responsibilities to the job of managing, in the words of the minister William P. Lovett, "a frontier town of the gold rush period." Many people wondered if it was ungovernable.

Frictions across the long-established racial divide were a source of particular concern, and sure enough, when the conditions were right, they went off like "dynamite," as a writer for *Life* magazine predicted in September 1942. It is hard to exaggerate the scale of the ensuing destruction and the damage done to the morale and social fabric of the city. The thousands of people arriving from the South, white and black, found the rules of Jim Crow in effect in Detroit, too, but now workers and their families found themselves jammed daily into uncomfortable proximity as they competed for jobs, housing, and recreational space and stood in lines for just about everything. Tempers flared, and a barely concealed atmosphere of racial tension pervaded every aspect of life in the wartime Arsenal.

The revolt of white neighbors over the opening of the integrated Sojourner Truth Homes in early 1942 was a warning of things to come, as were the ugly "hate strikes" staged by white workers over the hiring and promotion of blacks at Ford and Packard. Fueling the danger were voices in the local media spouting the vitriol of southern racists and immigrant Catholics. The big explosion unfolded over two steamy days and nights in late June 1943. The precise origins—the spark that set off a spontaneous combustion—will never be known with certainty. But it is clear that, as in so many civil disturbances, one or two minor incidents served to blow the lid off deep-seated, long-simmering animosities. Before anyone could stop it, the fire spiraled into a conflagration.

As darkness approached Sunday evening, June 20, at the end of a long day in ninety-degree heat, fistfights broke out between young black and white men packed in a gridlock of cars and bodies on the Belle Isle Bridge. Like a force of nature, the violence took on a momentum of its own, propelled by sensational (and false) rumors as it spilled into the city proper. A black man raped a white woman, someone loudly announced. White thugs threw an African American mother and her child to their deaths in the Detroit River, others cried, with equal volume.

Adding to the bad blood that night was the presence of two hundred or so off-duty sailors stationed at the nearby Brodhead Armory on East Jefferson. Alcohol fueled and looking for trouble, they were only too happy to launch themselves into the melee once it came into their sights.

The police were undermanned and overwhelmed, and soon downtown itself was a war zone. The sounds of sirens and broken glass filled the air, and Black Bottom and Paradise Valley, the vibrant main streets of black Detroit, were under siege. Brandishing the crude tools of the mob—bricks, tire irons, sections of metal pipe, and a few guns—gangs of white men pushed their way up Woodward Avenue, ready to bludgeon any black person who got in their way. People were pulled from movie lines and out of streetcars and savagely beaten. Motorists of both races scrambled for their lives as the self-styled vigilantes overturned and torched random vehicles while bystanders cheered them on.

The scene reminded the *Detroit Free Press* columnist Malcolm Bingay of episodes that haunted him from his youth in the Deep South: "On the streets of Detroit I saw again the same horrible exhibition of uninhibited hate as they fought and killed one another—white against black—in a

After a night and day of interracial rioting in July 1943, federal troops rolled in to quell the disturbance. According to news reports, the city was cordoned into four zones, and order was quickly restored. Image courtesy of the Detroit Historical Society Collection.

frenzy of homicidal mania, without rhyme or reason. Their faces were all the same, their lips drawn back, their teeth bared like fangs, their eyes glazed—bestial faces bereft of all human expression."

No one knew when the chaos might play itself out or how far the swath of destruction would reach. With loaded hunting rifles, men in the suburbs stood watch on lawns and front porches while their young children cowered in the darkness. The commander at Selfridge Field ordered the black Tuskegee pilots stationed there confined to the base until further notice. Meanwhile, Mayor Jeffries and Governor Harry Kelly vacillated about their next moves, hoping to be spared the embarrassment of calling Washington for help.

The madness rolled on through dawn as Detroit's Bloody Sunday turned into Bloody Monday. "It was a real race riot," recalled James Cummings, an African American eyewitness quoted in this author's *Detroit in World War II*. "It was not like this in 1967, where it was mostly looting. In 1943 they had boundaries set up which, if you would pass, you would certainly get killed or hurt."

It is important to remember that for every story of the horror that unfolded in Detroit at the start of that second wartime summer, there were instances, too, of people reaching out to one another across the color line. On June 22, 1943, the *Free Press* reported, "Riot Foes Fraternize in Hospital," looking for signs of hope amid the carnage. These were breaches of etiquette similar to those occurring in war zones overseas, each a spontaneous brotherhood of the wounded in which old habits and taboos lost their meaning. The sheer unexpectedness of these moments made them newsworthy:

> Receiving Hospital was probably the one place Monday where Negroes and white men met on amicable terms. Bleeding Negroes and whites sat side by side, even talking together, as the staff of 200 nurses and 60 doctors and interns battled tirelessly to staunch the flow of blood and patch up broken bodies. A few minutes earlier the injured had been the hunted or hunters in the rioting (just) blocks away, but now the fight was over. Dazed and mostly silent, they sat there mopping faces with blood-tinged handkerchiefs or strips of torn shirt until the doctors could get to them.

The Motor City madness did not abate until Monday evening, June 21, when the boots of six thousand federal troops hit the ground, bayonets fixed, tanks and trucks with machine guns rumbling alongside them in support. It was easy to forget that there was another, larger war going on outside the city. Belated as the show of force was, it worked, and martial law took hold. It was an eerie scene as soldiers patrolled the near-deserted streets of a place that liked to call itself the Arsenal of Democracy.

Governor Kelly instituted a nightly curfew and put a ban on all liquor sales. Detroit Tigers baseball games were canceled, and for days the air reeked of charred wood and tear gas. Businesses remained shuttered, and schools, post offices, and other municipal buildings stayed closed. Residents of black neighborhoods waited it out inside their homes as their communities endured a protective lockdown.

In the end, the official death toll was thirty-four, the majority of the victims African Americans. The actual body count was almost certainly higher. Six hundred were injured seriously enough to be sent to the hospital, including a number of police officers, and the court docket for the week recorded over one thousand arrests. Property damage ran into the millions of dollars, and damage to the city's image—something statistics could not measure—was profound and lasting.

There were political casualties, too. Mayor Jeffries was eventually turned out of office, in part because of his halting response to the days of anarchy in his city. Troops stayed for months to keep the peace, bivouacked on Belle Isle, the lawn of the Detroit Public Library, and any other public space that could be made to accommodate them.

The postmortems and finger-pointing started even before the smoke cleared. Some people attributed the disaster to "war nerves." President Roosevelt knew it was more complex than that, but he declined to give the Fireside Chat on race that his wife and other advisers privately urged him to make. Always keeping his eye on the goal of winning the war, he was most concerned about the threat to munitions production that such disorders posed. It was estimated that Detroit's output fell 6 percent during its "Bloody Week."

An Open Letter on Race Hatred, a radio play aired nationally on the CBS network a month after the riot, posed the question in the most pointed terms: "How many of your sons will die for the lack of the tanks and planes and guns which Detroit did not make?" the narrator asked. The tragedy demanded reflection and soul-searching by all Americans. "We lost Bataan—gallantly. We surrendered Corregidor—with honor. We were defeated at Detroit by ourselves." Even worse, the contagion was spreading. Disturbances flared in Harlem, Chicago, St. Louis, Galveston, El Paso, and dozens of other cities over the course of that long, hot, wartime summer.

The president lamented, too, the aid and comfort given to the enemy by newswire photographs of rampaging mobs and overturned cars aflame. Indeed, the strife in Detroit was a staple of German and Japanese propaganda for at least the next year. Nazi-controlled Vichy radio in France, quoted in the July 3, 1943, edition of the *Afro-American*, called the riot a product of "the internal disorganization of a country torn by social injustice, race hatreds, regional disputes, the violence of an irritated proletariat, and the gangsterism of a capitalistic police."

Congressman Martin Dies, chairman of the infamous House Un-American Activities Committee, came to a different conclusion, charging that the Motor City violence was the handiwork of deep-cover Japanese provocateurs. He presented no evidence in support of the theory, however.

Inevitably, there were those who were eager to lay blame at the doorstep of the First Lady. Critics had long condemned what they saw as her "meddling" on race issues, and they had not forgotten the warmth of the reception she received on a visit to Black Bottom in 1935, when she turned the first shovel for the new Brewster-Douglass housing project.

"In Detroit, a city known for the growing impudence and insolence of its Negro population," a letter to the editor of the *Jackson (MS) Daily News* declared, "an attempt was made to put your preachments into practice, Mrs. Roosevelt." Now she had "blood on her hands."

To understand what lay behind the '43 Detroit riot, however, it is not necessary to conjure up Axis agents or defame crusading social reformers. The root problem was segregation and the attitudes that supported it. The *real* instigator was Jim Crow.

Fortunately there were plenty of people who did not succumb to the furies of the mob, individuals who went out of their way to help fellow citizens in danger, and, again, their stories needed to be told, too. The *Open Letter on Race Hatred* program dramatized a series of episodes that, taken together, brought the point home. A quick-thinking white woman hides a black passenger under her seat as marauders sweep through a streetcar. Students at integrated Northeastern High walk home together after their graduation ceremonies, their numbers a protection against harm. And three off-duty sailors stop a gang from assaulting a black pedestrian downtown. "I'm just payin' off a debt!" one of them explains, his jaw set as he rolls up his sleeves. He was acting in the name of an African American shipmate lost in the Pacific.

Out of the ashes, there were other signs of hope in postriot Detroit. Schools, churches, UAW locals, and other civic organizations sponsored town meetings aimed at preventing a relapse, and a big crowd packed a "Double-V" civil rights rally in Olympia Stadium. It fell to the next generation to build on these promising foundations.

A Streetcar Named Disaster

Tommie M. Johnson

Tommie Johnson was interviewed by William Winkel, September 22, 2016, and her transcript was edited by Joel Stone, November 28, 2016, to fit this volume's physical limitations. The complete original transcript can be accessed via the Detroit Historical Society's electronic portal (detroithistorical.org).

I came to Detroit from Gary, Indiana, as an infant in December 1925. I can't remember too much about the late 1920s. The early 1930, I remember I went to Garfield School on Frederick Street, between Rivard and Russell. It was right across the street from our house. Our mother could watch us cross the street and go into the school building, so she did not have to get up. She liked where we lived. But when I think about school, I enjoyed the school and at that time, we were—blacks were very much in the minority in the Detroit Public Schools.

We lived over a block of stores there on Rivard, and I know the people who lived next door to us were Serbian, because I remember that Eddie Rockovich was in my same class. So that's the kind of neighborhood it was around the school at that time: very mixed, with blacks in the minority.

I felt very comfortable in my neighborhood because my mother's family was very clannish. I had an aunt who lived on Ferry Street, off Rivard. I had another aunt who lived on Hastings there by Frederick. My grandparents lived on Frederick. And so I felt very comfortable in that particular neighborhood to the extent that I never worried about anybody bothering me or picking on me or anything like that, because first of all—there were six children in my family, and my mother's sister had six, and her oldest four were boys. So nobody ever picked on us. I used to worry about my brother being picked on, because we were five girls and one boy. But because we were cousins and everybody knew it, nobody bothered us. I guess you'd say we had our own village. Garfield went from prekindergarten to the ninth grade, in school, and I know we always lived within walking distance.

I always felt comfortable in my neighborhood. I really did. Now I don't know—I guess, had I been a male, I might have felt differently. But at that time, I felt very comfortable.

One time I can remember my father didn't come home. My aunt's husband said, "Let's check the hospital, and let's check the police station." And sure enough, he'd been picked up by the police because they said that they had received information that a man with a limp had stolen a lady's purse or something like that. But when the lady came in, she said, "Oh no, that wasn't the man who stole my purse."

I think that happened to my father a couple of times, because my father liked to walk, and when we lived on Farnsworth and Rivard, he worked at Fisher Body. We didn't have a car, and I guess transportation at night was not so good, even then. He worked afternoons, I think, as far back as I can remember.

— —

I don't have memories of the Sojourner Truth incident, but the 1943 race riot? I remember that very distinctly.

If I felt racial tension, I heard it from my grandfather, because he was always up and around. One of his favorite beats was Hastings Street. He knew just about all the shopkeepers along there and used to do errands for them. Back then people didn't have checking accounts and banking accounts and so forth. When one of the shops had to pay a water bill, you had to go down to the Water Board building to do it. So he would do things like that for them and knew more about what was going on in the city in terms of friction. My brother may have known more, because people let boys have more freedom than girls had.

I think I was in high school at the time, at Northeastern. I think blacks were 10 percent or so of the population. I don't remember any big problems there, with the schools or with the students. I don't remember any fights, at least cross-culture fights. The Polish guys fought the Polish guys, and the black guys fought the black guys.

— —

Later, I knew there was tension because you could read about it in the paper. We had the *Michigan Chronicle* and the *Pittsburgh Courier*, two black newspapers. In 1943, I had a part-time job working for the *Pittsburgh Courier*'s Detroit edition, downtown on St. Antoine at Adams Street.

Well, when that riot broke out, we met at the editor's home. And I remember he asked me to take some information down to the *Free Press*—I guess they had some pictures or some stories or something that they had picked up—and so he asked me would I take them? I said, "Well, yeah, sure. I'll take them." The other young lady who worked there looked at me kind of strange, but she didn't say anything.

So I got on the Woodward streetcar, and by the time I got to the downtown area, there was a lot of commotion, and it was all white. And I was on the streetcar there, and there was a white lady on the streetcar, and she said, "You better duck down. Duck down under the seat so they won't see you." So I did, and sure enough, they stormed the streetcar, these white fellows did, yelling and carrying on. But they didn't see me and let the streetcar go on through.

I got down to the *Free Press* and gave them the material I had. And then I said, "Now how am I going to get back out of here?" Maybe I should take one of those buses that go west of Woodward. So I got on a bus, and over on that side of Woodward, there was no problem—no trouble, no gatherings, no anything. I got off when I came to Farnsworth, and then I ran home from there.

I didn't tell my parents anything about it, because they would have had a fit with this guy. But the full-time secretary for the paper, the next time I saw her, she said, "You were crazy to take that stuff downtown like that. You saw that he wasn't going to take it!" And I said, "Well, I didn't know what was going on down there!" But it was a big mass of white people storming all the streetcars and whatnot on Woodward Avenue at that time.

It shocked me because I didn't expect it. Back then you heard things on the radio, and you read in the paper and so forth, but just to see this whole mass of people on Woodward Avenue . . .

Part II

A Deteriorating Situation

Following World War II, Americans were ready to revel in their victory and settle into the normal domestic routines that they remembered. It was not long, however, before those routines were upset by postwar realities.

Nearly one in five war workers had been drawn to urban centers across the nation, dramatically shifting demographics in places such as Detroit and Los Angeles. Decentralization of industry and postwar recessions similarly shook the economic status quo. Some of the young men and women who had seen the world in the military and had access to college through the GI Bill began to reimagine their country as more inclusive.

Communism was the new enemy threatening the United States, prompting a Cold War with the Soviet Union, frustrating and costly anticommunist military actions in Korea and Vietnam, and an internal witch hunt led by US Senate demagogues. The space race represented a technological struggle for global supremacy, a race that America initially was losing.

Music, theater, and movies sought new directions, while television grew into a whole new entertainment option. New recording technologies and record labels, along with growing investments in youth-focused radio, allowed new musical forms like rock-and-roll, doo-wop, and "race" records to gain wide distribution. Broadway stages offered uplifting musical spectacles like *Showboat*, *Oklahoma*, and *Camelot*, while off-Broadway plays by David Mamet, Arthur Miller, and Lorraine Hansberry exposed the nation's grittier side for the first time. Cinemascope and 3-D extravaganzas made the big screen bigger, and Walt Disney projected his all-American dream in movies, TV, and an out-of-this-world amusement park. Americans, who had been myopically focused on winning the war, were suddenly thrust into an era that offered too many options: some familiar, some uncomfortably new.

Radical rhetoric and mass protests from blacks, whites, American Indians, youth, communists, and environmentalists engendered conflict, animosity, and retrenchment. The advent of a drug culture and urban poverty exacerbated crime. Urban renewal and freeway construction carved up traditional neighborhoods, even as the national highway system made transcontinental automobile travel easier.

Detroiters experienced all of this, even as the auto industry experienced paroxysms that saw Packard and Studebaker close their plants. Portions of Graham-Paige, Hudson, Nash-Kelvinator, Willys, and Kaiser-Fraser ended up as American Motors. The mergers and closings cost Detroit tens of thousands of jobs, even as the "Big 3"—Ford, Chrysler, and General Motors—were turning out some of America's most iconic vehicles. The advent of suburban shopping centers eroded retail in the central city. Detroit's streetcar system, once an efficient public-transportation staple, ceased operation in 1956.

In 1963, the assassination of President John Kennedy stunned Americans to their core, inflaming an undercurrent of uncertainty. As in an earthquake, people felt that the floor was moving.

The Deindustrialization of Detroit

Thomas A. Klug

In a chapter titled "The Future of Cities," the 1968 report of the National Advisory Commission on Civil Disorders (also known as the Kerner Commission) declared, "We are well on the way to . . . a divided nation. . . . One predominantly white and located in the suburbs, in smaller cities, and in outlying areas, and one largely Negro located in central cities." It went on to describe the stark economic inequalities that accompanied the sharp racial separation occurring in major metropolitan areas of the United States. "Most new employment opportunities," it observed, "do not occur in central cities, near all-Negro neighborhoods. They are being created in suburbs and outlying areas—and this trend is likely to continue indefinitely." The commission's report did not dwell on *how* central cities had once sustained meaningful employment for numerous workers and became landscapes of economic decay, abandonment, and concentrated poverty—while suburban areas on their peripheries flourished and grew. It was clear, however, that this process predated by many years the urban upheavals of the mid-1960s.

"Detroit's decline has been going on for a long while," noted an article in *Time* magazine in October 1961. Ever since Detroit's industrial heyday as the Arsenal of Democracy during World War II, the country's leading automotive city had suffered a serious loss of manufacturing capacity and blue-collar employment. Between 1947 and 1967, the number of production workers employed at manufacturing sites in Detroit shrank from 281,500 to 149,600, a drop of 131,900 (47 percent). During the same period, production-worker employment outside the city in Wayne, Macomb, and Oakland Counties grew from 186,700 to 244,700, an increase of 58,000 (31 percent). The worst period of industrial job loss for Detroit occurred during the 1950s. As the historian Thomas J. Sugrue remarked in *The Origins of the Urban Crisis*, his definitive study of postwar Detroit, "The 1950s marked a decisive turning point in the development of the city—a systematic restructuring of the local economy from which the city never fully recovered."

The economic restructuring of Detroit was not simply the result of general economic change, sometimes called modernization or progress. It happened because the captains of industry made strategic choices about where and how to produce automobiles and automotive components. Moreover, they made their decisions within a particular historical framework. The autoworkers' revolt of the late 1930s, marked by a wave of sit-down strikes against General Motors and Chrysler and the emergence of the United Automobile Workers (UAW) union, transformed Detroit into a fortress of the industrial union movement. The last bastion of employer autocracy, Ford Motor Company, fell to the UAW in 1941 following a lengthy and methodical unionization campaign. Organized autoworkers challenged industrialists' claims to run their enterprises as they saw fit. From the perspective of employers, observed Neil Hurley in *Land Economics* magazine, February 1959, "the most unpredictable labor market in the entire economy is to be found in the automobile industry and the most mercurial labor center is unquestionably Detroit." The postwar managerial counterattack against an empowered Detroit working class dovetailed with decisions by manufacturers about the location of factories and the adoption of new labor-saving technologies.

The postwar period saw a complicated choreography of moves by companies about where to produce manufactured goods. Between 1946 and 1956, General Motors, Ford, and Chrysler spent $5.9 billion on new plants in anticipation of a surge in postwar consumer demand for automobiles. Part of the sum went into the construction of facilities in the suburbs of Detroit, where land was cheap and plentiful. According to a 1956 regional-planning study, the Big 3 built twenty new plants in the Detroit area, with five more planned or under construction. All of them were located in the suburbs. Resources also poured into updating older plants and acquiring existing facilities, especially within the city. In 1953, for example, Chrysler purchased nine Detroit plants of the Briggs Manufacturing Company, the recently defunct auto-body manufacturer and supplier. The last new auto factory built in Detroit, Chrysler's Plymouth plant at Mt. Elliott Street and Lynch Road, had opened in 1929. Its single-story, steel-framed main assembly building was nearly half a mile in length and was reputed to be the world's largest automobile factory under one roof. It stood in contrast to the older, typically four-story, automobile factories in the city that were obsolete by the 1950s. The Plymouth plant pointed to the efficient manufacturing layout of the future—a future that was realized along the industrial corridors in the suburbs.

The Mound Road industrial corridor in Macomb County developed astride the New York Central railway, which bisected two major arterial highways, Mound to the west and Van Dyke Street to the east. The corridor began to take shape in 1938 when Chrysler built its ultramodern Dodge truck assembly plant on Mound above Eight Mile Road in rural Warren Township. In the chapter "Detroit: Linear City," from *Mapping Detroit*, Robert Fishman notes that, as the United States moved to rearm, "Mound Road became the favored site for some of the most massive war production plants anywhere in the world." Most notable was Chrysler's Detroit Tank Arsenal between Eleven and Twelve Mile Roads, which opened in 1941. Industrial expansion continued after the war as new automobile and defense plants and their network of suppliers filled in the zone. Perhaps the crowning jewel was the completion in 1955 of the new General Motors Technical Center ("the Versailles of Industry," according to *Life* magazine in May 1956). Between 1950 and 1956, manufacturing employment in the Mound Road corridor jumped from twenty-two thousand to sixty-two thousand. A similar industrial corridor emerged after the war in western Wayne County, along the railway line north of Plymouth Road. Between 1949 and 1955, Ford, Chevrolet, GM Hydramatic, and Fisher Body established new plants in suburban Livonia. Manufacturing employment in the Plymouth Road corridor increased from sixty-eight hundred in 1950 to twenty-eight thousand in 1956. Altogether, by 1958 just over one-half of the manufacturing jobs in the Detroit region were in Macomb and Oakland Counties and those portions of Wayne County outside of the central city.

As manufacturers moved production from Detroit to the suburbs, they also looked to sites beyond the region and even the state. A case in point is the postwar restructuring undertaken by the Holley Carburetor Company. In 1951, Holley left its aging main plant on the west side of Detroit and relocated to Warren. Eight years later, it transferred its aircraft-division work to a factory in Clare, in mid-Michigan, a move that affected about one thousand employees in the Detroit area. Meanwhile, carburetor manufacturing shifted to Holley's plants in Paris, Tennessee (opened in 1948), and Bowling Green, Kentucky (opened in 1952).

The Big 3 restructured operations during the 1950s by bringing body and parts manufacturing into company-owned plants. The loss of contracts put inordinate pressure on independent suppliers. After Murray Body Company lost its contract with Ford, it closed in 1955, leaving behind a large, six-story structure (today's Russell Industrial Center). Similar action by Chrysler forced Motor Products Corporation to shut its Mack Avenue plant in 1956, which ended six hundred jobs. In 1959, after Midland-Ross lost its Chrysler frame business, it laid off twenty-five hundred and closed the former Midland Steel factory on Mt. Elliott. Reductions in subcontracting by General Motors cost jobs, particularly in Michigan, as independent suppliers saw their work integrated into GM parts plants, many of which were located outside the state.

A sharp drop in Detroit-area employment also came when Ford moved parts and engine manufacturing away from its Rouge complex in Dearborn to factories chiefly in Ohio. The effects on the Rouge were dramatic. With eighty-five thousand workers in 1945, Rouge employment fell to sixty-two thousand in 1949, fifty-four thousand in 1954, and thirty thousand in 1960. Hardest hit by Ford's decentralization drive was the Motor Building, which saw much of its work transferred to the new Cleveland engine plant, and the production foundry, which was where a considerable number of African Americans long worked. The historian Nelson Lichtenstein, writing in *Life and Labor: Dimensions of American Working-Class History*, says that Ford's actions "decimated the workforce in two of the largest and most militant buildings at the Rouge." It was hardly a coincidence that UAW Local 600, the aggressive and left-led union of Rouge workers, had long been a thorn in the side of Ford management. In 1947–48, Rouge workers represented 57 percent of UAW membership at Ford; a decade later, they constituted 30 percent.

If decentralization represented one way to "reset" relations between management and labor, the new technology of "automation" was another. At one level, automation represented the latest form of technological innovation in the auto industry (commonly known as "Fordism") that reached back to the introduction of moving assembly lines and highly specialized machine tools during the 1910s. What postwar automation did in the auto industry was mechanically connect sequences of machine tool operations by reducing the need for workers to move heavy castings from one machine to the next. Automation, however, did not just lessen the burdens of heavy and dangerous labor for workers. In that same postwar context, writes Sugrue in *Origins of the Urban Crisis*, "automation was primarily a weapon in the employers' anti-labor arsenal. Through automation, employers attempted to reassert control over the industrial process, chipping away at the control over production that workers had gained through intricately negotiated work rules."

It was in the making of automobile engines that automation made its greatest advances. Ford's heavily automated engine plant near Cleveland, which opened in 1952, received considerable public attention because it boosted output while dramatically reducing the costs of labor. Closer to home, the Plymouth Mound Road engine plant in Detroit—a wartime production facility that Chrysler bought from Briggs in 1953 and subsequently repurposed—opened as an automated engine plant in 1955. The Cross Company of Detroit built and installed the $2.5 million, quarter-mile-long, automated apparatus that turned out assembled V-8 engines with 25 percent fewer workers than standard assembly-line operations.

Corporate battles for production and sales left casualties in their wake, which had devastating effects on Detroit. The country's six small, independent automakers did not have the resources to retool for expensive annual model changes, nor did their diminishing market share (down to 4 percent in 1955) enable them to realize the cost benefits of automated technology. In 1954, therefore, Hudson merged with Nash (eventually becoming American Motors Corporation), and Packard merged with Studebaker. At the start of the decade, the Detroit plants of Hudson and Packard had employed 25,000 and 16,000 workers, respectively. Within three years of the mergers, these plants had closed. The geographic impact was spectacular and highly concentrated. According to Sugrue, the Michigan Employment Security Commission reported that between 1953 and 1960, the city's east side lost ten plants and 71,137 industrial jobs.

The economic effects of plant closings rippled through Detroit's retail sector and housing stock and left swaths of the city's commercial arteries and working-class neighborhoods in decay. The city's fiscal health deteriorated as industrial and commercial investments, white homeowners, and the related tax base flowed to the suburbs. The hardest hit was the city's working class and most especially recent African American migrants from the South who continued to settle in the city. Their predecessors had made gains in securing blue-collar industrial employment, but many of those job opportunities evaporated during the 1950s as factories closed, work moved out of Detroit, and automation took its toll on the demand for labor. By 1960, Sugrue argues, young African American men in Detroit found themselves entrapped in a deindustrializing central city, feeling both hopeless and angry about their poor chances of securing meaningful employment.

At the time, it was difficult to see that these developments signified any long-term trend for Detroit. Regional planners, for instance, tended to bury the hollowing out of the central city in statistics about the overall growth of the wider Detroit region. Others could take comfort in the fact that cycles of boom and bust had long been part of the DNA of the auto industry and the Detroit economy. Experienced people knew that periods of stress were always followed by periods of plenty. The fairly mild recession of 1953–54, for example, was followed by the extraordinary year of 1955, when US automakers turned out an all-time high of 9.6 million cars and trucks. The subsequent Eisenhower Recession of 1957–58 was just one of four recessions between 1949 and 1960. Officially it lasted only eight months; but it crushed the auto industry, and its impact on Detroit was especially severe and prolonged. In April 1958, the month the recession technically ended, the national unemployment rate stood at 6.7 percent. The rate in the Detroit area, however, was 15.1 percent, and as many as 40,000 out of the 230,000 unemployed workers had run out of their jobless benefits. A. H. Raskin, writing for the *New York Times* in May 1958, visited Detroit and was shocked by what he saw. "The abandoned shells of once flourishing plants," he wrote, "stand as acre-broad tombstones for companies that could not meet the test of survival in the war for market supremacy." For Raskin, the sizable investments in the downtown district, with its "glistening Civic Center" along the riverfront, stood in sharp contrast with the rest of the city. "These manifestations of well-being, even opulence, leave the visitor ill prepared for the misery that is Detroit's other side. It is to be formed in the human waste pile of the unemployed."

Raskin and other keen observers also pondered whether manufacturing levels in the city of Detroit would come back even after the Big 3 (also known as "Detroit") returned to prosperity. "The basic reason why Detroit is in trouble, apart from the current auto sag," *Time* magazine reported in April 1958, was that "the auto companies have been gradually moving out of Detroit for more than a decade. . . . And in the remaining auto plants automation is steadily shrinking the need for workers." In a sign that Detroit's future as a manufacturing center might follow that of New England, which saw its textile industry head to the South, the US Labor Department in 1959 placed the city on its list of areas of "chronic labor surplus."

City planners and officials under mayors Albert Cobo and Louis Miriani (January 1950–January 1962) responded to the dismantling of Detroit's industrial fabric with the tools they had available to them. They assembled blue-ribbon panels of community leaders, including representatives from both business and labor, to promote industrial redevelopment and diversification. Studies and conferences took up the "flight of industry." Investigators queried manufacturers about the reasons that propelled them to quit the city.

Harold Black, in his 1958 "Detroit: A Case Study in Industrial Problems of a Central City," noted that labor costs and taxes mattered, but a top issue was the lack of suitable land for factory expansion, truck deliveries, and off-street parking for employees within the crowded industrial districts of Detroit. Strides were made to deal with closed "ghost plants." In 1960, the New York syndicate of Helmsley-Spear bought the seventeen acres of buildings and land of the Murray Body factory. Some plants were privately purchased and converted into warehousing. The sprawling Packard plant on East Grand Boulevard, empty since 1954, was "cut down" into manufacturing and storage space for small industry. Chemical Processing Inc. set up shop there in late 1958 (it remained there for fifty-two years), and by 1960, it shared the Packard site with three dozen other industrial enterprises. Other long-standing factories disappeared from the map of the city before the end of the decade. In the mid-1950s, the venerable Detroit-Michigan Stove Company (which had roots dating to 1864) merged with the Welbilt Corporation of Queens, New York. Welbilt closed the Detroit plant in the spring of 1957, leaving behind fifteen empty industrial buildings along East Jefferson near the bridge to Belle Isle. Vandalism and fires soon plagued the unsecured site, prompting the city to take legal steps against the company. But then a six-alarm fire left the structures in ruin, and in May 1959, the remnants of the stove plant were razed. That same year, the Hudson factory at East Jefferson and Connor came down.

Planners and officials also responded to long-term industrial decline by clearing land for factories. The logic behind these efforts was simple: if the city could not force companies to remain in Detroit, perhaps it could give them an incentive to stay by offering them publicly subsidized cheap land for new facilities within the city. Under the guise of urban renewal, the city used its power of eminent domain to take private property in areas designated as "slums" or "blighted" and to clear and sell the land to private developers, who would then offer tracts to light-industrial enterprises. Two such projects were launched in the 1950s. The first was the West Side Industrial Project, which targeted seventy-five acres of the Corktown neighborhood due west of downtown. It started in 1957 after several years of delay due in part to determined opposition from Corktown's predominantly Maltese and Mexican residents. While the federal government covered two-thirds of the cost of the Corktown initiative, the city financed the second one without federal aid. It focused on a district northeast of the downtown core: the Milwaukee Junction area, the home to a dense constellation of industrial properties that dated to the late nineteenth century. The initial project, however, encompassed a mere seventeen acres. Given the magnitude of Detroit's loss of manufacturing, neither attempt at industrial revitalization added up to much. In *Redevelopment and Race: Planning a Finer City in Postwar Detroit*, the urban-planning historian June Manning Thomas notes that city planners in 1956 had identified 2,540 acres of industrial land as "extremely or considerably deteriorated."

The unprecedented expansion of the US economy from early 1961 until late 1969, which coincided with Jerome Cavanagh's tenure as mayor of Detroit, erased many doubts about Detroit's economic viability. Nationally, unemployment fell from 6.6 percent in 1961 to 4.6 percent in 1965. Detroit may have experienced its most prosperous years ever. Visions of manufacturing decline vanished as auto production hit twelve million cars and trucks in 1965 (up from seven million in 1961). Auto sales soared, as did corporate profits. Employment at the Big 3 surged. Chrysler's Hamtramck assembly plant (commonly known as Dodge Main) took on an additional five thousand workers during the mid-decade boom. The Detroit unemployment rate plummeted from 10.9 percent in 1961 to 4.3 percent in 1964. When in early 1966 the national rate fell to 3.5 percent, joblessness in Detroit and other Great Lakes manufacturing centers dove below 2.5 percent. Worries about labor shortages (and inflation) appeared in the business press. In Detroit, a roaring economy along with $47.7 million in federal money granted to the city to wage a war on poverty brought unemployment among African Americans down to 3.4 percent in 1965 (compared with 17.4 percent in 1961), while the percentage of African American households in poverty declined from 21 percent in 1965 to 16 percent in 1967. Urban redevelopment plans sprouted, with $143 million spent on twenty projects by 1965. Detroit's tarnished image as a place to do business improved. The city's finances turned around with the enactment in 1962 of a 1 percent income tax on residents and on nonresidents who worked in the city—a tax that fell on individuals, not on businesses. The hemorrhaging of jobs during the 1950s faded from view as some companies sought plant sites in the city. In 1965, Chrysler started construction of the Huber Foundry at Mt. Elliott and Lynch. As a sign that maybe

Detroit could compete with southern locations, in 1963, one small auto supplier, the Crescent Brass & Pin Company, *returned* to Detroit after five years in Americus, Georgia. According to the *Toledo Blade* on September 8, 1963, the company cited the lack of skilled workers and supporting machine and tool shops as the reason for abandoning its experiment in the South. As a sign of revival, in 1963, Detroit came off the federal list of economically distressed cities. The following year, Mayor Cavanagh could confidently tell New York financial leaders that Detroit was in the throes of a "comeback."

A more critical mind, however, would have seen Detroit's boom years of the 1960s as something akin to a mirage sustained by heavy doses of wishful thinking. First of all, the Detroit of the Big 3 was not the same thing as the working population of Detroit. According to a 1964 study by the UAW Research Department, the output of the motor-vehicle industry grew 42.5 percent from 1956 to 1963, and employees saw their real compensation grow an average of 2.7 percent per year. Yet the actual number of production workers required fell 7.7 percent due to productivity enhancements and the use of overtime, which increased 3.9 percent over the same period. By not having to hire additional workers and pay them benefits, companies saved money with overtime labor. Overtime work certainly fattened the paychecks of autoworkers. But it also precluded the hiring of those who needed a well-paying job (a kind of "silent firing"). The UAW calculated that in 1965 the average of 5.9 hours per week of overtime among the employed saved the auto industry from hiring people for one hundred thousand jobs. Management practices, therefore, baked into the economy a certain level of structural unemployment.

Second, the Detroit region was not the same thing as the city that lay at the core of the region. The two did not benefit the same way from the prosperity. The number of production workers in the Detroit area grew from 295,800 in 1958 to 394,300 in 1967 (33 percent). Yet virtually all the growth occurred outside the city. Whereas the number of production workers outside the city grew by 62 percent during these same years, the city added only 3 percent. During the boom years between 1963 and 1967, 56,400 production workers were added to the suburbs, but only 8,200 within the city. Chrysler and Ford built new factories in Sterling Heights in Macomb County. Meanwhile, Chrysler's aging plants in the city churned out production with high concentrations of African Americans (65–70 percent) in their workforces. (These were the very same obsolete factories that faced the next significant bout of economic restructuring during the 1970s and

Manufacturing Employment of Production Workers in the Detroit Area and the City of Detroit, 1939–1977

Year	Workers in Detroit area	Workers outside Detroit	Workers inside Detroit	Detroit's share of area workers (%)
1939	315,200	133,300	181,900	57.7
1947	468,200	186,700	281,500	60.1
1954	434,400	202,100	232,300	53.5
1958	295,800	150,700	145,100	49.0
1963	329,700	188,300	141,400	42.9
1967	394,300	244,700	149,600	37.9
1972	367,000	241,200	125,800	34.3
1977	369,600	262,100	107,500	29.1

Source: US Department of Commerce, Bureau of the Census, *Census of Manufactures* (1947–77).

1980s.) In 1958, city and suburbs split the number of production workers just about evenly. By 1967, the city's share had fallen to 38 percent. Fifteen years of deindustrialization had eroded the city's capacity to support manufacturing employment.

More importantly, despite general improvements in the labor market in the mid-1960s, the rate of joblessness for African Americans remained three times that of whites. In 1967, the annual rate in the Detroit area was 4.5 percent; black unemployment was 10.9 percent, white 3.2 percent. The geographic concentration of racialized unemployment and poverty revealed things to be a lot worse. In Detroit's poverty zone, according to Robert Conot in *American Odyssey*, the effective employment rate was more like 30 percent. In July 1967, the unemployment rate in the Detroit area jumped to 6.2 percent—at which time, Sidney Fine estimates in *Violence in the Model City*, joblessness among young African Americans (eighteen to twenty-four years of age) was 25–30 percent. Raskin, again writing for the *New York Times* in December 1967, stated that efforts to address the "hard-core unemployed" through federally funded job-training programs seemingly trained blacks for unemployment—for manufacturing jobs that steadily moved to the distant suburbs and for construction jobs from which they were systematically excluded by building-trades unions.

In 1966, Mayor Cavanagh told a subcommittee of the US Senate that over the next ten years, Detroit needed *$10 billion* in federal money to mount a successful fight against poverty. (Instead, between 1968 and 1975, Detroit's Model Neighborhoods program received $73.3 million.) The July 1967 riot/rebellion in Detroit also unmasked hard, costly, and politically unpalatable truths about class and racial inequality in the major metropolitan areas of the nation. However, coming as it did during a period of national affluence, it also reinforced what has proven to be an indelible yet mistaken belief that the economy of Detroit and its vital manufacturing base were fundamentally sound before 1967.

Joe's Record Shop

Marsha Music

Marsha Music, aka Marsha Battle Philpot, was interviewed by Tobi Voigt, September 21, 2015. The complete original transcript can be accessed via the Detroit Historical Society's electronic portal (detroithistorical.org). On July 21, 2016, she recalled the events of July 1967 in her opening address at the Detroit 67 Community Open House, held at the Detroit Historical Museum. Marsha graciously edited those transcribed comments and her oral history transcript for this volume.

My father, Joe Von Battle, opened a record store on Hastings Street in Detroit in 1945. He gathered up the records from his home, where he lived with his wife and four children, and opened shop. He sold records from opera to Elvis, Frank Sinatra to Nat King Cole—but Joe's Record Shop was known for blues music. He ran the store with his son, Joe Jr., and his clerk, Shirley Baker—a striking young beauty who later became my mother. He sold the blues to many of the black people who were still, after three decades, coming up in droves from the South, to be segregated into the Hastings Street and Black Bottom community.

He opened just two years after the 1943 race riot had ravaged many commercial storefronts on Hastings, a street full of immigrant—mostly Jewish—shopkeepers and black business folk and residents. Detroit was dynamic and musical; there were dozens of record shops in the city. My father was notable for not only selling records but for establishing several record labels and national distribution deals with Chess, Savoy, King, and other companies and for launching the recording career of the Rev. C. L. Franklin and his daughter Aretha.

By 1948, my father created a recording studio in the back of his shop and recorded artists who walked in off of Hastings Street—John Lee Hooker, Johnny Bassett, Washboard Willie, Little Sonny, and many others. It is believed that he was the first independent black record producer in post-war America.

In 1953, Joe Von Battle went a few blocks up Hastings Street to hear an amazing preacher at the New Bethel Baptist Church. Rev. C. L. Franklin's style of demonstrative, musical preaching was a prototype of today's black preaching; he was known as the Man with the Million-Dollar Voice. After Rev. Franklin's Sunday-night radio show and my father's radio show on CKLW that followed it—where they both played sermons by Franklin— calls would come in to the record shop from all over the country: "Send me that new Rev. C. L. Franklin on the fastest train coming!" My father shipped records by mail order, but the demand for these recordings became so great that Phil and Leonard Chess of Chicago (whom my father had preceded in the recording business) handled the national distribution. Black congregations were hungry for Franklin's messages on faith, hope, and power not just for the hereafter but to cope with the harshness that they faced on this earth—in Detroit and beyond.

-- --

One of my dad's first recordings was "Hastings Street Opera," a classic Detroit piano blues record. Bob White, an itinerant poet, walked up and down Hastings Street talking and rapping. He was known as the Detroit Count, and he made this record in which he recounted all the bars and clubs on Hastings Street. It's a joking, novelty record, and he signifies about my dad's store, "Joe's Record Shop . . . he's got everything in there but a T-Bone steak." He declares this in jest, but he came to it honestly; when business was slow, my father would sell straw boater hats or tall sugarcane stalks outside the shop.

The sugarcane was a sweet treat, the very idea of it a marvel to us kids, for we northern-born youngsters were disconnected from much having to do with the earth or farming or the hard life that many of our relatives had lived in the segregated, sharecropping South. We were terrified and fascinated about anything approaching that old life, even dad's old "country" blues friends. Even the most friendly or hilarious had a certain gravitas; we had a respect and awe of their unspoken past lives. We knew that there was something going on in the South that was much different than what we had experienced. They didn't talk about it, trying to protect us from the terrors and humiliations of their old, southern lives—and to protect us from the terrible knowledge that in some ways, life in Detroit hadn't changed much in that respect, at all.

My mother wasn't born in the South. She was born in Detroit and raised in an enclave of blacks on the west side, off of Tireman Avenue—a Polish neighborhood. My dad was a Macon, Georgia, man, and this was the source of endless foolishness between them. My mother, though ever gracious to others, had an upturned nose about his "country" ways, his food, and his blues and southern friends.

-- --

By the fifties, the music was changing; it was the beginning of rock and roll, and many blacks' tastes were changing to the new, modern music. My mother didn't like those "country" men like Muddy Waters and Howlin' Wolf, singing about the train going through town. A new record company called Motown was making the smooth, exciting music that my mother loved.

By 1959, two gentlemen from France, Jacques Demetre and Marcel Chauvard, came to Detroit to write about the blues in America. When they arrived, they knew the place to go was Joe's Record Shop. One of the now-iconic photos that they took is one with John Lee Hooker and his guitar. They were capturing the end of an era.

In 1960, my father was compelled to relocate his record shop, as the Chrysler Freeway was being constructed right through Hastings Street. For years, there was seething resentment in the community about the urban renewal, aka "Negro removal," that had ended Black Bottom and Hastings Street, eliminating not just buildings but a generation of entrepreneurial experience and wealth. Though most black businesses could not survive the demise of Hastings, some who did—like my father—ended up on 12th Street, so there was a kind of a built-in community when we got there. But the growing change in the culture was evident: the transition from the South to the North; a greater schism in social classes; even the music we sold changed—now everybody wanted to buy the new urban sounds of Motown.

In this vortex of social and musical change, my father became sick with Addison's disease, an affliction of the adrenals that was finally stabilized by a new miracle drug called cortisone. His convivial tastes of Scotch whisky at the back of the shop with friends made a sharp turn into alcoholism.

Though his transition to 12th Street was tough, Joe was still "the man" in the record biz. Berry Gordy, whom my father had preceded in business by fifteen years, would come by Dad's record shops on Hastings and in the new neighborhood. Many Motown artists would come by, like the Motown bassist James Jamerson and vocalist Mary Wells. Jamerson had played on Dad's blues records, one with an artist named Washboard Willy, a percussionist who had a whole multi-instrument contrivance. But now Jamerson played his slick bass sounds in the Hitsville House, down the street and around the corner on West Grand Boulevard.

-- --

Musically, industrially, artistically, spiritually—there was so much going on in the city it seemed about to burst with energy and art. Even so, there was a bristling tension in the air, combined with the heat of the summer—itself a harbinger. The presence of the police in the black neighborhoods in Detroit had always been oppressive; their power was brutal, arbitrary, and precincts were feared as dens of torment. Though Detroit wasn't the segregated South, there were neighborhoods where we could not live, stores and shops—even downtown—where we were not welcome, and jobs for which you better not even think you were going to be hired.

Black Detroiters were terrorized in the riots of 1943, mostly over competition with whites for housing. Our parents watched in incredulity as whites left the city's magnificent homes. In the 1960s, blacks were pushed from Black Bottom along Hastings Street to neighborhoods where they were boxed in again by segregation, albeit in the vintage homes of the east side and the handsome brick homes and flats of the west. In 1967, Vietnam veterans were returning home from yet another US war where blacks had shed blood for our country, yet many were denied housing and jobs. Under the surface of solidness—of the neighborhoods, the musicality of the churches, radio stations, and record companies—the black community heaved with bitterness, even as city officials called Detroit "The Model City."

In July of 1966, the lid blew off on the east side, on Kercheval Street. A revolt against police brutality was quickly quelled with a rainstorm and arrests, a victory that gave officials a false sense of Detroit's invulnerability to civil unrest. The "'66 mini-riot" was a precursor of things to come.

On Saturday afternoons, at the record shop, I stuck my head out the door and watched in awe as new, black militants strode up 12th Street in berets and leather and dashikis. They were regarded, variously, as troublemakers (by my father) or superheroes (by me) and everything in between (by the community). Their presence was evidence of a new jubilant, vigorous Black Pride and signified growing anger and impatience with inequality. It was a time of great social upheaval, and my father's drinking grew worse; my thirteen-year-old world was spiraling into turmoil and rebellion.

-- --

It was July. It was Saturday night. It was hot. The telephone rang in the middle of the night; someone had called my father and said that "something" was happening on 12th Street. We knew what "something" meant. He jumped out of bed, got his gun (most businessmen carried), and headed over to 12th Street. We (my mother, myself, and three siblings) went back to sleep after a while, worried about Daddy.

Our house was in Highland Park, a tiny city within the City of Detroit, a couple of miles—and a world away—from 12th Street. When we woke again in the morning, we ran out onto John R Street and looked west toward 12th; over the horizon, we could see a sky full of black smoke. We didn't know all that was going on, but we knew that our lives would never be the same.

My father came back home and told our mother what was going on, and by that time, we had seen on TV that there was a "riot." We were terrified with the thought that he and the other business folks on the block were guarding their stores and writing "Soul Brother" signs, in a plea for solidarity that was brave, pitiful—and futile.

Television stopped reporting on the "disturbance" early on, but reports were coming in from friends, relatives, and neighbors. Other streets were consumed in the unrest: 14th Street, Linwood, Dexter, the main arteries of the west side—soon, east-side streets too. The looting was spreading, and it was clear that it was not just a "criminal element" but regular working folks, too. A lot of whites were in the streets looting, although that was rarely reported. One thing for sure, it was no "race riot"—race against race. It was rioting within a rebellion, against whatever power there was.

The conflagration continued for days. In our neighborhood in Highland Park, we were far away, relatively speaking, from the mayhem on 12th Street. Life in our neighborhood was tense, as the news spread, but our streets, full of middle-class minimansions and shady elm trees, were as peaceful as always. It was an utter shock—even in the midst of the mounting tension— to look out from my ruffled-curtained bedroom and see a massive green tank slowly, incongruously, rolling its way up quiet John R. Incredulously, across the street from our house on California Street, soldiers looked out from the balcony of the Monterey Motel onto our Arts and Crafts houses and manicured lawns, bayonets over their shoulders as they lolled around smoking cigarettes on R&R, like in a bizarre dream. Our mother cautioned us not to wave.

After the first days, the anger and tension of martial law in Detroit permeated both cities, and soon, the unrest and looting reached Hamilton in

Highland Park. Our neighborhood, on the other side of our small town, remained unchanged but for a curfew and the daunting presence of the military.

-- --

My father had been on 12th Street, standing guard in front of his shop with his gun and his "Soul Brother" sign. After the first day or so, the authorities stopped letting business owners guard their shops, and my father returned home defeated. He never shook the feeling that by halting his efforts to protect his store, they had guaranteed its destruction. Days later, they allowed Daddy to return to a smoldering 12th Street. He took my uncle, my little brother, and my cousin—the first look at the damage was deemed a job for men and boys. But the next day, he took me. The noise and smoke and burnt buildings made 12th Street hellish. We walked through the wet, fetid debris of what had been one of the seminal record shops in Detroit.

I trailed Daddy silently as we trudged through charred rubble and melted vinyl records. Some of the most significant voices in recorded history were in those fire-hose-soaked reel-to-reel tapes, unwound and slithering like water snakes. Thousands of songs, sounds, and voices of an era—most never pressed onto records—were gone forever. I believe Daddy died that day.

My father's alcoholism gravely worsened, after his life's work and provision for his family was destroyed—by looters; by the explosion of the pressure cooker of racism and discrimination; by the move from Hastings to a new and different location, with a new modern music; by the turning of his beloved first record shop and studio into a freeway service drive. He returned home from his ruined 12th Street store and proceeded to drink himself to death. Though Joe Von Battle was not pronounced dead or buried until 1973, he died on that day in 1967.

Benefit of the Redoubt

Jeffrey Horner

We just got tired of running, and we didn't want to have to run again.

—Lillie Mae Wiley, Virginia Park Association

On the evening of July 23, 1967, the greatest Detroit Tiger ever went two-for-three in a winning effort in the second game of a home doubleheader and, after having learned of a major disturbance near his old east-side neighborhood, left the stadium while still in uniform in a quixotic attempt to help restore order. William Wattison Horton, just six years earlier, was a baseball phenom at nearby Northwestern High School; he has always credited family, friends, and coaches from the Virginia Park neighborhood for his professional career that began right out of Northwestern. That day his old neighborhood was in flames.

The Virginia Park neighborhood was initially developed as a Jewish district in the 1920s. When Detroit's most populous black district, Paradise Valley, was designated as blighted and then razed under urban renewal and the Interstate Highway Act in the late 1950s, many evicted residents moved to the 12th Street commercial district of Virginia Park, where many held jobs with Jewish-owned businesses.

According to Thomas Sugrue in *The Origins of the Urban Crisis*, pre–World War II black residents were concentrated in four areas of the city, with about 75 percent living in the Paradise Valley and Black Bottom districts, east of downtown. With the destruction of these neighborhoods and following a period of significant postwar demographic growth, Virginia Park became a majority-black district by the mid-1960s, in many respects serving as the new home for those who had been displaced by urban renewal from Detroit's lower east side.

According to the National Advisory Commission on Civil Disorders,

On either side of 12th Street were neat, middle class districts. Along 12th Street itself, however, crowded apartment houses created a density of more than 21,000 per square mile, almost double the city average.

The movement of people when the slums of Black Bottom had been cleared for urban renewal had changed 12th Street from an integrated community to an almost totally black one, in which only a number of merchants remained white. Only 18 percent of the residents were homeowners. Twenty-five percent of the housing was considered so substandard as to require clearance. Another 19 percent had major deficiencies.

The path to Virginia Park was a cauldron of day-to-day trials, gross indignities, threats to one's livelihood, and employment and housing discrimination, much as it had been throughout modern history for African Americans. This essay examines the quotidian circumstances, systemic discriminations, and the imbalance of resources leading up to and helping to cause the events in Detroit in July 1967. It closes with a critique of the solutions prescribed by the National Advisory Commission on Civil Disorders in its landmark report released in 1968, also known as the Kerner Report.

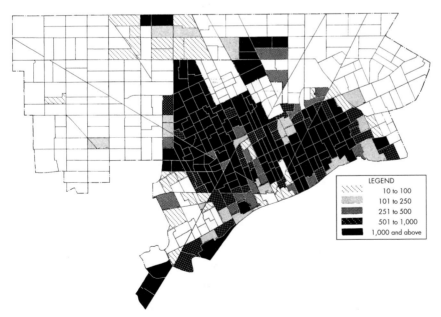

Black population, 1960. Based on US Bureau of Census Statistics, prepared by the Research Division Commission on Community Relations.

Kerner Report Findings

While several full-length books have done an excellent job of summarizing the events and causes of Detroit's 1967 rebellion, including Sidney Fine's *Violence in the Model City* and Hubert Locke's *The Detroit Riot of 1967*, this chapter focuses primarily on the fundamental inequities listed in the Kerner Report's first and second levels of intensity leading up to July 1967 in Detroit.

The Kerner Commission, appointed by President Lyndon Johnson days after order was restored in Detroit, sought to investigate the events, causes, outcomes, and commonalities of twenty-four major incidents in twenty-three cities in the United States throughout the 1960s. In the commissioners' final report, they ranked causes of endemic civil insurrections in black urban communities throughout the United States:

First Level of Intensity
1. Police practices
2. Unemployment and underemployment
3. Inadequate housing

Second Level of Intensity
4. Inadequate education
5. Poor recreation facilities and programs
6. Ineffectiveness of the political structure and grievance mechanisms

Third Level of Intensity
7. Disrespectful white attitudes
8. Discriminatory administration of justice
9. Inadequacy of federal programs
10. Inadequacy of municipal services
11. Discriminatory consumer and credit practices
12. Inadequate welfare programs

Police Brutality and Disparate Treatment of Blacks

According to the Kerner Report, the most immediate and direct societal inequity was disparate treatment of African Americans by local police forces in comparison to treatment of whites. Given the city's intransigence toward integrating its police forces commensurate with its racial populations and its infamous history of poor race relations between black residents and white police, this finding was hardly surprising.

A most thorough and penetrating history of this conflict is offered in Joe Darden and Richard Thomas's *Detroit: Race Riots, Racial Conflicts, and Efforts to Bridge the Racial Divide*. As they point out, its antecedents are directly related to enforcing segregation:

> In some ways, the white police force in the black ghettos functioned as the first line of white defense against the invading "black hordes" that, if not checked, would overwhelm surrounding white neighborhoods. White police brutality, therefore, often functioned, whether deliberately or not, as an effective method of racial social control. During this period, when the black population was rapidly increasing in Detroit and bursting through the seams of the ghettos to which black people were restricted, white police brutality could (and often did) maintain the racial status quo when all other efforts to check black movement failed or were weakening in the face of black protest.

On March 21, 1953, the *Michigan Chronicle*, a black-owned newspaper, described police brutality in the most recent ten years as "the symbol of everything that was wrong with Detroit" and reported that NAACP officials "spent most of their time processing complaints against the police department."

Efforts to eliminate or minimize instances of racially charged police brutality were largely feckless and had been long before the *Chronicle* editorial. Darden and Thomas write,

> In late August (of 1939) the Committee to End Police Brutality, still under the leadership of the NAACP Detroit president, Dr. James J. McClendon, staged mass protest meetings on nine playgrounds throughout the city. Speakers discussed the objectives of the meetings and listed incidents of police brutality. People were encouraged to sign petitions for the removal of the police commissioner from office. The next month the committee submitted a petition to the Detroit Common Council (now City Council) requesting that the Council investigate the policies and practices of the police department, an investigation that, the committee was convinced, would lead to the firing of the police commissioner.

Suffice it to say that the police commissioner kept his job, and reports of police brutality continued apace. Perhaps no statistic better exemplifies the police force's antipathy toward blacks than this one from the 1943 riot: "White rioters numbered in the thousands, while blacks numbered in the hundreds, [yet] the police killed 17 blacks (some were shot in the back), but not one white. On Woodward Avenue, a major thoroughfare on the edge of the ghetto, white mobs beat blacks under the very eyes of the police" (Richard Thomas, *Life for Us Is What We Make It*).

The intractability of racial order at the end of a police baton was so ingrained in Detroit that Wayne County Sheriff Roman A. Gribbs, running for mayor two years after the 1967 riot, won on a law-and-order campaign platform. Stepped-up policing practices and the controversial Stop the Robberies, Enjoy Safe Streets (STRESS) program enacted by Police Commissioner John Nichols were politically disastrous and contributed in part to Mayor Gribbs opting not to run for reelection in 1973. His successor, Coleman A. Young, pledged to disband STRESS and other racially selective policing practices and to better integrate the police force. In a city of over 660,000 blacks, he won overwhelmingly.

Housing and Employment Discrimination in Detroit

Finding a suitable residence was an onerous challenge for those who had been displaced by urban renewal, much as it had been throughout the city's history. While the proportion of blacks had grown to over 40 percent of the city's population, they were still met with hostility in most neighborhoods. Recent in the minds of many were the deadly 1943 race riots, ignited largely by black residents seeking housing in majority-white neighborhoods on the east side and increasingly integrating factory floors. Tensions in neighborhoods and factories had roiled for years, prompting *Life* magazine to publish a marquee story, "Detroit Is Dynamite," ten months before the '43 riots. The story depicted housing conditions for blacks as tenuous and deleterious, and *Life*'s publisher limited the story's distribution to North America, presumably to suppress its possible use as anti-American propaganda by Axis powers. When the fuse reached its terminus, Belle Isle, its east side and downtown exploded into war, with numerous outbreaks of hand-to-hand street fighting, murder, arson, vandalism, and property crimes resulting in thirty-four dead (mostly black), hundreds arrested, and significant property destruction.

Causes of the severe concentration of the vast majority of the city's black residents into a handful of districts included public- and private-sector race discrimination, as well as a severe shortage of new housing. As pointed out by Thomas Sugrue in *The Origins of the Urban Crisis*, fewer than 10 percent of the city's 545,000 housing units were available to blacks in 1947. In addition, a 1945 housing survey reported an unbelievable 99.2 percent occupancy rate for the city, brought on by a virtual freeze on new residential construction and mobilization for the war effort.

Some new housing units were built as the Great Depression wound down, but blacks were not allowed to purchase them. In 1941, a six-foot concrete wall was built adjacent to the historically black Eight Mile and Wyoming neighborhood, a Federal Housing Authority–approved "compromise" negotiated between government and a housing developer to approve loan guarantees to banks writing FHA-insured mortgages to white homeowners on the other side of the wall. Blacks, already limited in finding safe and secure housing, were literally walled off from the new homes in an adjacent neighborhood.

Geographic housing constraints for blacks were so severe that on November 23, 1946, *Collier's* magazine foretold the problems that occurred in the 1960s: "Unsolved, the Negro housing dilemma costs Detroit heavily in other ways than jittery nerves. Badly in need of a medical center, express highways, parks and other deferred civic improvements, Detroit must wait indefinitely for them. The land they will occupy now houses hundreds of Negro families who can't be evicted because there's no place for them to go."

It is difficult to fully disentangle the sources of racial animus aimed at blacks. But one major dimension arose on crowded factory floors during World War II. Historically, blacks fortunate enough to be hired for automotive factory work were given what Sugrue has characterized as the "meanest and dirtiest jobs," although managers were nimble at elevating black workers to higher positions when it suited their needs. As described by George Galster, in presentations of his 2012 book *Driving Detroit*, the Packard Motor Company, seeking to heighten racial tensions among its mostly white workers in order to sow dissent within the union local, integrated black workers with whites on shop floors, forcing a wildcat walkout by twenty-five thousand white workers. According to Joe Darden, Richard Hill, June Thomas, and Richard Thomas in their seminal work *Detroit: Race and Uneven Development*, one hate-striker commented on the indignity of having to work alongside blacks: "I'd rather see Hitler and Hirohito win than have to work next to a nigger."

Indeed, workplace discrimination was commonplace in many northern states, which had not adopted the state-sanctioned discrimination laws allowed by *Plessy v. Ferguson*, known as Jim Crow. Throughout the South, separate but equal was the law of the land; while in the North, it was the practice of the land.

As discussed by Reynolds Farley, Sheldon Danziger, and Harry J. Holzer in *Detroit Divided*, in 1940, the Ford Motor Company's local workforce of eighty-five thousand was over 20 percent black, and, remarkably, more than half of all black men employed in the metro area worked at Ford. While Detroit's role as the Arsenal of Democracy in World War II changed the employment calculus for blacks in factories, employment discrimination was rife in other sectors.

In nonindustrial employment sectors, blacks faced limited opportunities and, if they were hired at all, were given the least desirable jobs. According to Sugrue, blacks fared best in municipal positions, filling 36 percent of city jobs in 1946, roughly commensurate to the city's population. Many of these positions were as lower-paying janitors, groundskeepers, and sanitation workers. Other industries were less receptive to hiring blacks. Retail sales positions were all but closed to them except for backroom work, as retailers were fearful of their white customers having to interact with black clerks and salespeople.

Apprenticeship programs in trade unions were also all but closed to blacks. This dynamic was especially pernicious, given that most apprentices had a long and higher-paying skilled-trades career after training. As cited by Sugrue, the Detroit Urban League reported that as recently as 1966, there were 41 black apprentices in all skilled-trades unions out of 2,363 apprentices, a rate of 1.7 percent. That percentage declined from over 2 percent ten years earlier.

Schools, Recreation, and Politics

While Detroit Public Schools had no official segregation policies, significant evidence suggests that the Board of Education pursued unofficial policies aimed at promoting racial harmony through segregated schools. In the 1930s, the school board transformed Sidney Miller Intermediate School near the Black Bottom residential district into a high school and allowed students to transfer. Jeffrey Mirel, in *The Rise and Fall of an Urban School System: Detroit, 1907–81*, writes,

> From its inception, Miller fed into Eastern High School. During the depression, when high school enrollments soared, an increasing number of black

students from Miller went on to Eastern. By September, 1933, Eastern, like most of the Detroit high schools, was severely overcrowded. Unlike the other schools, however, Eastern was also racially integrated. Apparently unwilling to maintain Eastern as an integrated high school, the board transformed Miller into a senior high and announced a liberal policy for students who wished to transfer to other schools. Since the Miller attendance area was almost completely black, the transfer policy enabled the few white students still in the area to leave the school. While the board justified the creation of the new high school and the transfer policy as legitimate responses to overcrowding, both actions, in effect, created a segregated, black high school in Detroit. The importance of race in these decisions is underscored by the fact that, despite the severe overcrowding of all the high schools in the city in the 1930s, no other intermediate schools were elevated to senior high status and, with the exception of Western High School (which was rebuilt after a fire in 1936), no new high schools were constructed during this period. In short, the creation of Miller High School was a clear case of deliberate school segregation.

Private youth and adult recreation options were arguably even more limited than school and employment opportunities, and most were inferior experiences if offered at all. In the 1940s, the Bob-Lo Excursion Company, a private, "no coloreds allowed" amusement park, was forced to integrate by the US Supreme Court (*Bob-Lo Excursion Co. v Michigan*). Before this decision was handed down, Bob-Lo's ownership interests had relaxed its discriminatory practices to allow blacks and other undesirables to visit on Mondays only, seemingly because another park with similar offerings that was open to blacks was doing burgeoning business. Once Bob-Lo became fully desegregated, nearby Sugar Island Park shut down for lack of business. In the city of Oak Park on Detroit's northern border, the private Crystal Pool closed and was sold off to a shopping-mall developer when faced with having to integrate.

Black citizens seeking redress in City Hall were often met with indifference or buck-passing. The fundamental problem was that the nine-member Detroit Common Council was elected on an at-large basis, with each member representing the interests of the entire city. As such, residents of majority-black districts had to compete with the majority-white citywide population. The only black member in 1967 was Rev. Nicholas Hood Sr. Councilman Hood lived only a few blocks from 12th Street and, tellingly, received threats to his personal safety during the riot, causing him and his family to temporarily relocate to another part of the city.

With the passage of open-housing laws in the late 1940s, the forefront of local politics in the 1950s was local community groups fighting neighborhood integration. Albert Cobo, elected mayor in 1949, ran on an explicit platform of opposition to the "Negro invasion" made possible by open housing and public housing sites. He unsurprisingly swept the heavily defended white neighborhood subdivisions on the north side and surprisingly won the vote of UAW members who were more fearful of having to integrate with blacks than what a Republican mayor (and former city treasurer) might try to do to their paychecks. He was reelected in 1953.

During this time, angry black residents began to back increasingly radical players in labor unions and local clergy. Coleman Young's reputation in union politics as a street fighter was galvanized in the 1950s, when he defied the House Un-American Activities Committee during the Red Scare, going so far as to correct a southern congressman's vernacular use of the word *Negro*. He was elected to the state senate in 1964, serving there until elected mayor in 1973.

Albert Cleage was a Presbyterian minister who split with the church in the 1950s in a dispute over how to best minister to the city's disenfranchised black congregants. He then founded the Central Congregation Church to better meet the needs of his followers. It was renamed the the Central United Church of Christ, and following the '67 rebellion, he reformed it as the Shrine of the Black Madonna.

The Importance of an Invested Community of Stakeholders

> Home, boy,
> Home, boy,
> Everybody needs a home.
>
> —James Osterberg, aka Iggy Pop, "Home"

A mostly academic discussion has centered on the riot or rebellion question of the conflagration. Sidney Fine cited the incidents as a riot, given that chaos, disorder, looting, and lawlessness prevailed for days. More recent scholarship has described the incidents as a rebellion, caused more by police brutality, systemic employment and housing discrimination, and public and private social discrimination and less by immediate racial antipathies.

Given these adverse historical legacies faced by blacks in Detroit, there is another supporting dimension to the rebellion descriptor. While

Children gathered at a rally on Seward Avenue on July 12, 1967, eleven days before the neighborhood was struck by violence. *Detroit News* photograph, from the Detroit Historical Society Collection.

arguments for the aptness of the term *race riots* are buttressed by a 95 percent white police force overseeing a city fast approaching a 50 percent black population, a thought experiment presents itself: would the 12th Street incidents have occurred if the blind-pig raid and arrests had been carried out by exclusively black police officers? A strong case can be made that even if the raiding police were blacks who carried out their duties in the same manner, a similar incident of international renown would have ensued.

This is because the United Community League for Civic Action, the quasi-formal name of the raided establishment, served as a focal point of the community. As such, it served much as did bars and speakeasies in turn-of-the-century urban democratic strongholds, where the bartender was often highly influential, if not an elected official, trading information, gossip, favors, and whatever else one frequents social clubs for. While police reports cited the civic league as an unlicensed, after-hours drinking establishment (in a city more than familiar with the model dating to Prohibition), it nonetheless functioned as an important node of cohesion for a group of people long under siege from severe housing, employment, and police discrimination.

Benefit of the Redoubt

Therefore, it was a particularly gross and exacerbating indignity, after years of open discrimination and prejudice, to have an important social dimension of the community raided and shut down and its dozens of peaceful congregants handcuffed and taken away for booking. The sanctity of a regularly frequented place of social interaction in the black community was now destroyed, and neither baseball star Willie Horton, Congressman John Conyers, nor civil rights leader Dr. Arthur Johnson were able to halt the resulting tragedy.

However, none of this is to suggest that the incidents would not have occurred but for the raid on the civic league. Ronald Hewitt, a Detroit city planner, was interviewed in the movie *The 1967 Detroit Riots: A Community Speaks*. As an eyewitness to the events on 12th Street, Hewitt remarked, "Black folks' discontent, unhappiness, anger, rage—what happened could've happened anywhere. It just so happened to have happened up here on the corner of Clairmount and 12th Street. In fact, it had almost started a year before, in what was called the Kercheval incident, on the east side."

Like the 12th Street uprising, the Kercheval incident occurred on a hot summer night, when rioting broke out after several days of police occupation and stepped-up patrols, in response to allegations of black militants' peace disturbances. Rioting, looting, and civil disorder erupted following a car being pulled over and its occupants arrested. Accounts vary as to how order was restored after only a few hours, with some witnesses suggesting that what effectively quashed the disorder was the active presence of well-known community clergy members who convinced cooler heads to prevail.

Conclusion: Plans Forward

According to the National Advisory Commission on Civil Disorders,

> As the riot alternately waxed and waned, one area of the ghetto remained insulated. On the northeast side the residents of some 150 square blocks inhabited by 21,000 persons had, in 1966, banded together in the Positive Neighborhood Action Committee (PNAC). With professional help from the Institute of Urban Dynamics, they had organized block clubs and made plans for the improvement of the neighborhood. . . .
>
> When the riot broke out, the residents, through the block clubs, were able to organize quickly. Youngsters, agreeing to stay in the neighborhood, participated in detouring traffic. While many persons reportedly sympathized with

the idea of a rebellion against the "system," only two small fires were set—one in an empty building.

It is striking that despite the Kerner Commission's observation of the effectiveness of the Positive Neighborhood Action Committee in quelling violence and vandalism, not one of the commission's dozens of recommendations for action included direct community building. One is left to wonder whether, if the urban-renewal projects of a few years earlier had included as much community-development resources as community-destruction resources, Detroit's or other cities' civil insurrections would have occurred at all.

Indeed, many Kerner Commission recommendations (which actually called for an expansion of urban-renewal programs) advocated for yet more geographically diffuse policies for minority populations. While expansion of open-housing laws was a laudable objective given persistent residential segregation, it may have served to actually weaken existing majority-black neighborhoods by encouraging the abandonment of them.

Ultimately, preservation of primal human needs for safety, shelter, and sociability is what compelled Willie Horton to travel back in haste to 12th Street after the doubleheader. The city would have been far better off had governments, both before and after the uprising, taken heed the way Mr. Horton did to the importance of community fabric.

Defending the Divide

HOMEOWNERS' ASSOCIATIONS AND THE STRUGGLE FOR INTEGRATION IN DETROIT, 1940–1965

William Winkel

In 1940, Detroit was one of the fastest growing cities in the world. As the United States fought World War II, many thousands of people were attracted to the city's strong manufacturing sector, lured by the high wages that factory jobs offered. Southerners, both white and black, made the journey in droves. By 1948, over half a million had flocked to Detroit. The massive influx of new faces was not without great logistical challenges, as the city's borders did not grow to match its newfound population.

Housing in Detroit was a constant problem. One hundred thousand new units were built between 1945 and 1950. However, only 2 percent was available to people of color. The city's legally imposed restrictions confined blacks to older neighborhoods that were too small to accommodate the new arrivals. The primary black neighborhoods were known as Black Bottom and Paradise Valley, both located east and north of downtown. The black population in 1920 was 40,838, yet by 1940, the black population tripled to 149,119. This increase overwhelmed the available housing. In 1946, the Detroit Commission on Community Relations published a report titled "Race Relations in Housing," which stated, "Overcrowding today is often two or three times as great in the Negro areas as in neighboring white districts."

Members of the white community vowed to take action against the perceived threat of black expansion across Detroit. Accustomed to strict segregation, white residents organized homeowners' associations to protect their investments. Their entrenched belief was that the inclusion of people of color into their neighborhoods meant the end of stability. This fear, rooted in racism, was the primary driver behind white associations.

The purpose of this essay is to examine how economic interests and bigotry led to the formation and success of homeowners' associations over the course of three decades. This essay explores the relationship between homeownership and opportunity as well as the various institutional mechanisms utilized to impede black progress and protect white hegemony. The legacy of this era has permeated metro Detroit and defines the relationship between the city and the suburbs today. In order to understand the definitive features of modern Detroit, this relationship must be reckoned with.

1940–1949: Separation under Threat

Over the course of the 1940s, the racial status quo in Detroit was upended. As recounted in earlier chapters, World War II opened avenues for the black community. Aided by unions, the massive labor shortage, and President Franklin Roosevelt's Executive Order 8802, blacks were employed across the war industries. A UAW report titled "Negro Employment in Detroit Area" from 1944 found that "a 44% advance in wartime employment brought with it an advance of 103% in the total number of Negroes employed."

With greater purchasing power, blacks seeking access to middle-class neighborhoods were increasingly challenged by restrictive covenants. These legal devices, written into deeds to prevent sales of real estate to a particular segment of the population, were most commonly aimed at the black and Jewish communities but also targeted eastern Europeans, Irish, and Asians. Covenants were neither new nor unique to Detroit; they were used across the country as a means to enforce racial separation.

As the war industries ramped up production, workers needed housing. Public housing projects were deemed vital to wartime production. These projects, both single-family homes and apartments, were traditionally met with vehement local opposition. Residents feared abandonment once the war ended. The dynamic was most clearly exemplified at the Sojourner Truth housing project.

Opposition to black residents at Sojourner Truth, which was situated on Nevada Avenue between Fenelon and Justine Avenues in Detroit's predominantly white northeast area, became the segregationists' boot camp, gestating tactics, unified organizations, and political influence. The perceived threat to property values was touted as the call to arms and spurred a group of white residents to form the Seven Mile–Fenelon Improvement Association. The association launched a fierce campaign to ensure that Sojourner Truth remained white only. Opinions were injected into the debate through picketing and protesting at Common Council meetings, through an aggressive letter-writing campaign that flooded the offices of city officials, and by directly lobbying Washington lawmakers.

In the end, the federal government declared the Sojourner Truth housing project an integrated facility, but local agencies stood in opposition. The Detroit Housing Commission adopted language put forth in the Federal Housing Commission's 1936 *Underwriting Manual* declaring that "a project should not affect the racial composition of a neighborhood." Nor should it "be instrumental in introducing to the neighborhood character of property or occupancy, members of any race or nationality, or any industry whose presence will clearly be detrimental to real estate values," verbiage parroted by the Detroit Real Estate Board.

Tension increased when new residents, both white and black, were greeted by a billboard erected by the Seven Mile–Fenelon Improvement Association that read, "We Want White Tenants in Our White Community." Accompanying the billboard was a crowd of angry white residents that gathered to reinforce the message. The white mob was met by supporters of the black families moving into Sojourner Truth. Violence erupted. The clash left 40 injured and 220 arrested, with 109 remaining in custody to stand trial. Of those arrested and brought to trial, only three were not black.

The war accelerated the movement of blacks into white neighborhoods throughout the city. Damage done to those areas during the 1943 riot resulted in their eventual demolition. Urban-renewal projects after the war (known in the black community as "Negro removal" projects) hastened the redistribution of the black community across the city, even as restrictive covenants remained an impediment to free movement. However, the constitutionality of restrictive covenants was gradually being challenged across the country, including a case that began in Detroit. In 1944, the McGhee family purchased a home on Seebaldt Street on the west side. The previous owner ignored the restrictive covenant on the property and sold it to the McGhees, who were black. Prompted by neighbors, the Sipes family took the McGhees to court. The McGhee family was represented by the NAACP. While the McGhees were ultimately victorious, not all families were as lucky. On November 16, 1945, as the McGhees' case was pending, the Michigan Supreme Court upheld an order to remove a black family

Billboard erected by the white residents of the Nevada-Fenelon neighborhood protesting blacks being allowed at the Sojourner Truth housing project in 1942. Image courtesy of the Library of Congress.

from its new home on St. Aubin Street solely on the basis of the home's restrictive covenant.

By 1948, the opponents of restrictive covenants brought the matter to the US Supreme Court. *McGhee v. Sipes* reached the bench along with *Shelley v. Kraemer*, a restrictive-covenant case originating in St. Louis, Missouri, in 1945. In May, the Supreme Court ruled in *Shelley* that racially specific restrictive covenants violated the Equal Protection Clause of the Fourteenth Amendment. Despite the Court's ruling, the decision was resisted by local officials. The NAACP had to launch fresh litigation against the Detroit Housing Commission in order to get Mayor Albert Cobo and the city government to stop formally enforcing segregation.

The Supreme Court decision united white residents who were intent on preserving the all-white character of their neighborhoods. By the end of the 1940s, numerous homeowners' associations were established in Detroit, among them the Ruritan Park Civic Association, the Courville District Improvement Association, and the Seven Mile–Fenelon Improvement Association.

Defending the Divide

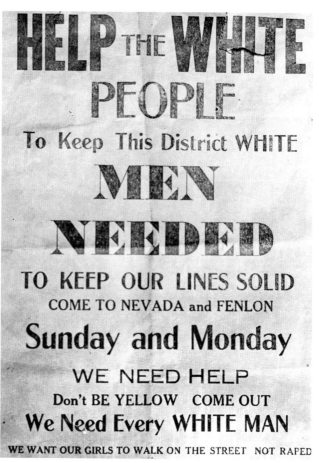

Propaganda distributed by segregationist whites in response to further black expansion throughout Detroit. Image courtesy of the Walter P. Reuther Library, Wayne State University.

At face value, a homeowners' association is tasked with protecting the stability of a neighborhood. Well-kept homes, neighbors suggested, ensured neighborhood tranquility and preserved home equity. By avoiding racially specific language (for example, "White Citizens' Council"), these groups were able to recruit moderates under the pretense of financial and domestic stability. However, their other motivations were never far from the surface. Printed on handbills, recruitment flyers, and protest placards, the goals of the homeowners' associations were quickly known throughout the city: "Help the White People."

At the beginning of the 1940s, black homeownership was less common than white homeownership, and the rate was lower in Detroit than in other cities. In 1940, only 14.4 percent of blacks in Detroit owned their own homes, below the national average of 22.8 percent. Black families paid above-average rent for below-average housing. Furthermore, the rent was a heavier burden because blacks earned less than their white counterparts did. The "Race Relations in Housing" report stated that black families were commonly "forced to pay $50 for a $40 home in a $30 neighborhood." Denied homeownership and overcharged for rent, black families were deprived of the ability to build home equity and wealth—the very equity and wealth that whites were allegedly defending through their associations.

Picketing became an increasingly common approach to intimidating city officials and noncompliant property owners. Using this approach, the associations ensured that their concerns remained in the spotlight. A good example is the case of Edward Brock, who owned two homes on the lower west side that he sold to black families. Once the word got out, Brock was picketed for a week by ten to twenty-five women of the neighborhood. The placards were devised not only to inform but to shame. Signs with messages such as "The Lord separated the races, why should Ed Brock mix them?" and "My home is my castle, I will die defending it" reflected the seriousness of the protesters' intent.

Shame became a primary tactic of the white community throughout the 1950s. Job loss, public humiliation, and property damage were a few of the threats that noncompliant whites received. The activist Rodney Redpath of the Dewitt-Clinton Association was pleased to report during an association gathering that the white man from Chalfonte Street who had sold to a black family was now happily unemployed. As the associations grew, shame was leveraged in leaflets and flyers aimed directly at disloyal neighbors who had not yet contributed.

In tandem with shame, threats of violence were employed. In November 1948, a block from the Sojourner Truth housing project, two men set an effigy ablaze. Such symbols clearly invoked Ku Klux Klan–inspired fear-mongering. By aligning with the southern terrorist group, which had a long history in Detroit, these men elevated tensions among residents, many of whom had recently emigrated from the South.

The real and threatened violence went largely unchecked by the Detroit Police Department. It was more than a truism that when the races clashed, blacks were arrested and whites were released. When the black real-estate agent James Morris called the police while he and his black clients were harassed and catcalled by a crowd of angry whites, law enforcement sided with the protesters and arrested Morris. The sense of invulnerability in the eyes of the law meant that white citizens' groups grew increasingly bold. The Detroit Police Department's attitude continued to reflect its demographics.

As homeowners' associations organized, so too did their opponents. The NAACP held the line in the courts and kept up the pressure on Detroit's civic leaders. *McGhee v. Sipes* was a carefully chosen, very public battle, but there was also subtle, behind-the-scenes pressure at City Hall. Working in conjunction with the Mayor's Interracial Committee, the Detroit Police Department, civil rights activists, and the Jewish Community Council, the NAACP sought to defend civil rights victories at the governmental level rather than in the streets.

When a friend of Arthur Johnson, a Detroit Public Schools assistant superintendent, purchased a house in a white neighborhood, a crowd of thirty-five whites gathered outside the home. Johnson, recalling the incident in his autobiography, *Race and Remembrance*, said that the police officers stated that they could not "disperse the crowd or offer protection." After the initial incident, Johnson informed the police sergeant that the NAACP would be monitoring the situation and would not let this go unnoticed.

In an unexpected twist, another foe of the homeowners' associations was the Communist Party of Michigan. The Communist Party stated that the associations were a threat to democracy and needed to be observed and, if necessary, thwarted. In a letter to the Mayor's Interracial Committee in 1948, the party's state chairman, Carl Winter, stated, "[The Communist Party] feels you can and should act in order to expose and defeat the un-American threat to our city represented by the anti-Negro incitement of the Courville District Improvement Association. . . . We assure you that the full support of our organization will be behind any action undertaken to defend and strengthen the civil rights of all the people in our society." The participation of the Communist Party inadvertently gave white separatists further evidence to suggest that the civil rights movement was part of a grand communist conspiracy.

1950–1959: Never Give Up, Never Surrender

The tumult of the 1940s sparked retrenchment, and homeowners' associations emerged determined to secure white property owners' rights and racial separation. The 1950s saw membership surge, organizations professionalize, and tactics shift.

Not surprisingly in a population recently at war, associations created formal top-down structures to maximize potential within the community.

They featured officers, boards, committees, and foot soldiers. The formal structures established some manner of status and respect, which amplified their reach.

Officers spoke for the association: interacting with City Hall, courting donors, and advocating the associations' principles. In addition to promoting the association, officers used these positions as gateways to elected office. Thomas Poindexter leveraged his role as founder of the Greater Detroit Homeowners' Association to make an unsuccessful attempt at Congress before gaining a seat on Detroit's Common Council in 1964. Having the support of elected officials was vital to the associations. In the 1950s, the associations had a firm ally in Mayor Cobo.

Besides the officers, the most visible and numerous members of the associations were block captains, who recruited members, collected dues, enforced association rules, and maintained watch over their sectors. Men and women of the community were welcomed equally. By utilizing a large pool of members, the homeowners' associations could fight on multiple fronts at once. While men worked the assembly line, women—generally homemakers and caregivers—worked the picket line. The social component of membership was enticing for many members as well. Over the course of three years, the Ruritan Park Homeowners' Association grew to eleven hundred of the twenty-four hundred homes in its area. Despite not having over 50 percent of the neighborhood enlisted, the association remained the most potent and powerful group in the community.

Aside from race, a common thread among association members was simple geography. "Homeowners between X Street and Y Street are welcome" was common on recruitment leaflets. In order to attract and retain the greatest number of white members, inclusive clauses would be added. Inserted near the end of the Federated Property Owners of America's Articles of Incorporation was the line "This corporation shall be non-profit, non-sectarian and non-partisan."

In addition to support from community leaders and private citizens, the support of local business owners was tremendously important. Partnerships with business leaders had significant payoffs, including discounted goods needed for protests, legal services, and more. In return, associations would include businesses in their newsletters and leaflets, encouraging others to support the cause by shopping at association-approved businesses.

The push for organization among the white citizens of Detroit brought new potency to their efforts. No longer were integration activists fighting individual community members; they were fighting against cohesive and well-funded organizations. Large treasuries were amassed in order to mount effective offensives and defenses. The Courville District Improvement Association sought to maintain a treasury of nearly $5,000 (almost $50,000 in 2016 dollars). A treasury of this size was not the norm, but it demonstrates the conviction of the association's membership.

As rosters grew, so too did the number of homeowners' associations, even as the white population of Detroit dwindled. Despite growing by 73,000 during the 1940s, the number of whites in the city shrank by 362,877 in the 1950s. In 1945, there were 56 homeowners' associations within the city limits; by 1956, the number of organizations nearly tripled to 143. Ironically, the growing number of associations generated competition for the ever-shrinking pool of potential members, creating friction between the groups. Accusations of disloyalty were published. Regarding higher black enrollment at Courville and Pershing schools, the Courville District Improvement Association published "Action! Courville!," which stated, "This neighborhood is divided in its loyalty somewhat at this writing by another Association the SEVEN MILE IMPROVEMENT also trying to solicit membership. May the better of the two win, however, our association is the one to support to keep your colored people below Six Mile."

By the late 1950s, the active competition between associations abated, and fights over membership led to the formation of umbrella homeowners' associations. Members understood that the white population of Detroit was plummeting and that resources needed to be consolidated in order to remain potent. The most prominent umbrella organization was the Federated Civic Associations of Northwest Detroit, which represented fifty groups. Two other umbrella organizations were the North East Council of Home Owners Associations, which represented twelve groups, and the Michigan Council of Civic Associations Inc., which represented eleven.

A contentious issue for the associations was construction of the interstate highways, particularly Interstate 375 leading directly out of downtown. This route did not bisect white neighborhoods as other portions of the new freeways would. Instead, the creation of I-375 would require demolition of the two main black neighborhoods in Detroit, Paradise Valley and Black Bottom. Ever since the project was first explored in the mid-1940s, homeowners' associations resisted. A flyer from the local election of 1945, circulated by the West Side Home and Property Owners' Protective Association and carrying the large headline "Attention West Siders!," denounced Detroit Council members for building a freeway through black neighborhoods. It warned that the construction may "cause a race riot larger than the last one."

Perhaps the greatest adversaries of the associations were the nonaligned members of the white community, a contingent by no means insignificant. The University of Michigan conducted the 1956 Detroit Area Study to gauge the white community's attitudes toward race and social issues. Eight hundred Detroiters were asked simple questions related to racial integration. The first question asked whether school integration should be permitted: 56 percent responded that blacks and whites should be taught together in the same classroom. Slightly more than one-third of the respondents replied that whites and blacks should absolutely be taught separately in different schools. The next question focused on after-school entertainment. Should black and white children be allowed to play together? Four out of ten responded that interracial playtime should be permitted; 13 percent of the respondents replied that they would forbid the practice.

In addition to the nonaligned whites, another Achilles' heel for the associations were members easily frightened by strategic blockbusting. Blockbusting was the process by which realtors scared homeowners out of the neighborhood and bought the homes at rock-bottom prices. A black family moving onto the block, a black woman walking a baby through a neighborhood, or a group of black children riding their bikes down the street was enough to make the skittish move out. This practice persisted in Detroit for decades, undermining the cohesion and property values of neighborhoods.

In the wake of *Shelley v. Kraemer*, racially specific language began to go by the wayside. "Undesirables" became the standard phrase for associations looking to tout their message. This change did not stop racially specific language from continuing to persist among association members. At a meeting of the Community Home Owners Association recorded in the *East Side Shopper*, former president Arthur Madar was asked to speak with nonmembers about the association's work. Madar stated, "The homeowners banded together two years ago to prevent a Negro family from moving into the community. . . . Our job was to keep the Negro family from moving in and we did a marvelous job!" Similarly, a meeting of the Ruritan Park Civic Association was recorded by the Detroit Urban League (DUL). After the visiting Common Councilwoman Mary Beck had departed, "the meeting then degenerated to [a] stage of keeping 'Niggers' out of the area."

This incident did not endear many other organizations to the cause. The DUL kept tabs on the meetings and activities of multiple associations throughout the late 1940s and into the 1950s, including the Ruritan Park Civic Association, the DeWitt-Clinton Association, and the East Outer Drive Improvement Association. In order to monitor these groups, the DUL would send members to association meetings, events, and fund-raisers. Detailed notes were compiled that included where, when, size, tone, and subject. The DUL used the information gathered at these events in order to devise plans and pursue opportunities to thwart the associations.

The DUL explored detaching associations from the community by barring them from schools and other public facilities. In order to deprive the associations of further political clout, the DUL pressured public leaders to abstain from association meetings and events. Pledging to serve the community and assist the disenfranchised, the DUL, in a report titled "Summary of Known Improvement Association Activities in the Past Two Years: 1955–1957," viewed associations as "not a manifestation of health, but of illness, and . . . not a return to the democratic spirit but a drastic turn from it."

1960–1965: The Push for Open Housing

Another 344,093 whites left Detroit over the course of the 1960s. In spite of the continued exodus, the associations still represented a massive block of Detroiters. As such, the battles fought throughout the 1960s were significant. The rise of Thomas Poindexter, the Homeowners' Rights Ordinance, open housing, and lucrative blockbusting all shaped the early sixties.

During the election of 1961, Jerome Cavanagh received over 85 percent of the black vote. On June 23, 1963, Cavanagh marched side by side with Martin Luther King Jr. down Woodward Avenue during the largest civil rights march to date. While it was clear that the associations could no longer expect mayoral support, the Common Council was still largely on their side.

In the face of Mayor Cavanagh's racially progressive politics, the council continued to act as a champion of the past. In 1962, the Common Council passed the Fair Neighborhoods Practices Ordinance. The ordinance, cited in Fine's *Violence in the Model City*, "restricted the number, location, and length of time that realty signs could be displayed and made it unlawful to refer to race in seeking property listings or in published or written realty advertising." Open-housing advocates saw it as hollow and weak, while homeowners' associations saw it as a gateway to further encroachment by minorities and big government.

Open-housing advocates moved first. Councilmen Mel Ravitz and William Patrick Jr. crafted staunch new open-housing legislation in 1963, which forbade discrimination in real-estate transactions on the basis of race, religion, or ancestry. The bill was defeated seven to two, Ravitz and Patrick being the only supporters. The defeat of open-housing legislation was expected; despite continued white flight, the white community in Detroit still held a massive majority.

Resisting the Ravitz-Patrick bill put the associations on the offensive, and they organized the Homeowners' Rights Ordinance. The sole purpose of the ordinance was to reestablish de jure segregation throughout the city. The ordinance granted a homeowner "the right to freedom from interference with his property by public authorities attempting to give special privileges to any group." The success of the ordinance would represent a significant victory in terms of both enforced segregation and public relations. The ordinance, the associations hoped, would stem the flow of separationist whites from the city.

Common Council member Thomas Poindexter, who gained his seat through his association ties, led the charge to make the ordinance a ballot issue. The associations' determined ballot efforts in support of the measure were even more effective. Thousands of members from various associations combed the neighborhoods vying for signatures. Over forty-four thousand Detroiters signed their names and placed the ordinance on the 1964 primary ballot. It passed by a ten-point margin, 55 percent to 45 percent. The victory was short-lived; the Wayne County Court ruled that the ordinance was unconstitutional.

Conclusion

The 1940s and 1950s witnessed the birth of our modern racial-political divide. The fears harbored by homeowners' associations were manifest in significant white flight. The exodus began in the 1950s and continued into the 1970s. As separationists departed the city, they took their tactics with them.

Into the 1960s, the tug-of-war continued until the racial tension nearly ripped Detroit in half. In an attempt to maintain the status quo, supported by a fraction of the community, homeowners' associations established a destructive precedent. The associations divided whites and blacks, divided neighborhoods, and set the tone for adversarial city-suburb relations as well.

Liberals and "Get-Tough" Policing in Postwar Detroit

Alex Elkins

On August 12, 1964, the *Wall Street Journal* declared Detroit a model city in preventing rioting and racial conflict. Since mid-July, thousands of African Americans had rioted against the police in New York—Harlem, Brooklyn, Rochester—a Chicago suburb, and three New Jersey cities. At the end of August, hundreds more would take to the streets in North Philadelphia. Yet the Motor City stayed quiet. Many people credited the liberal policies of Democratic Mayor Jerome P. Cavanagh and his two police commissioners, George Edwards and Ray Girardin. Throughout their tenure, all three denounced the "get-tough" policies of former administrations that too often subdued black residents through force and intimidation, attempting instead to enlist their cooperation in the war on crime. As in other liberal administrations, Cavanagh embraced the color-blind, technocratic ideals of post–World War II police professionalism. By adopting cutting-edge technology, equipment, training, and crime-fighting tactics, the mayor hoped the police might become a stabilizing presence.

Despite this shift from City Hall, the majority of officers in the Detroit Police Department (DPD)—from top inspectors to the uniformed ranks—rejected the liberal platform of color-blind, equal law enforcement. In African American neighborhoods, police continued to mete out extra-legal rough justice on a regular basis. Even middle-class black residents who had long requested greater protection from crime protested the often-unpunished harassment, beatings, and killings. The department's failure to enforce a professional ethos on the streets ultimately undermined the top-down reforms that were jointly sponsored by civil rights leaders to improve training, transparency, and discipline. More fundamentally,

Cavanagh and his top cops, although keen to disavow the racially charged stigma of "get-tough" approaches, repeatedly used the police to crack down on crime and disorder. By embracing the war on crime, including its central logic of "toughness," the Cavanagh administration's mixed messages set up a confrontation between the DPD and black Detroiters that culminated in the 1967 rebellion.

Crackdown in the Jim Crow Era

In 1960, only 143 of the 4,357 (3.3 percent) members of the Detroit Police Department were African Americans in a city that was nearly one-third black. According to a 1958 Detroit Urban League survey cited by Judge Damon Keith in *Baker v. Detroit* (1979), five of thirteen precincts had no African American officers, whereas 85 percent of black officers were assigned to five precincts. When Police Commissioner Herbert W. Hart attempted to integrate scout cars in 1959, white officers organized a slowdown, or a "blue flu," in protest. By the end of 1960, the department had integrated 24 of 118 scout cars and several precincts. No African American supervised a white officer until the middle of the decade. By 1968, the department was still only 6 percent black. There were nine black sergeants, two black lieutenants, and one black officer ranked higher than lieutenant. African Americans occupied only 2 percent of supervisory roles.

As a matter of custom and department policy, Detroit police officers used arrests for "investigation" to solve even routine crimes. An investigative arrest was a station-house detention, often on less than probable cause, for the purpose of interrogation. It was illegal but common. In 1958, the Civil Liberties Committee of the Detroit Bar Association reported that the DPD had arrested 73,827 persons in 1956 but had formally charged only 40,641. Police held about 45 percent, or 33,186, for investigation, while more than a third, or 26,696, were "released without charge." In 1956, three-quarters of the DPD's arrests for crimes like murder, rape, and robbery were for "investigation." According to Loukas Loukopoulos, in 1963, the final year the DPD published data on the practice, police made 38,812 investigative arrests—over 4,000 more than in any year since 1949. For the most part, the police used these illegal tactics in poor, predominantly minority neighborhoods.

Police leaders defended investigative detentions as a vital expedient in the war on crime, especially in abolishing the vice syndicates—an argument they invoked to continue using the tactic, albeit to a lesser degree, in the 1960s. They also defended, and did little to restrain, the racially charged conduct of officers toward African Americans, which ranged from racial slurs to retaliatory arrests to reckless, sometimes fatal, shootings.

Harold Norris of the Detroit branch of the National Association for the Advancement of Colored People (NAACP) wrote in the October 1958 edition of the *Crisis* that the two most common complaints against the police that the branch had received between 1956 and 1957 were for physical assault and racial slurs. African Americans alleged that police frequently told them to say "sir" when "answering a white man." Black citizens who invoked their rights were often called "smart niggers" by police and then beaten or arrested, sometimes both. Police covered up extralegal conduct by charging citizens with resisting arrest, vagrancy, or disorderly conduct.

In December 1960, the US Commission on Civil Rights (CCR) held a public hearing on the police in Detroit. Black critics of the DPD almost uniformly referred to a "policy of containment." Arthur Johnson, the executive director of the Detroit NAACP, giving testimony about "police and the blacks" to the US Civil Rights Commission, listed the following as the core complaints of black Detroiters: "unreasonable and illegal arrests, indiscriminate and open searching of their person on the public streets, disrespectful and profane language, derogatory references to their race and color, interference with [interracial] personal associations," and "violent, intimidating police reactions to their protests against improper treatment." The DPD left little doubt about its approach during the crackdown of late December 1960 and early January 1961, following the murder of two white women in an already-bloody year. The two suspected killers were black men. According to Ed Cray in *The Enemy in the Streets*, Commissioner Hart initiated a "crash program." He put police on a six-day work week and ordered them to "arrest all suspicious individuals." The NAACP's Harold Norris, addressing police policies, suggested that Mayor Louis Miriani encouraged officers "to alert themselves to those persons who were in odd places at odd hours without any reasonable expectation" ("Recent Detroit Police Policies"). The *Detroit News* offered a large cash reward for information that led to the killers' capture. In the first forty-eight hours, police made 600 arrests. Over two weeks, they arrested up to 1,500 black men, 780 for investigation. Most were held overnight for questioning, some for days. The DPD also made 150,000 "street contacts"—field (or alley) interrogations—in black neighborhoods. On January 11, Hart ended the "state of emergency." The killers had not been found.

The crackdown mobilized black residents. In January, seventy-five community and civil rights organizations endorsed civilian control of the DPD on the model of Philadelphia's Police Advisory Board. In a December 1959 *Free Press* article, Hart warned that civilian review would induce police "laxity"; parroting the Fraternal Order of Police, he said the board was "crippling morale" in Philadelphia. Nevertheless, the Wayne County AFL-CIO Council, with four hundred thousand members, came out in favor of civilian review, prompting Miriani to set up the Community Relations Bureau within the DPD to investigate complaints. It was too late for him. In the fall, the young liberal Cavanagh upset Miriani to become mayor of Detroit; 85 percent of black voters chose the anticrackdown candidate.

Civil Rights and Police Professionalism

To lead the DPD, Cavanagh chose George Edwards, a prominent civil libertarian and state supreme court justice. In Edwards's two years as commissioner, he tripled the hours of human-relations training at the academy, organized precinct-community meetings, imposed tighter supervision of the use of force, formally banned police use of racial epithets, and expanded the authority of the Community Relations Bureau over brutality cases. Edwards's successor, Ray Girardin, a longtime crime reporter, extended these reforms. In January 1965, fulfilling a long-standing request of black residents, Girardin integrated the Big Four cruisers, which patrolled high-crime neighborhoods armed with shotguns, tear gas, and gas masks. He added twenty hours to academy training in human relations—bringing the total to fifty—and authorized the renamed Citizens Complaint Bureau to investigate cases at its own initiative and report its findings directly to the commissioner.

Efforts to enforce professional, color-blind standards and increase transparency earned praise from civil rights organizations and black residents. Cavanagh's commissioners confidently asserted during their tenures that the DPD had regained the trust of African American residents and had reduced the chances of urban rebellion. Despite limited success, however, both Edwards and Girardin overestimated the efficacy of top-down reforms and underestimated the degree to which the rest of the department would pursue its own agenda.

In May 1965, Cavanagh used his leverage as a member of the White House Task Force on Urban Summer Problems to secure $213,000 from the Office of Economic Opportunity for an ambitious in-service training program to—according to the operating grant—"develop in police officers an appreciation of the civil rights of the public" as well as "the ability to meet, without undue militancy, aggressiveness, hostility, or prejudice, police situations involving minority groups." The in-service program used a curriculum designed by private consultants: a mix of lectures, role-playing, and guided discussions. Each session was attended by several dozen officers, lecturers, CCR staff, and one or two black residents.

As reported in exit surveys, the vast majority of police participants found the training useless. Officers gave stock answers on civil rights questions and became animated only when trying to understand how recent US Supreme Court decisions might affect their work. Some discussions were disheartening to CCR staff. For the hypothetical scenario "Fights and Riots," police refer to a Mexican suspect as a "spic" and punch him in the face after he spits on them. Officers in the seminar ignored the lesson of how a racial epithet could escalate a situation. Some repeated the slur; all approved of the violent retaliation even though, according to a staff log from one of the training session, "It might be illegal." Between July 1 and October 31, eighteen hundred Detroit police officers from high-crime precincts graduated from the in-service training program. Richard V. Marks, the secretary-director of the CCR, was optimistic that the training would professionalize the department by helping police officers accommodate recent changes in the law and departmental policy and accept the sweeping cultural changes precipitated by the civil rights revolution. On the streets, police continued to operate by the get-tough logic of the war on crime, which, significantly, some liberals also endorsed.

"Crime in the Streets" and Liberal Get-Tough Policing

"Crime in the Streets" was the banner theme for Detroit's 1965 election. The Republican businessman Walter C. Shamie ran against Cavanagh under the slogan "Four Years of Fear Are Enough!" Four conservative council incumbents—Mary V. Beck, Thomas L. Poindexter, William Rogell, and Anthony J. Wierzbicki—stated in a July 13 *Free Press* editorial that the mayor had "handcuffed police by refusing to back them in the use of force." As a result, Rogell said, "People are afraid to go out on the street at night." Poindexter even introduced an ordinance "to protect and secure respect for police officers," which would have made it a crime to "insult" or "ridicule" the police. In November, the liberals prevailed. Shamie lost by a two-to-one margin. Wierzbicki was out, and in a sign of rising black political power, Poindexter lost to a liberal black minister, Nicholas Hood.

Although not a winning electoral issue, street crime was becoming a major public concern. In 1965, the city had 201 homicides—an increase of 47 percent over 1964 and the highest total since Prohibition. In the midst of that upswing, in April 1965, the *Detroit Free Press* published a full-page article, "Our Police Today: Frustrated, Bitter, and Resentful," which quoted unnamed officers who blamed the crime increase on pressure from civil rights groups and recent Supreme Court decisions restricting their arrest and search powers. Indeed, voices coming from various governmental agencies were often contradictory. The federal ruling *Mapp v. Ohio* in 1961, which barred from state criminal trials evidence seized in violation of the Fourth Amendment, was contravened by the Michigan Supreme Court, which held that an amendment to the state constitution gave police permission to conduct on-the-street searches of suspicious persons. Even Detroit's liberal mayor proposed a citywide stop-and-frisk law, which was almost immediately opposed by civil rights groups. Concerned about "the public spectacle" of street searches, Detroit NAACP president Rev. James Wadsworth said, in an interview with the *Free Press* writer William Sudomier, that the police already saw all blacks as criminals who "have no rights as far as white men are concerned." Instead of dragnet tactics, Wadsworth said, the city should hire up to one thousand officers. By April 1966, after months of tension, the mayor had distanced himself from stop-and-frisk.

Black Detroiters had long asked police for greater protection from crime and disorder in their neighborhoods. In the mid-1960s, middle-class black residents in particular wanted something done about street prostitution, which had links to organized crime, police graft, and robberies. In April 1965, at Girardin's request, the city passed a get-tough ordinance that punished known prostitutes caught soliciting in public up to $500 and ninety days in jail. The American Civil Liberties Union (ACLU) and NAACP testified at public hearings that the law would lead to police abuse and civil rights violations. Many black residents and business leaders, however, welcomed the measure, pushing for an additional provision to punish customers, who tended to be white men.

For many Detroiters in the 1960s, including the mayor, professionalizing the police department was an urgent civil rights issue. Cavanagh saw the police institution as a potential agent of justice for African Americans and the poor, the groups most victimized by violent crime. "The war on crime is a real war," Cavanagh said in a July 1965 statement. "As in any war, victory calls for dedicated soldiers. But it also calls for the best possible training and equipment." With these words, on July 1, 1965, the mayor unveiled the new Tactical Mobile Unit (TMU), an elite squad to respond quickly to emergencies, such as riots or serious crimes. Each car carried two officers, equipped with walkie-talkies, shotguns, and tear gas. The TMU used "saturation patrol," a strategy that relied on a show of force to deter crime and disorder. The TMU gave the department a more aggressive street presence. In its first month, the new unit made 348 arrests, over half for traffic-related offenses such as driving without a license. In August, Cavanagh added five prowlers to the initial fleet of eleven. The following March, the DPD doubled the TMU to 132 officers and twenty-six cars.

The Cavanagh administration's plans for a more professional police department in some ways conflicted with the interests of civil rights groups that resented the powerful, insular autonomy of the DPD. In the fall of 1964, after the riots in other cities and a string of brutality cases in Detroit, activists demanded greater civilian input in police discipline proceedings. The Citizens Complaint Bureau was run entirely by police. Only the three-member Board of Inquiry, set up by Edwards in 1963 to investigate police killings, had a civilian member. Over the winter of 1965, civil rights groups failed to convince Girardin to appoint two more civilians to reverse the ratio. Instead, the mayor and his commissioners encouraged black community leaders to allow the State Commission on Civil Rights, formed in 1964, to act as a public review board.

The watchwords of mainstream liberal thinking on police reform in Detroit and elsewhere in the 1960s were "training" and "discipline." White liberals and to some extent black leaders were interested primarily in controlling explicitly racial conduct and preventing riots. As such, middle-class progressives tended to deemphasize the everyday experience of get-tough policing. The public spectacle of the frisk, though nonviolent, still carried the threat of force and often was a humiliating, demeaning experience for the young working-class men most often targeted with this tactic.

Street Justice and Get-Tough Policing

Black Detroiters had good reason to fear being shot by police. Between 1958 and 1961, twelve African Americans died at the hands of police. Every officer was white. Each death was ruled a justifiable homicide by Wayne County Prosecutor Samuel H. Olsen. The law and departmental policy gave officers wide leeway to take lethal action against a fleeing felon. The DPD maintained this policy into the 1970s and rarely punished officers for firing their weapons at civilians, even in circumstances in which their lives were not in jeopardy.

At 3:00 a.m. on July 5, 1963, Patrolman Theodore Spicher shot a black sex worker named Cynthia Scott three times, twice in the back, as she tried to walk away from an attempted arrest. Spicher said Scott had slashed his hand with a knife, a statement disputed by witnesses. Even though Spicher did not have probable cause to make an arrest and his life was not in danger, Olsen cleared him three days later. In late July, so did Edwards. In late August 1964, police arrested Barbara Jackson, a black sex worker, for allegedly stealing money from a customer, a charge that turned out to be untrue. In the station house, officers assaulted Jackson, including bashing her over the head with a flashlight. Jackson filed a complaint with the NAACP and the State Commission on Civil Rights. In retaliation, police arrested Jackson and held her for four hours and tried to coax her boyfriend to testify against her. The DPD gave the arresting officer a reprimand for the assault, but the harassment went unpunished.

Black officers who spoke out against the rough justice of their white colleagues faced workplace harassment and put their careers at risk. In September 1965, Patrolman Kenneth Johnson, who was black, watched a white fellow officer use a nightstick to strike a black fifteen-year-old named Howard King in a station-house garage. King suffered a broken hand and a serious head wound. Johnson made no mention of the beating in his first report. A second report was requested, and Johnson mentioned the beating. This time he was subsequently suspended. For testifying against a brother officer, Johnson was harassed, transferred, and eventually taken off the street. The DPD also reprimanded him for filing a false report. No white officer in the case was similarly punished.

At about 8:30 p.m. on August 9, 1966, a Big Four cruiser pulled up to the corner of Kercheval and Pennsylvania Avenues. Hanging out there were seven members of the Afro-American Youth Movement, an offshoot of the Adult Community Movement for Equality (ACME), a black militant organization. Police ordered them to disperse. Four left, but three stood their ground. They resisted arrest and shouted to the one hundred bystanders, "Whitey is going to kill us," "This is the start of a riot," and "Black Power." Some onlookers tossed bottles at police cruisers and store windows; several youths attacked white motorists. Rumors spread that police had killed or injured a black man during the initial arrest. Within the hour, at least 150 police—including the Tactical Mobile Unit—patrolled the area, carrying rifles affixed with bayonets. The "mini-riot" included some rock throwing and mostly abortive attempts to firebomb stores but no looting. It continued the next two nights.

The mayor and the police congratulated themselves on preventing a larger rebellion. Civil rights leaders praised the department's restrained, color-blind professionalism. The DPD, at Girardin's urging, had drawn up riot plans in August 1965, after witnessing the catastrophe of Watts, in which Los Angeles police had backed off at the beginning. In a 1966 letter to Gordon Rowe, Girardin wrote that the DPD riot plan prioritized a "maximum initial response" and the centralized coordination of tactical teams, community leaders, emergency supplies, and the courts. Police executed this plan during the Kercheval disturbance. Officers partnered with civil rights groups and toured the area together. On the third night, August 11, they authorized civilian "peace patrols" to encourage people to stay off the streets. Police also maintained their own heavily armed "saturation patrols" until the fifteenth. The mayor and city newspapers interpreted Kercheval as a triumph of enlightened liberal planning: it was, according to the *New York Times* writer Anthony Lukas, "the riot that didn't happen."

The riot, of course, did happen, but a larger one was averted. In fact, many residents of the Kercheval area—the site of the widely praised Fifth Precinct Police-Community Relations meetings held on a consistent basis over the preceding few years—wanted police to drive young men from street corners. In surveys after the incident, a majority of residents acknowledged the reality of police brutality but, more fervently, wanted protection from street crime and disorder, mentioning corner loiterers in particular. But most middle-class African Americans stopped short of endorsing get-tough measures. The Miriani crackdown was a sore memory for every black Detroiter. No amount of privilege or public standing had offered adequate shelter from the 150,000 street stops police had made. No black person had been safe—neither the NAACP's Arthur Johnson nor the prominent black pastor and civil rights activist Hubert Locke, whom Girardin appointed as his administrative assistant in 1966.

For African Americans, the street frisk was particularly onerous. It was a humiliating, public ritual. Too often officers were discourteous or overtly racist. Too often they had no legitimate basis for suspicion. Although the Kercheval uprising was relatively small scale, it was one sign of growing working-class insurgency against the police, a reaction that had been gaining momentum in black neighborhoods across the country. Almost all the recent summer riots had begun with a crowd challenging police authority at the point of arrest. The urban poor began treating the police as if they were an invading army, trampling on their rights. In a front-page story on July 14, 1965, the *Detroit Free Press* reported with approval that Wayne County Prosecutor Olsen would seek a new state riot law in response to "a recent wave of attacks on police by teen-age hoodlums and agitators seeking to foil arrests." In almost every case, young men, black and white, led the fight. They resisted arrest. A crowd gathered. Some taunted the police; some threw bottles. From there, the cases varied from escalation to dissipation.

Given the record of beatings, killings, and harassment, many young, poor, and black residents looked on routine police actions, such as a traffic stop, with suspicion. In June 1963, O. Lee Molette of the Group on Advanced Leadership (GOAL), a black activist organization, invited the US Commission on Civil Rights to return to the city to investigate the enforcement of traffic laws. The group alleged that police conducted "dozens of illegal searches and seizures" of black residents "daily" and that the Traffic and Recorder's Courts penalized blacks more harshly than whites for traffic violations. It was not only the "average" black resident caught up in this dragnet, Molette insisted, but "Negro professionals with proper identification [who] have also been systematically subjected to this humiliating and unconstitutional police practice."

Conclusion

In the spring of 1967, the politics of policing and crime hit a crisis point in Detroit. In April, Councilmember Mary Beck started a recall campaign against Cavanagh—one of two that spring—to protest his liberal police policies. Hours after Beck announced the recall, a white teenager was stabbed to death in Cobo Hall, the new convention center; police suspected two black teenagers. The horrific crime and the moral panic that followed, reminiscent of the Miriani crackdown, bolstered Beck's desired war on crime. The recall campaign petered out in June. Between May 16 and July 11, the Detroit Police Officers Association used its new bargaining power to initiate a work slowdown, or "blue flu," intent on a salary increase. By June 19, 847 officers, or 20 percent of the DPD, had called in sick. Ticket enforcement dropped by nearly 67 percent, and Girardin suspended 186 officers.

That spring, block clubs in black neighborhoods redoubled their demands for police protection. In March, two hundred residents attended a "Citizens Mass Meeting against Crime" at St. Agnes Church on 12th Street. They asked police to crack down on prostitution, blind pigs, corner loitering, and street litter. Their final resolution, as recorded by Susan Holmes of the *Free Press*, urged citizens to "support the police and wage individual crusades against crime." Coincidently, the DPD had been targeting illegal bars in the area over the past year. Between February 1966 and July 23, 1967, police attempted to raid a blind pig at 12th Street and Clairmount Avenue nine times. On the morning of July 23, they were finally successful.

Cavanagh entered office in 1962 promising to solve the racial crisis by improving relations between African Americans and the Detroit Police Department. He appointed two commissioners who executed hallmark postwar liberal police reforms: in-service training in human relations and civil rights; efficiency-optimizing, highly trained mobile tactical teams; new channels of citizen redress; and an overall emphasis on color-blind, technocratic administration and street policing. Black residents, however, knew firsthand the brutal, unethical ways that officers used their discretion on the beat, and they also saw that the police problem was rooted in the political economy of the city. They were locked out of safe neighborhoods, good jobs, and better schools. In the civil rights era, black Detroiters expected the police, as the state, to ensure equal treatment under the law. When even the liberal police department permitted its officers to harass, brutalize, and kill black citizens with near-complete impunity, the irony was too tragic to bear.

Part III

A Riot by Any Other Name

Black Day in July. The Canadian songwriter Gordon Lightfoot used the Detroit scenario as a metaphor for the racial eruptions across the United States—over 160 total, at least 24 considered severe. Detroit's story is one of uneasy relationships gone sour, in the neighborhoods and across the city. The narrative is clouded in disparate data, divergent memories, and hardened opinions. Gradually, however, various truths emerge.

Late on some evenings, particularly on hot summer nights, 12th Street was alive with a variety of activities that were not always legal or moral. Participants might have included the people who lived in nearby homes and ran the active businesses that lined 12th Street, Linwood Street, Grand Boulevard, and Grand River Avenue. These were solid, often religious people in moderate to low income brackets. In reminiscences, they recall the neighborhoods fondly, as transitional locales but good places to grow up. The homes were nice brick bungalows and flats, well constructed, surrounded by mature trees—elms in particular—and occupied mostly by young families. The daytime neighborhoods and retailers maintained an uneasy relationship with the nighttime enterprises.

Within the city, the politics of City Hall suppressed open housing and police issues until the Democrat Jerome Cavanagh was elected in 1962. At thirty-three, he was the youngest person to hold the Detroit mayor's office, and he did it with strong African American support. His progressive approach was favored in Washington, DC, by President Lyndon Johnson, John Kennedy's successor in 1963. When Cavanagh started criticizing the administration for spending more money in Vietnam than in American cities, his relationship with the White House cooled.

Michigan's Republican governor George Romney was an auto executive who brought fiscal reform to state government. As a social moderate, he was considered a friend to the civil rights movement within his party but had a less-than-positive relationship with the Johnson administration. Having pursued the presidency briefly in 1964, he was considered a rival approaching the next election cycle.

When violence erupted on July 23, 1967, its severity in Detroit neighborhoods ebbed and flowed, confusing governmental officials at all levels. Conflicting information and political maneuvering slowed state and federal reaction time, allowing the upheaval to spread. Despite a rumor-control hotline set up for citizens by the mayor's office, communication suffered. Discrepancies between reports from the police, the military, and eyewitnesses added to citizens' doubts about government competency and further strained relationships.

Chronology of Events

This timeline was developed from a number of primary sources, including activity logs created by the mayor's office, police reports, and a chronology published by the assistant secretary of defense Cyrus R. Vance, with additional input from numerous secondary sources. Naturally, not all the sources agreed. Every effort was made to offer only verifiable information.

Saturday, July 22

10:30 p.m.   Undercover police officers Charles Henry and Joseph Brown, members of the vice squad, sought to gain entry into the blind pig at 9125 12th Street and Clairmount Avenue. They were turned away.

Sunday, July 23

3:00 a.m.   The Motor Traffic Bureau (MTB) and the Tactical Mobile Unit (TMU—riot police) went off duty. Mounted police were also off duty on Sundays. At this time, only 203 police officers were on duty citywide.

3:45 a.m.   Officer Henry joined a group of young ladies and slipped into the blind pig. Henry ordered a beer.

3:55 a.m.   After ten minutes, Henry did not emerge. Waiting ten minutes was the signal that a purchase had been made. The vice squad moved in.

4:00–4:40 a.m.   A crowd gathered as police brought the arrestees out to the sidewalk for transportation to jail.

4:40 a.m.   Police completed placing the arrestees into the police wagons and departed.

5:00 a.m.	Lieutenant Raymond Good of the Tenth Precinct arrived at 12th Street. He reported several hundred people in the streets and withdrew police units.
5:10 a.m.	The Tenth Precinct received the first burglar alarm.
5:20 a.m.	Police Commissioner Ray Girardin was phoned on the emergency line at his home. He then called Mayor Cavanagh.
6:00 a.m.	Police made the first looting arrest.
	Two black plainclothesmen were dispatched to 12th Street to gather intelligence.
	Commissioner Girardin arrived at police headquarters and initiated the department's riot plan. The night patrol remained on duty, leave was canceled, and shifts were extended to twelve hours.
7:00 a.m.	The Detroit Police Department notified the Michigan State Police, the National Guard, the Wayne County sheriff and prosecutor, and the FBI.
7:45 a.m.	Commissioner Girardin ordered Belle Isle sealed off.
7:50 a.m.	The crowd grew faster than the police presence: 360 police to 3,000 civilians. As the crowd became more violent (bottle and rock throwing), police decided to attempt a sweep.
8:24 a.m.	The first fire broke out at a shoe store at 12th and Blaine Streets. The shoe store was in a building that also housed five other stores and eighteen apartments.
8:55 a.m.	The CBS radio affiliate in Detroit, WJR, aired the first national broadcast about the riots. It was the only report for several hours.
9:00 a.m.	Damon Keith, cochairman of the state's Civil Rights Commission, called the general manager of WJR and requested that the station not report on the riot and persuaded other radio stations as well. Keith made similar requests of the *Detroit News* and the *Detroit Free Press*. He also requested that the news outlets refer to the riot as a "civil disturbance." Mayor Cavanagh also called

prominent news agencies to quell coverage. A media blackout of coverage began.

The *Time* magazine contributor Ed Bailey called a *Time* correspondent and said, "It's here, baby."

The Mayor's Committee for Human Resources Development decided to reach out to community leaders, churches, and civic organizations in an effort to curb the riots. Preachers were asked to include calming and antilooting messages in their sermons.

9:30 a.m.	The TMU and the MTB were partly mobilized and were lined up "shoulder to shoulder," with plastic shields and their bayonets unsheathed, on 12th Street.
10:00 a.m.	The administrative assistant to Commissioner Girardin, Hubert Locke; the deputy superintendent of Detroit Public Schools, Arthur Johnson; Congressman John Conyers; the lawyer and activist Damon Keith; clergymen; businessmen; and black community leaders gathered at Grace Episcopal Church in an attempt to stop the riot by organizing peace patrols.
	Operation Sundown: Major General Laurence C. Schnipke and Major General Cecil L. Simmons of the Michigan National Guard sent Brigadier General Noble Moore to Detroit, should the National Guard become necessary.
10:45 a.m.	Robert J. Danhof, Governor George Romney's legal adviser, called Cavanagh to advise him that state assistance was available; 380 guardsmen of the 156th Signal Battalion were already posted at the Detroit Artillery Armory on Eight Mile Road. Cavanagh stated that "no help was needed," but the state decided to keep the guardsmen there rather than release them for the day.
	Police began a disorder log. First entry: "Large crowd, can't control, officer in trouble. Getting attacked by mob."
10:57 a.m.	Colonel Frederick Davids, director of the Michigan State Police, issued a mobilization alert for seven state

police districts in response to the information supplied by criminal informants. The information did not match what DPD provided, and Davids decided that the DPD intelligence was faulty.

11:00 a.m.	Four squad cars of police withdrew from the disturbance area to the Herman Kiefer command post to permit the entry of the peace patrols.
	Security at police headquarters was significantly heightened.
	For an hour, police did not intervene on 12th Street but only observed.
11:15 a.m.	The peace patrols attempted to persuade the rioters to disperse and go home. Their efforts fell on deaf ears. Conyers and Johnson verbally clashed with an angry crowd at 12th Street and Hazelwood Street. Their message was aggressively ignored.
Noon	Hubert Locke told Girardin that police had lost control of the situation, and it was now a "lost cause."
1:00 p.m.	Mayor Cavanagh, acting under optimistic intelligence, stated that the civil disobedience on 12th Street would soon be under control. Reporters informed him otherwise.
	Firefighters attempted to put out the fires on 12th Street after four separate alarms went off, but they were physically rebuffed by the crowd.
1:20 p.m.	General Moore arrived in Detroit.
1:42 p.m.	Firefighters with no police support again attempted to put out fires on 12th Street but were pushed back. An all-black fire crew was assembled to fight the fires on 12th Street, but they too were attacked and pushed back. Girardin later viewed this as the "decisive turning point" of the riot.
2:00 p.m.	Mayor Cavanagh announced that he requested assistance from the Michigan State Police.
	A Windsor television station aired the first television report about the unrest.

The police on 12th Street requested permission to use tear gas, but the request was denied due to high winds.

Girardin advised Colonel Davids that the city did not need the assistance of the state troopers. Girardin was not convinced that they had a "full blown riot" on their hands. Despite this, Superintendent of Police Eugene Reuter requested the state police provide Detroit with all assistance possible.

2:15 p.m. Moore, Reuter, and DPD Deputy Superintendent John F. Nichols determined that the National Guard's assistance was required.

3:30 p.m. Looting spread to Linwood Street.

4:00 p.m. Moore requested that Schnipke authorize mobilization of the 156th Signal Battalion, but Schnipke determined that the mayor had to make the request.

The first case of arson at Grand River and Warren Avenues was reported.

4:10 p.m. Mayor Cavanagh requested Governor Romney to authorize the use of the National Guard in Detroit.

4:20 p.m. Romney committed the National Guard to Detroit.

4:30 p.m. A 3-777 signal was sent citywide. This signal summoned all city firefighters to their stations. Fire stations reported that 95 percent of crews reported on duty within hours.

The Detroit Fire Department was forced to abandon a one-hundred-square-block area west of 12th Street.

4:40 p.m. Commanding officers were ordered to remove all guns from gun shops in their commands. Hundreds of guns had already been stolen.

5:00 p.m. Police announced that the quarantine of the unrest had failed. Unrest spread to Joy Road and Grand River Avenue.

5:25 p.m. Widespread looting was reported along Grand River Avenue.

5:27 p.m. Calls were received reporting breaking and entering in the area of Seven Mile Road and Livernois Avenue.

Looting began in the early-morning hours of Sunday, July 23, waned with daylight, then resumed in earnest on Sunday afternoon. The ebb and flow of violence confused governmental officials attempting to determine appropriate countermeasures. This photo shows 12th Street looking south from Philadelphia Street. Image courtesy of Thomas Diggs.

5:30 p.m.	DPD ordered all precincts to send their black officers to the riot scene to replace the white officers.
5:44 p.m.	Looting was reported at John R. and Canfield Streets.
6:04 p.m.	Vandalism spread downtown along Washington Boulevard.
7:30 p.m.	Richard L. Williams, assistant director of the Mayor's Committee for Human Resources Development, said the situation was under control. Then word spread that the police had a no-shoot policy.
7:45 p.m.	Cavanagh stated that the situation was "critical" but not yet "out of control." He then announced a 9:00 p.m.– 5:30 a.m. citywide curfew.
8:15 p.m.	The first newspaper accounts of the riots hit the streets.
9:10 p.m.	Eight hundred of the state's 1,459 troopers were assigned to Detroit.
9:35 p.m.	Sniper fire directed at firefighters was reported in the 12th Street–Lawrence–Collingwood neighborhood.

| 10:25 p.m. | The mayor and the police commissioner ordered all gas stations in the city to be closed. |
| 10:50 p.m. | Governor Romney ordered the guardsmen from Camp Grayling to mobilize. |

Store owners guarded their properties with everything from rifles to swords. One store owner was killed by looters, and at least three looters were killed by shopkeepers or security guards. Image courtesy of the *Detroit News*, from the Detroit Historical Society Collection.

Monday, July 24

Midnight | Governor Romney declared the cities of Detroit, Highland Park, Hamtramck, Ecorse, and River Rouge to be in a state of emergency. He issued an executive order forbidding anyone other than law enforcement officers to carry firearms, ammunition, explosives, or inflammable materials. The order also closed all places of amusement and all places selling or dispensing alcoholic beverages and imposed a 9:00 p.m.–5:30 a.m. curfew. Assemblies of more than five people were illegal.

12:14 a.m. | Ferndale police informed the DPD that they were keeping a full-strength watch along Eight Mile Road.

1:10 a.m. | A fire was reported at Dexter Avenue and Davison Street.

1:33 a.m. | This entire block was now engulfed in flames.

2:40 a.m. | Romney called US Attorney General Ramsey Clark at his home. Romney told Clark that five thousand federal troops "might" be required in Detroit if "conditions did not improve." Romney then asked if a formal telegram would need to be sent. Clark responded that an oral request would be sufficient and that Romney should not "worry about formalities." Clark then called President Johnson. The president authorized the "alerting" of army units. Clark relayed the authorization to Secretary of the Army Stanley Resor, who then ordered Chief of Staff Harold K. Johnson to begin planning the operation.

3:00 a.m. | Cavanagh and Romney announced the request of five thousand federal troops. The mayor said, "We would rather be overcommitted than undercommitted."

4:00 a.m. | Romney announced that he planned to reevaluate the request of federal troops with key advisers.

4:20 a.m. | Resor told Clark that the National Guard was confident in its ability to control the situation. Nonetheless, General Johnson of the US Army readied the 82nd Airborne at Fort Bragg and the 101st Airborne at Fort Campbell.

5:00 a.m.	Romney was informed by Clark that a formal request of troops must be submitted.
5:50 a.m.	Resor asked Clark when he wanted troops to be deployed to Selfridge Air Force Base. Clark responded that he did not know because he did not want to "press the governor."
6:45 a.m.	Cavanagh activated city assistance for emergency food and shelter provisions.
7:00 a.m.	DPD reported that over four hundred people had been injured since midnight.
	Romney and Cavanagh toured the city.
8:30 a.m.	Romney sent telegrams to President Johnson and Clark recommending immediate deployment of federal troops. Cavanagh supported this decision. Clark responded that the governor must "request" troops, not "recommend" troops.
9:30 a.m.	Cavanagh said, "At no time was an order issued that police were not to use weapons available to them." He also stated that he saw "no evidence of outside agents."
9:40 a.m.	Looting was reported to be citywide.
9:45 a.m.	Romney sent the updated telegram. Clark approved the language and told Romney to send it to the president.
11:02 a.m.	The president ordered federal troops to Detroit. Johnson told Secretary of Defense Robert McNamara "to prepare troops for movement," and then McNamara informed Resor "to load the troops on the aircraft." President Johnson ordered troops to stay at Selfridge Air Force Base until further orders. Federal troops were in Detroit to "support and assist," not to "supplant" local agencies.
12:10 p.m.	Police reported that the situation in the Fifth and Seventh Precincts was out of control.
1:20 p.m.	Deputy Secretary of Defense Cyrus Vance arrived at Selfridge Air Force Base and then departed for DPD headquarters.
2:00 p.m.	Vance met with Cavanagh, Romney, Girardin, and other top officials for a briefing on the unrest.

National Guardsmen and Detroit police gathered at the Tenth Precinct on Monday, July 24, 1967. Image courtesy of the *Detroit News*, from the Detroit Historical Society Collection.

5:15 p.m.	Cavanagh, Vance, US Army General John Throckmorton, and Romney, along with local leaders, toured the city in a five-car convoy. The streets were largely empty at that point, leading Throckmorton and Vance to believe that the riot was largely over and winding down. The convoy toured the hardest hit areas of the city for roughly two hours. The only incident during the inspection was a flat tire.
	Vance and Throckmorton received similar feedback from other federal agencies investigating the situation.
8:15 p.m.	Cavanagh, Romney, and Vance held a press conference. Vance announced that there was insufficient evidence to support the need of federal troops in the city. Cavanagh wanted federal troops.
	Damon Keith, cochair of the Michigan Civil Rights Commission, urged the implementation of federal troops and declared that the unrest was not a "race riot."

9:15 p.m.	Only eight police officers were left on reserve. All others were committed.
9:54 p.m.	All police were ordered to retreat from 12th Street and the Tenth Precinct.
10:25 p.m.	Sniper fire increased, pinning down police and police reinforcements across the city.
11:00 p.m.	Vance, Throckmorton, Cavanagh, and Romney concluded that local agencies failed and that the situation was out of control.

Mayor Jerome Cavanagh addressed the media in the Common Council chambers. He is flanked (*left to right*) by US Army General John Throckmorton, Deputy Secretary of Defense Cyrus Vance, and Governor George Romney. Photograph by Jerry Heiman, *Detroit Free Press*. Donated by the City of Detroit Department of Information—Photography Department, from the Detroit Historical Society Collection.

| 11:10 p.m. | The four men recommend to the president that federal troops be deployed in the city. |
| 11:20 p.m. | President Johnson signed the proclamation and the executive order authorizing the use of federal troops in Detroit. |

Tuesday, July 25

| Midnight | President Johnson addressed the nation regarding the riot in Detroit and the commitment of federal troops. The president was joined in the address by McNamara, FBI Director J. Edgar Hoover, and Clark. |
| | Hubert Locke stated that "veteran police officers were convinced that they were engaged in the worst urban guerilla warfare witnessed in the United States in the twentieth century." |

Federal troops of the 82nd Airborne Division were shuttled by chartered buses to various staging points near the conflict zones. From the Detroit Historical Society Collection.

Federal troops, led by an M41 Walker Bulldog tank, convoyed south down Jefferson Avenue past East Grand Boulevard and Belle Isle. Photograph by Fred Plofchan, *Detroit Free Press*. Donated by the City of Detroit Department of Information—Photography Department, from the Detroit Historical Society Collection.

4:00 a.m.	Throckmorton ordered all paratroopers and guardsmen to unload their weapons and place their ammo in their pockets. The order was, "You will unload all weapons. You will put the round[s] in your pocket[s]. You will not fire at looters. You will return fire on snipers only on the command of a commissioned officer."
8:00 a.m.	Romney urged businesses to go back to work. Cavanagh and Vance agreed.
10:00 a.m.	Governor Romney permitted the sale of gasoline from noon until 5:00 p.m. This was limited to only five gallons per customer and was allowed to be put only into vehicles. Bars and entertainment venues were still shuttered. The public schools elected to remain closed also.
9:00 p.m.	Sniper fire restarted near 12th Street and Clairmount Avenue.
9:54 p.m.	All police were ordered to retreat from 12th Street.
10:01 p.m.	Police were ordered to retreat from the Tenth Precinct.
10:20 p.m.	Sniper activity went on the offensive.

Chronology of Events

Cyrus Vance and General Throckmorton addressed reporters. Photograph by Fred Plofchan, *Detroit Free Press*. Donated by the City of Detroit Department of Information—Photography Department, from the Detroit Historical Society Collection.

11:00 p.m.	Police, firefighters, and state police were ordered out of the area between West Grand Boulevard, Clairmount Avenue, Woodrow Wilson Street, and Dexter Avenue. The units pulled back in preparation for a National Guard sweep of the area.
11:11 p.m.	The fire station at Livernois Avenue and West Chicago came under heavy sniper fire.

Wednesday, July 26

1:00 a.m.	Throckmorton and Vance toured the city again. Vance stated, "No organized leadership of riot is evident."
2:15 a.m.	A clerk from the Wayne County morgue phoned Detective Joseph Zisler of the Homicide Bureau to say that

there were three dead bodies in the Manor House annex of the Algiers Motel.

8:30 a.m.	Gas-station hours were extended, and people were urged to return to work. Officials agreed that an adequate number of troops were on the streets.
9:15 a.m.	The first reports of price gouging surfaced.
11:00 a.m.	The governor warned of price gouging and appealed to merchants.
12:05 p.m.	Judge Vincent Brennan stated that 90 percent of arrestees had been charged with entering without breaking, 5 percent with violation of curfew, 5 percent with assault with a deadly weapon, carrying a deadly weapon, or possession of stolen property.
2:55 p.m.	Sniper fire dramatically increased across the city: Hamilton Avenue and Lawrence Street, Leslie and Lawton Streets, Livernois and Warren Avenues, Hazelwood Street and Second Avenue, the 2200 block of Blaine Street, Taylor and Woodrow Wilson Streets, Woodward Avenue and Collingwood Street, and Clairmount Avenue near the Lodge.
4:30 p.m.	Vance toured the east side: all quiet. He stated, "It is now possible to move back to normalcy."
5:00 p.m.	The Common Council passed a price-control ordinance.
7:45 p.m.	Police patrols moved back into Woodrow Wilson Street, Dexter and Clairmount Avenues, and West Grand Boulevard.

Thursday, July 27

Early morning	Michigan State Police officers were withdrawn.
	The 4th Infantry Division was assigned to the First, Seventh, and Thirteenth Precincts. The 82nd and 101st Airborne Divisions were withdrawn.
9:30 a.m.	1,671 people were in custody in Detroit's sixteen precincts.

Over seven thousand people were arrested, generally for looting or curfew violations. Most were taken to temporary detention facilities throughout the region. Some spent days confined on buses. Photograph by Jerry Heiman, *Detroit Free Press*. Donated by the City of Detroit Department of Information—Photography Department, from the Detroit Historical Society Collection.

Noon	Vance suggested lifting the curfew, and Romney complied.
1:20 p.m.	Groups representing citizens asked for the curfew to remain in effect.
7:15 p.m.	The curfew was reinstated by the governor.

Friday, July 28

11:00 a.m.	Romney specified that the state of emergency and related restrictions were unchanged for the weekend. Romney said, "The task before us is enormous, but not for government alone."
2:50 p.m.	The National Guard began its gradual withdrawal.

| 5:00 p.m. | Each Detroit precinct was assigned an observer from the Civil Rights Commission. |
| 8:15 p.m. | DPD announced that a prisoner information center had been established for the public at headquarters. |

Saturday, July 29

| 11:00 a.m. | Governor Romney authorized the release of fourteen hundred prisoners from custody. The majority of these people were curfew breakers. Curfew was extended to include 9:00 p.m. to 11:00 p.m. |
| 5:40 p.m. | Cavanagh announced that emergency bonds would be issued to provide funds to pay police officers, firefighters, and other city employees who worked overtime during the disorder. |

Mayor Cavanagh and US Senator Philip Hart toured the afflicted areas of the city and listened to the residents' concerns. Image courtesy of Berl Falbaum.

Sunday, July 30

2:00 a.m.   Twenty-three hundred troops encamped at Chandler Park.

Monday, July 31

8:21 a.m.   Curfew hours were reduced from midnight to 5:30 a.m. Alcohol could be served from 7:00 a.m. to midnight.

12:30 p.m.   Superintendent Reuter advised that police officers return to eight-hour shifts, but with no leave and no furlough.

Tuesday, August 1

12:05 p.m.   Curfew restrictions were lifted.

4:00 p.m.   National Guardsmen were ordered to withdraw from streets by 9:00 p.m. A full pullout was scheduled for noon on Friday, August 4.

Wednesday, August 2

6:42 p.m.   Vice President Hubert Humphrey arrived at Detroit City Airport.

Thursday, August 3

8:55 a.m.   Perimeter defense of Detroit police headquarters was removed.

Steel Meets Flint

HOW TO START A RIOT

Joel Stone

This narrative is based on the recollections of two men. Neither can be taken as absolute truth; the "fog of war" was heavy in Detroit, and no two accounts completely reconcile. Facts and events that the men cite align closely with those of other eyewitnesses and police records. There are some details here not mentioned in other accounts. This should not cast doubt on the veracity of the memory but add depth to the record. Anthony Fierimonte's version was collected through personal conversations and captured in an oral-history video recording on file with the Detroit Historical Society in 2015. William Scott's reminiscences were included in *Hurt, Baby, Hurt,* published by New Ghetto Press in 1970 in Ann Arbor, Michigan.

The flashpoint of the uprising in Detroit was a police raid on an unlicensed, after-hours drinking club. In contemporary parlance, it was a "joint" or a "blind pig." While the people arrested were being taken away, an irritable crowd was provoked to action when someone threw a bottle at a cop. The rest is history.

In the process of developing the *Detroit '67* project, two important people came to light. One was the arresting officer, the guy who broke down the door of the blind pig. The other was the man in the crowd who threw the bottle and then started screaming at police. One was the flint. The other was the steel.

The two men, both young, were representative of their segments of Detroit society. Significantly, both loved learning. Otherwise, their personalities, backgrounds, family lives, and career paths are a study in contrasts. They were a metaphor of the city in the moment when polar opposites passed each other on 12th Street—meeting for only a second—and profoundly changed the psyche, history, and future of an entire region.

Neither was a bad man. They did not intend to start the largest civil disturbance of the era. They were in the moment and reacted as they might have been expected to, as most of us would have reacted under the same circumstances. Perhaps by putting a human face on the "spark," we can gain further insight into the event.

– –

Tony Fierimonte was from the northeast side of Detroit. Christened Antonio Luigi Giuseppe Fierimonte, his surname means "fair mountain." He quipped that his mother expected him to become pope—not an unusual expectation in Italian families but probably not likely for this fun-loving, jovial, slightly irreverent lad. His father worked as a mechanic for the city's Department of Street Railways—the DSR—which ran streetcars and buses. Tony grew up in St. Bartholomew Roman Catholic parish and eventually went to the local high school.

John J. Pershing High School was typical in that it was a three-story, moderately Art Deco building named after a national war hero, built in 1937 to serve newly constructed neighborhoods near the city limits. Pershing was *not* typical in that the neighborhoods it served were both black and white. The school was built in an area known locally as Conant Gardens; it had once been owned by Shubael Conant, a merchant, an abolitionist, and the founder of the Detroit Anti-Slavery Society in 1837. He placed no race-related deed restrictions on the property, and as a result, it became the premier neighborhood for upscale African Americans to build homes in the 1920s. It was one of the few places in Detroit where blacks could get Federal Housing Administration loans. The "Gardens" was home to doctors, lawyers, engineers, and other professionals, and Pershing High was the formative home for the likes of Duke Fakir and Levi Stubbs of the Four Tops singing group from Motown Records, the actor Tim Meadows, the basketball legend Spencer Haywood—and Tony Fierimonte.

While at Pershing, the young man entered the police cadet program. A buddy's dad worked in a "Big Four" unit—three plainclothesmen and a uniformed driver. Tony recalled them cruising in large cars—DeSotos or Buicks—not the standard Ford patrol sedans. Out of high school, he entered the Detroit Police Academy, graduated first in his class in 1962, and probably could have chosen any precinct in the city. When asked where he wanted to work, he demurred—wherever he was needed.

He was assigned to the Tenth Precinct, in a brand-new building on Livernois Avenue at Elmhurst Street. It was one of two precincts where the force was integrated. Commissioner Ray Girardin's push to get more black officers into the force and into the neighborhoods was being met with opposition from many white cops. There were sick-outs and a reduction in ticket writing, which affected municipal revenue. Some officers quit. Tony did not have a problem with it. He was a Pershing Doughboy.

The Tenth Precinct served a mixed neighborhood. Much of it was white, both Christian and Jewish. A significant portion of it was black, newly shifted from the old Black Bottom neighborhood, which was removed in the 1950s. The homes were beautifully built, mostly brick, many duplexes with upper and lower units. Like lots of the neighborhoods in Detroit, the structures were situated close to one another, with only the width of a driveway between. Streets were lined with massive elm trees that created a cooling canopy—except in late summer, when they stifled breezes altogether.

The southeastern quadrant of the precinct was a neighborhood in transition. Residents were mostly black, and the population density was twice the city average. This was the western end of the very tony Boston-Edison district and included the LaSalle Gardens, Virginia Park, and Petoskey-Otsego neighborhoods. Livernois and Dexter Avenues and Linwood and 12th Streets were the major north-south streets, lined with businesses. Bottom to top, Grand Boulevard, Clairmount Avenue, Joy Road, Elmhurst Street, and Davison Avenue were the east-west arteries. The businesses were owned by a culturally diverse group of entrepreneurs, with predominantly Jewish ownership of the properties. The heart of the district was home to the classically styled Central High School and the Roman Catholic archdiocese's Sacred Heart Seminary complex, as well as the Jewish Congregation Shaarey Zedek and Central United Church of Christ under the leadership of the political firebrand Rev. Albert Cleage (the church and its pastor later were renamed the Shrine of the Black Madonna and Jaramogi Abebe Agyeman, respectively).

The Tenth Precinct was also home to William Walter Scott III. Sometimes.

— —

William, or Billy, was born to this neighborhood. He knew that his middle and last names referenced a famous dead writer, but that was almost all that tied him to the past. His home lacked stability for much of his childhood, and at school, he had difficulty learning. Scott's father, who worked at Dodge Main for a while, was a tough-love type of guy. His mother was attentive and caring but very frail from a heart ailment. When his dad lost the auto job and began hustling numbers on the street—a popular illegal lottery—he had his hands full with an ailing wife and Billy's brothers and sisters. At ten years old, Billy found himself enrolled at the Hawthorne Center in suburban Northville, a state mental health facility about seventeen miles from home. It might as well have been a thousand miles.

Hawthorne Center was one of the first child psychiatric institutions in the nation. It opened in 1956 on a fifty-eight-acre campus in the rolling country west of Detroit. Initially, about sixty students were housed in cottages near a main building, which also served perhaps fifteen outpatients. Boarding patients received food, health care, education, and clothing, while a team of psychologists, psychiatrists, physicians, and educators addressed issues ranging from reading difficulties to severe schizophrenia.

Billy was the only African American at the center. He was quiet, perhaps a little scared, and he blended in—or faded to the background. As a child, he had no comprehension of why he was there. He made friends and enjoyed the steady routine of the program. He missed his family, especially his mom. For the three years he lived at Hawthorne, his family never came to see him. The route was not difficult—straight out Seven Mile Road to Haggerty— but it was a long trek for a family without reliable transportation.

At thirteen, Billy was transferred to Boys' Republic, a few miles away in Farmington. As its name might suggest, it was described as a self-governing school for delinquent boys. Instead of being new, the Boys' Republic lineage dates to the progressive 1890s, when it was considered prudent to get young offenders out of adult jails. Everything was still provided to Billy, and there was still a routine; but this was much less a home than a place for young men who were better off not in prison. Family contact was minimal. Billy occasionally got home on holidays; during one Labor Day visit, his sickly mother passed away.

In the summer of 1963, the fifteen-year-old was sent to a foster home. An older couple on Detroit's near east side gave him a bed in a room that he shared with another boy. Billy was able to attend classes at Eastern High School, interacting with other students and getting his first exposure to girls. Belle Isle, Detroit's summer playground, was a mile or so away. The foster parents, though, were tough on him. Or at least the woman was; the man did not seem to care. Billy finally had enough and split.

He sought out his father and moved in with him in time to enroll at Northern High School. He hit a bit of a groove—got into sports, graduated, and started looking to college. It was then that he discovered how poor his education had been. While working in bottom-tier jobs, he took remedial classes and studied in the evening. Late at night, he would occasionally walk with his older brothers down 12th Street.

There was a thrill being on the street. During the day, it was lined with modestly successful businesses—shoe stores, drugstores, convenience stores, appliance stores, cleaners. The Chit Chat Lounge and a few other legitimate clubs were hopping, but bars were in short supply because it was hard for African Americans to get the necessary licenses. However, if you knew where to go, there was good music and cold beer to be had. As the night wore on, the street scene became more electric. Adults could get almost anything they were interested in along that strip, for a price. Everyone knew it. Locals knew it. Suburbanites knew it. And the cops knew it.

When Billy and his brothers were out on their walks, they were aware of the local police presence. They hated the "Big Four"; everyone did. But there were also regular patrol units and undercover assets roving. A black man walking the street took a gamble. Statistically, it was a good bet that he would be stopped at least once a year somewhere in the city; on 12th Street, the odds were higher.

-- --

Tony Fierimonte had been on the job less than two months. He was walking the beat on 12th Street by himself, without a radio, when Sergeant Cardinelli pulled up. "Hey, kid. You want to go undercover? You'll be arresting prostitutes, going at the illegal gambling casinos, blind pigs." This was real police work. Tony could not jump on board fast enough.

It was an odd shift, working a 9:00 p.m. to 3:00 a.m. shift every other month and days in between. The main targets were the numbers men. People picked numbers—three or four generally—and the daily winner was determined by various horse races. Different bookies had different systems. No matter who was selling the number, the business was mostly owned by the mafia.

Tony did not mind working the weird hours, and he did not mind working the Tenth Precinct. To him, it was easier than the white neighborhoods. Catch someone there playing fast and loose with the law, and he or she would claim to know a judge or some higher-up at City Hall. Worse was when they begged because the arrest would ruin their marriage, their job, their life. In the black neighborhoods, it was, "Hey, you busted us. That's it."

Tony had been working the area enough that he had numerous informants. It was not too hard. If you owned the house behind a blind pig or a bordello, the noise and traffic would be incentive enough for you to call the

A police raid on an illegal after-hours drinking establishment, or blind pig, sparked a week of violence. It was located in the headquarters of the United Community League for Civic Action on the second floor of Economy Printing at 12th Street and Clairmount Avenue. This photograph was taken in early August as City of Detroit workers cleaned up the neighborhood. From the Detroit Historical Society Collection.

cops. And there were folks who needed favors who would cooperate. One of these gave Sergeant Arthur Howison's squad a tip on the party upstairs at 9125 12th Street on July 22. Tony worked for Howison.

Precinct "cleanup crews"—the vice squad—had been to this address a few times before over the past eighteen months. They knew there were numbers, and they knew there was booze. Otherwise, this was not a dangerous place: no hard drugs, perhaps a little gambling. This should be a routine bust—if they could get through the door.

— —

Billy's dad had a brother, the only college graduate in the family. This uncle became active in local politics and saw results: Mayor Cavanagh was elected because he received 85 percent of the African American vote in 1963. It represented a powerful victory for black voices. Father and uncle saw an opportunity to effect change and formed the United Community League for Civic Action (UCLCA) out of a storefront on 12th Street, just north of Clairmount Avenue. Being less ideological than those who were in the nascent Black Power movement, they focused on getting people to the polls to vote instead of overthrowing the government. Once their voting bloc was organized, its profile caught the attention of various politicians eager to do what Cavanagh had done. They instilled money into the UCLCA, and the brothers were able to make the league more of a club. In nonelection years, when donations from the candidates were slim, the club survived by hosting meetings at which people bought drinks. At first, this fund-raising indiscretion was ignored.

Billy's dad called his place the Club. After a while, the Community League name became ponderous and perhaps ironic. He knew that the group could be leveraged for profit and prestige, but it was not effecting any serious political change. Billy worked for his dad as the doorman and was becoming equally discouraged. Despite his efforts at higher learning, he could not get a decent job—*any* job was hard to find. The deck seemed steeply stacked against him.

Mid-July 1967, Billy got lucky. He secured a spot on the afternoon shift in one of the auto plants. It was not going to exercise his brain, but it would pay the bills; and he could save for the next semester of college. Also, he enjoyed coming to the Club after work as a patron, not a doorman. It was Saturday night, his shift was over, and he was looking forward to closing out a week with friends. He had heard there were a couple of neighborhood guys just back from Vietnam, and their buddies were throwing them a party.

Billy had to park a block or so away; it was a busy night on the strip. This area was hopping after 2:30 a.m. Bars closed, and the legitimate clientele mixed with the less legitimate for a while. Walking down 12th Street toward the Club was hot. Earlier in the day, the temperature had reached 86 degrees with a bit of a breeze from the southwest. After midnight, the temperature had not fallen much, and the humidity hung heavily in the air. Billy noticed something going on ahead, lots of lights. He picked up the pace.

— —

Tony's unit rolled out of the station about 10:00 p.m. Sergeant Howison was working relief for the night, putting in overtime. The forty-three-hundred-man force was represented by only a few hundred bodies that night. Lots of guys were on vacation.

Patrolmen Charles Henry and Joseph Brown, both black, were the other two guys in the car. This team had made raids together before. Crowds would always gather to watch the fun—it was something for them to look at. There was a process, it happened, and everyone went on with their lives.

At least that was how it felt if you were a cop. For the arrestee, it could mean the difference between a good career and a lifetime of résumé red flags and uncomfortable questions.

Working off the tip, Howison's team headed for the address on 12th Street. Officers Henry and Brown tried to get in. They had a good pitch—Brown was a basketball player from Cincinnati looking for a good time—but were turned away. The unit moved on and investigated a number of other potential joints and prostitutes. It was getting near time to wrap up for the evening when they drove past the first joint. A couple of classy ladies were heading in that direction, so Henry suggested they try hooking up with the ladies and get into the party. It worked, and he was able to buy some beer. The game was afoot.

The department had a ten-minute rule. If the undercover guy did not come out of the building in ten minutes, it was a signal to the other officers. They had either made a buy and the bust was on, or they were having some other issue and needed help. Another unit had joined the team, and Tony figured it was going to be easy. Then they could not get past the front door.

Today, raiding parties carry small battering rams. In 1967, they depended on a strong shoulder, which was not working. As Tony remembers it, men in a passing fire truck offered their fire ax. In short order, the door was breached, and they pounded upstairs with badges out, announcing the bust.

A number of things happened that they did not expect. First, the joint was packed. Instead of a couple of dozen folks, they found over eighty. Second, the patrons were not happy about the party ending so soon. They were welcoming a couple of guys back from the war, guys who had risked their lives for their country, and this is how they were treated? Pool balls began flying, and the police retreated—all but Henry, who was playfully detained. Tony remembers taunts of "You're not taking anybody to jail" coming from threatening smiles, although Henry was eventually allowed to leave.

The third thing they did not expect was that the alley-side access door was inoperable; they would have to go out the front. Glass was raining down on the street as furniture and things were thrown out of windows of the two upstairs units. Predictably, the noise was drawing a crowd. Tony called for support and two or three paddy wagons for prisoner transport. A group of recent academy graduates on special patrol were detailed by their sergeant to help, and a Big Four cruiser rolled up, sure to intimidate—or rile up—any crowd.

The paddy wagons were the fourth surprise. It was after 3:00 a.m. The evening shift was gone, and the overnight force was reduced to just over two hundred men citywide. About 10 percent of that was already on-site. Getting even one fourteen-person van was going to take an hour. The teams slowly brought the arrestees downstairs and shuttled them to the precinct in squad cars. At first, the gathering throng was only curious, staying on the opposite side of the street, shouting friendly taunts at their handcuffed friends and not-so-subtle jabs at the police. Finally one police wagon arrived and then another, and the process accelerated. The officers were anxious to be out of the neighborhood and got pushy with some of the folks getting in the vans. This further antagonized the crowd. People became increasingly abusive, and the taunts became increasingly aggressive. A bottle flew from the mob and smashed to the pavement near one officer. More bottles flew. One shattered the rear window of the big Buick, just as the vans were pulling away.

— —

Billy saw the crowd opposite the club. There was a paddy wagon and a few squad cars, and he knew what was happening. He had been there for a previous raid. Everyone was having a great time, dancing so the floor swayed. Mr. James Brown blared from the jukebox. The gambling room was doing great business. Then one of the guys pulled a badge from his pocket, his partner locked the front door, and everyone started to dance—they did not want to waste the jukebox tunes. The crowd stayed calm as the arresting officers called in the backups and paddy wagons. Everyone was loaded up; taken to the precinct; ticketed for loitering, illegal occupation, selling liquor, or gambling; then kept for a few hours and released. That was how it usually went. While waiting in line for transport, Billy lit a cigarette and questioned the cop's right to tell him to put it out. It earned him some quiet time in the Club's office, a hard smack to the head, and humiliation at the hands of this black cop.

That memory was burning on his soul as he approached the Club tonight. His dad and sister were in there. So was Eddie, the brother-in-law who replaced him at the door. Billy began to cross the street and shouted at two of the officers guarding the door. He knew that the cops had to use the front door because the alley-side door did not open. He approached the cops suggesting in terse terms that they should get their white selves out of the neighborhood. Initially bold, the police officers began to approach this rabble-rouser. The crowd counteradvanced, and the officers retreated. The shouting picked up as people were hustled down the stairs, the arrestees themselves objecting loudly and firing up the crowd even more.

Hardy Drugs stood at the corner of 12th Street and Clairmount Avenue, across the street from the blind pig where confrontations with police began. It was one of the first buildings damaged when looting began. Image courtesy of Thomas Diggs.

Eventually additional patrolmen formed a cordon around the police van, with nightsticks drawn. Billy, in the vanguard, had a hard time not advancing; the crowd was surging forward. To clear some space, he hopped on the nearest squad car and exhorted the mob. With the strength of youth and adrenalin, he had them cheering the arrestees and badgering the police. Invectives, slurs, and curses exploded from him, loud and untempered. He saw the cops pushing his sister and father—some of the last people out of the building—and it became even more personal. He ran to the alley, grabbed a bottle, and threw it at the first cop he saw.

As it happened, he missed, but the sound of the glass shattering cleared the street. It naturally made the crowd shrink back, and police officers instantly advanced, stopping when they realized that most people were not moving. Law enforcement regrouped and was pulling out when a number of bottles came from the roof of the building across from the Club. One took out the Buick's rear window. Pistols came out of holsters. The paddy wagons left as more bricks and bottles flew. In a confused retreat, the police completely withdrew from the scene.

The crowd was jubilant. Billy said he felt free, observing a spirit that had possessed everyone—a fearless "unification of the rebellious spirit of man." A rebellion had occurred. The king's troops had been driven away. It lasted for only a few minutes, until he saw what the police had done to his father's club. They had ransacked it, randomly destroying anything at hand. Revenge replaced rebellion.

Along with a buddy and Eddie (who had jumped out the window when the raid came down), Billy stormed down to the corner, picked up a trash bin, and flung it through the drugstore window. If they can bust up his place, he could bust up theirs. The alarm went off. The crowd ran away.

— —

Back at the Livernois station house, Fierimonte was the arresting officer of record and had paperwork to do. The prisoners had been taken downtown, and he got only sporadic reports from the field. When his lieutenant returned from a reconnaissance cruise, he had been hit in the head with some type of projectile. Police cruisers were limping in with broken windows and dented hoods. Judging the size of the crowd, Lieutenant Ray Good activated a protocol that brought all off-duty personnel back to work. The calls filtered up the chain of command to the top. Girardin got it about 5:20 a.m. Cavanagh was aware a few minutes later.

Tony was eventually appointed to antisniper duty. He describes using the Buick with the rear window gone and mounting a .45 mm machine gun in that void. As a tank, it was a joke. He noted that the Detroit Police Department, the Michigan State Police, and the Michigan National Guard were unable to stem the tide. Things did not begin to slow down until troops from the US Army's 82nd and 101st Airborne units entered the fray early Tuesday morning. The tanks sent a no-nonsense message that patrol cars could not. Looting ended quickly. Sniping continued through Thursday.

— —

Once the drugstore was opened, Billy returned to the Club, grabbed all the beer—it was going to go warm without ice—and started to pass it out on the street. He encouraged people to take what they wished, and soon they did. More windows were broken. The looting expanded. Billy walked around in a daze for hours, gathering clothes, directing traffic, scaring white kids who happened by. About eight in the morning, he was worn out but headed down to police headquarters to find out about his dad and sister, who were in the main jail. The judge would see them sometime after noon and probably let them go.

Billy went home to bed. A few hours later, his house was on fire. His family—dad and sister were home by then—moved as much as they could to the street and then watched the entire block burn. Dad loaded up the car and left the boys to fend for themselves. Billy stayed for the night with a friend, got up the next morning to find a newspaper—he wanted to know how the press had covered the rebellion—and was subsequently rounded up by police for being on Grand River Avenue near where looting was occurring. According to his account, he spent the next fifteen days jailed in parking garages, city buses, a bathhouse, and a hospital.

He finally came before a judge and was simply told to go home—no conviction, no explanation. Once released, he admitted that, even though he was horribly bitter and angry, the cops had broken the rebellion out of him. As he walked up 12th Street, he realized that the strip had been similarly broken and would never be the same again. The spirit had been driven out of both of them.

– –

Soon afterward, Tony was among the first to enroll in classes in police-community relations. Within the DPD, he rose through the ranks to become a commander. He took advantage of the Law Enforcement Assistance Act to pay his tuition at Wayne State University, eventually getting a doctorate in psychiatry and teaching community relations. Following retirement, he set up a practice working with troubled police officers. He dabbled successfully in real estate in Michigan before settling in Florida.

– –

Billy returned to his factory job, only to find that he had lost it during his incarceration; his excuse fell on deaf ears. He had enough saved for the next semester of college but found he had to use it to supplement living expenses. Working through his anger, memories of July 1967 were set to paper. One essay won an Avery Hopwood Award from the University of Michigan in 1969 and allowed him to continue his studies. His full recollection, *Hurt, Baby, Hurt*, was published in 1970. Billy Scott also moved to Florida.

In the Center of the Storm

Hubert G. Locke

Hubert Locke was interviewed by William Winkel, August 17, 2016, and his transcript was edited by Joel Stone, November 21, 2016, to fit this volume's physical limitations. The complete original transcript can be accessed via the Detroit Historical Society's electronic portal (detroithistorical.org).

I grew up in what is known by black Detroiters as the old west side—the geographic area roughly served by Northwestern High School. It was one of three segregated areas in the city of Detroit in which black families could buy homes and bounded by Epworth on the west, West Grand Boulevard on the east, Tireman on the north, and Warren on the south.

In spite of the fact that it was segregated, it was a wonderful old community, very much intact. Many of the large churches of black Detroit were there, and one of the institutions was the Nacirema Club. (Nacirema is "American" spelled in reverse.) All my friends as I was growing up were in that neighborhood. We went to a church, as I recall, out of the community that was over on the east side; that was my parents' church. Other than that, we simply didn't have occasion to go outside of the neighborhood. Everything we wanted or needed or were interested in was in that area.

My dad worked his entire life after 1937 at Ford Motor Company, in the Open Hearth Building at the Rouge Plant. My mother was a housewife until the Second World War, and she worked at the old Ex-Cell-O plant on Hamilton at Oakman Boulevard. I remember it being a very tense period, but there were no problems in our part of town, . . . in the old west side. I don't remember there being any problems over there. One of the jobs I had in high school, I worked in the local grocery store that was at the corner of Stanford and Tireman. The owner was white and served both the black populace, who lived south of Tireman, and the white populace, who lived north of Tireman. So I was hauling groceries in the white area every evening after school and especially on the weekends. I never had any problems. But I'm saying all of this in the context of life within a very segregated city. We didn't have problems primarily because we lived by ourselves, had our own institutions and cultural exposures and opportunities, so there wasn't any need to see much of the city. There were two movie theaters, I remember, in the old neighborhood.

When I went to college, of course, I went to Wayne State, so that was really my first sort of exposure to the wider city and culture. Although I had a number of Jewish friends at Northwestern, I am suddenly being exposed not just to the university but this whole cultural center area, so that suddenly the world of the art museum opened up for me. I was president of the freshman class in 1950. We'd take ski trips up to Grayling and Gaylord, Michigan, in the winters. It was a wonderful time for me. In fact, I later served on the staff at Wayne for a couple of years and thought I'd never leave the boundaries of these six blocks.

I was politically active during my time as an undergraduate at Wayne State. This was the McCarthy era, among other things. I remember we had all sorts of anti-McCarthy activities going on during that period. I left in 1955, went to Chicago, took a degree there, and came back to Detroit in 1959. The city was booming, of course, in that period. There just was not the occasion for a lot of tension in that period, at least as far as I can recall.

A grant prompted my return to the city in 1959 and my becoming the executive director of what was known as the Citizens Committee for Equal Opportunity. It was part of the growing effort in the city then to begin to deal with some of its racial problems and some of the spin-offs of that situation. There was a critical election in this town [that] resulted in the dumping of the then-mayor Louis Miriani and his replacement by Jerry Cavanagh.

Things were heating up then, I think it's safe to say, in Detroit. The defeat of Miriani was particularly critical in that regard because there had been a couple of very tragic assaults on white nurses coming down to the medical center. The press, of course, was making a big cry about that, and Miriani made it a huge part of his reelection campaign: he was going to get the rapists off the street. What he did, really, was he announced what amounted to a crackdown on street crime, which of course meant a crackdown on black males. The police department went after it with considerable eagerness, so that any black male found walking in this area after dusk, in the evening, was going to be arrested—if not arrested, at least stopped, detained, patted down, roughed up—and that became an election issue in '62. It was that issue that swung the black vote toward Jerry Cavanagh.

Cavanagh came on board with the determination to try to do something about racial problems in the city. We were just beginning to get the spill-over effect of the desegregation of Detroit, so there was a lot of population movement throughout the city. That was creating some pockets of tension as black families moved into previously all-white areas. The Citizens Committee was euphemistically called the Bishop Emrich Committee, for the Episcopal bishop who chaired it. I can't recall how I got selected for that job, but I went to work for the Citizens Committee and stayed there for three years. I went back to my post at Wayne State and in 1966 went to the police department. That part I remember well.

That was a direct outcome of my work with the Citizens Committee. We had four major areas of concern in Bishop Emrich's committee: education, housing, public accommodations, and police-community relations. Because of the tension, we spent the greater majority of our time on police-community relations. I resigned in '64, '65, to go back to Wayne. And I got this call from the mayor, who invites me to sit down with him and Ray Girardin, then the commissioner of police, and their pitch was, "Look, you and the Citizens Committee have focused so much time on the problem of police-community relations, and you worked at it from the outside. We want you to come at it on the inside and help deal with it within the department," to which I said politely, "Mr. Mayor, you're out of your cotton-picking mind." Who in his right mind would go in the Detroit Police Department, which had, at that time, a pretty bad reputation as far as police-community relations were concerned?

Well, Jerry Cavanagh was a very astute politician. He immediately turns around and calls—who was it? Dick Austin, John Conyers, Buddy Battle from the labor union? Anyway, he calls these guys together, and he says, "Look, you've been knocking my head about the police-community relations problem. I'm trying to get Locke to come in the department; we are creating a post for him to work on this problem." I got called one evening shortly thereafter to a meeting in Dick Austin's basement recreation room. "Look, we don't know what Cavanagh is up to, but if he wants you to come inside the police department, you go." So I went, and I was there for two years.

When I went in the department, there were 137 or 139 black officers in a department that had 4,000 sworn officers. Black officers were all in the patrol ranks [with] two exceptions that I remember: one had risen to the level of precinct captain, and Bill Hart, who later became the chief of police, was in the vice squad.

I began with the most obvious problems, one being the low number of black officers in the department, and just began to look at it systematically from the whole recruitment process, through the exam, testing, to swearing in. I discovered that a number of young black males were going to the department, passing the screening exam, written exam, got to the medical exam, of all things, and were flunking it. I went to the medical office to see what the problem was, and the doctor said, "Oh, it's very simple. Blacks have flat feet, and they can't do patrol." I said, "But nobody walks the patrol beat anymore! They ride around in scout cars!"

I went back and told the commissioner what I'd found. He almost tore his hair out but said, "Hubert, if we were functioning at our ideal in this whole recruitment process, what do you think we'd be taking in in each entry class?" I said, "Well, the city's population is now close to 25 percent black, so if we're going to reflect the population of the city, we ought to have entrance classes that are approximately 25 percent black officers." He sent that word to the recruitment office and said, "I want to set that as a target." From that next class on, we were taking in exactly 25 percent! Exactly 25 percent. We set up police-community relations councils in each of the precincts. We were making some small but steady progress, chipping away at what had been a huge, glacial problem in the city.

I don't know that the white community was unhappy with the police department, but it certainly had a bad reputation in black Detroit. As a small note on that, in those days, part of the patrol tactic was to have in each precinct what was known as the felony car. The felony car was euphemistically known in the community as the Big Four, because it was an unmarked police car, usually a big Buick or something, in which four officers rode around who handled the felony runs in each precinct. This inevitably brought them into direct contact and conflict with a lot of young black males as they would make street stops and whatever. I remember that in those first few months in the department, I developed the habit of riding in one of those felony cars every Friday and Saturday night. Friday, I'd work from eight to five, get a bite to eat, and come back and go out with the felony car and ride 'til three in the morning, knowing that at least the felony car in which I was riding wasn't going to have any bad stories about police conduct.

Were police-community relations improving? I suppose the answer depends on who you ask. I think some felt at least things were turning around, heading in the right direction. Others would probably say no, nothing changed at all. I tend to think, for whatever it's worth, that there was at least movement. Things were not in a static mode during that period. Of course, we're talking about '66. I went in the department in March of '66. Fifteen months later, the riot erupts, so we didn't have much time to make a lot of progress.

We gained a lot of credit on our handling of the Kercheval incident [in 1966], because the rest of the nation was blowing up at that point. Watts had occurred, if I recall correctly, and Cleveland, and then suddenly, we think it's our turn. But we had two or three things going for us that night. One, it happened on a Tuesday night, and if I recall correctly, there may have been a baseball game in town that night. For some reason, there was a higher than normal contingent of officers on duty downtown. So when we got the alert, shipping them up to Kercheval wasn't much of a problem. Number two, the guys who were behind the Kercheval incident weren't the best planners in the world; whatever they had in mind, getting stirred up, didn't stir up very easily. The third thing—I will never forget—is that at about nine or ten o'clock that night, a rainstorm broke out, and that put a damper on Kercheval, wiped out the protest completely.

Detroit, suddenly, began to gain the reputation nationwide as the city that knows how to handle civil disorders. Officers were rather pleased with themselves, having handled Kercheval, particularly because of the growing problem nationally. They really thought that they had done something extraordinary. I remember that period as one in which the officers said, "Maybe there is something to this police-community relations business."

I can't say that we were caught unawares. One of the incidents I remember particularly: I was out riding, again, with the Big Four on the weekend before July 23, the weekend prior to the outbreak of the riot. We raided a blind pig—or busted is the more appropriate term—busted a blind pig on Linwood. The technique was for the vice squad to go, hit the place about two or three in the morning, arrest the people who were there, and take them on downtown for booking. We expected to find only a dozen or twenty people in the place. There were seventy or eighty people, and we had difficulty getting transportation for these people from the point of arrest downtown. I remember going back to headquarters that Monday and saying, "We gotta work out a different way of handling this." A week later, what happens but it repeats! The whole scenario repeats itself again.

— —

Nick Hood, who was the pastor at Plymouth Congregation, called me. I can't remember how that came about, but he called me early Sunday morning, and within minutes thereafter—it may have been almost at the same time—I get a call from Conrad Mallet. Conrad was the assistant to Cavanagh and was my next-door neighbor, and his son, Conrad Jr., was the neighborhood paperboy. He had gone up on 12th Street to pick up his supply of papers from wherever the drop was, came home wide-eyed as could be, and said to his dad, "Something's going on up on 12th Street." Conrad calls me, I hop in my car, because we lived at Boston between 12th and 14th, so it was a matter of four blocks for me to drive up there and see what's going on. I called headquarters, and they were just beginning to get alerts as to something going on. That's very well stuck in my mind.

I went directly to headquarters, after I got in the car and saw what was going on. I left home on Sunday—I think it was about four o'clock in the morning—I didn't get back home until Tuesday night. Didn't get any sleep or bathed or washed my face, as I can recall, until Tuesday evening. From then on, it was just one thing after another in the department, trying to get on top of this. My first response was to call Arthur Johnson, who was then head of the NAACP, and John Conyers, alerted them, and we agreed to meet at 12th and Virginia Park. Both Art and John were going to try to appeal to the crowd. I had some bullhorns brought up from headquarters. We got in the back of a convertible, and John and Art are going down 12th Street, urging people to cool it and get off the streets, etcetera. People were shouting back at them; it was clear they weren't in the mood.

That was where we found the first tactical problem. Officers formed a V formation, a wedge, and would move up 12th Street block by block, trying to clear it. But at each cross street, the crowd would simply swarm around behind the commercial establishments on 12th Street, go down the alley that paralleled 12th Street, and come up behind the officers, pelting them with anything they could lay their hands on. That technique just proved to be fruitless, and we abandoned it early on.

At that point, I recall us trying to get a cordon around I think it was Linwood and Woodrow Wilson, the Boulevard and Clairmount, to see if we could just contain the crowds, keep other people from flowing into the mix. But they began to set fires very rapidly at this point, not only on 12th Street but over on Linwood and, I think, by Grand River; early, by noon or so, we had fires burning there. It was just chaos, impossible to get a hold of.

Mayor Cavanagh made the decision to implement a no-shoot order with the police department. In retrospect, I can address that only in the perspective of current police-citizen problems in the country. If the shooting of one black civilian by a police officer can set off incidents such as occurred in Ferguson, Missouri, and elsewhere, you can imagine what would have happened if officers had been allowed to use their weapons in that crowded situation. It would have been a bloodbath, I'm sure—absolutely sure. The department, the officers in the department, any number of officers in the department—that's a more accurate way to put it—deeply resented that order. But I certainly applaud him for making it, and I think it was absolutely the right thing to do, without question.

— —

In a situation like this, the police department immediately goes into attack or command mode. As I recall, the prevailing attitude was that we've got another Kercheval on our hands, and we'll get on top of it. But I think that rapidly dissipated as we found such things as our tactics weren't working and that the call-up [of off-duty officers] wasn't going as it ought to.

Sometime Sunday afternoon, we had already called Governor Romney, who dispatched state patrolmen [and] the National Guard as well. I remember that after dusk that evening, going up on the rooftop of 1300 Beaubien, police headquarters, looking out over the city and just seeing fires raging in all parts of the city, in the west, out east, as well as along 12th Street, I knew that we'd lost it at that point. I think everybody else knew that, in the department; certainly the command staff in the department did. We began to talk about federal troops at that point.

I forget when the request for federal troops was made, but I remember the politics surrounding that situation. The 82nd Airborne were staged at Selfridge Field, up in Mt. Clements. Lyndon Johnson, then president, sent his emissary Cyrus Vance under specific orders not to release those troops until George Romney made a public acknowledgment that the situation was more than he could deal with. I can remember the back-and-forth in the department between Vance and Romney and Cavanagh, all trying to get those troops released. It was late Monday before that finally occurred.

How did the police department feel when the National Guard did move in? They were grateful. I'm sure there were a few in the department who were convinced that if the mayor lifted his no-shoot ban, they could get the thing controlled within minutes, but that was not the outlook nor the response of any sensible person in the department at the time. They wanted as much help as they could get, as early on as we could get it. The troops represented a massive presence, with tanks rolling down the streets, etcetera. If I remember, the federal troops were exclusively assigned to the east side of the city.

It was tense [on the west side] because of the National Guard. In many instances, it was the first time these youngsters had been in Detroit, let alone had faced something of this sort, so they were nervous as hell. The men in the department, I think, were both grateful for their presence but had really mixed feelings about their presence. By Monday night, the fact that we had both state police, National Guard, and, if I remember correctly, after about ten o'clock that night, the federal troops on the street was an event of great relief to us all.

A quick side note: I had that May indicated to Commissioner Girardin that I wanted to go back to Wayne, and he said, at the time, "Look, Hubert, we're expecting trouble this summer. Would you stay on at least during the summer months?" And I said, "Okay, I'll stay through August. Let me get back for the fall term." So I was anticipating going back, and more importantly, the department was anticipating problems; so anyone who suggested we were somehow caught by surprise or caught with our pants down or whatever just does not know what the inside—what the atmosphere internally was.

I did leave a month after. I left at the end of August. Much of the attention then had turned to the three officers who were arrested in the Algiers Motel. The incident itself was on a Wednesday. Thursday, I got a call from Nate Conyers, who was then a young attorney at offices in the Guardian Building. He called me at headquarters and said, "Locke, I've got two women here in my office who just told me a story that if it's half true suggests you got a real problem in the department." I left my desk, drove over to the Guardian Building, interviewed the two women, who were in the motel when all this took place, came back to police headquarters, and reported what I had heard to the commissioner, who immediately called Vince Piersante, chief of detectives, with orders to find out what had gone on. Vince, I remember, called George Bloomfield, retired head of the Homicide Bureau, and assigned him to go after them. Bloomfield came back within a very short period of time and gave the commissioner and Piersante the information and evidence that led to the indictment of those men for first-degree murder. I think to this day that's still the only case of a police shooting in the nation which has resulted in indictment for first-degree murder of a police officer. Clearly the department at that point had not lost its moral compass and was seriously anxious to get on top of it.

Many people have been on my case, and critically so, for calling it a riot. There are those who'd prefer to call it civil disorder, which I think is more neutral, though many more who prefer to call it an uprising or rebellion or all sorts of other descriptors. Quite frankly, they're entitled to their interpretation, political interpretation, if you will. The one thing I insist on is that it was not a race riot. What happened in this city in 1943 was a race riot. I mean, black men were being yanked off Woodward streetcars and being beaten in the street, etcetera. But I've got photos in 1967 of looting going on along Linwood: guys walking down the street carrying a huge sofa—two black guys in front, two white guys behind. I declare it to be one of the most integrated events we'd had in this city up until that time. The snipers whom we arrested—we didn't arrest a lot of them, but the ones we did arrest were white. It was just a very mixed affair. To describe it as a race riot is just fundamentally and historically inaccurate.

Rebellion, Revolution, or Riot

THE DEBATE CONTINUES

Ken Coleman

Lanky and brown-skinned, he looked like a member of the Detroit Pistons, who played home games in this building. But you immediately got the sense that he was not Dave Bing, the star point guard from Syracuse University, whom the team drafted seventy-nine days before. He took to Cobo Arena's stage podium like a lion ready to feast. His Afro was his well-coiffured mane; his words were his roar: "Don't you ever apologize for a black person who throws a Molotov cocktail, and don't call those things riots, because they're rebellions."

He spoke of the civil unrest that had rocked Watts, a predominantly black section of Los Angeles, riveted Harlem on Manhattan Island in New York City, and roiled through several other locales in recent months.

It was exactly one year before Detroit's civil unrest and about two weeks before an incident on Kercheval Street—four miles away on Detroit's east side—broke out like a rash.

Stokely Carmichael, the twenty-five-year-old national chairman of the Student Nonviolent Coordinating Committee, addressed the group of about five hundred people, most of whom were black. The gathering, co-sponsored by the Baptist Ministers Conference and the Council of Baptist Pastors of Detroit and Vicinity, had been expected to draw a larger crowd in the nine-thousand-seat arena.

"We have to be able to take care of ourselves, because the white people won't," stated Carmichael, who was born in Port of Spain, Trinidad and

Tobago, but grew up in New York City and had recently coined the phrase "Black Power." "We must move to disband the white power structure which beats us up every night."

On the other hand, the *Detroit Free Press* columnist Sydney Harris rebuffed the notion that the uprising was a rebellion:

> Some political figures have called them "insurrections" or "rebellions" or even "revolutions"—which only shows how little they know about social movements.
>
> Insurrections, rebellions and revolutions are purposeful acts with clear goals: to overthrow a government, to obtain food or jobs or lower prices, to seize the instruments of production or warfare. And they are always "led"— whereas the Negro riots are a form of spontaneous combustion arising when resentment has been smoldering long enough.

July 1967 in Detroit: An Academic Point of View

The question has been debated, discussed, and dissected more than the cause of the set of events itself. Was it a rebellion, a revolution, or a riot? Was it a spontaneous reaction to the busting of a blind pig at the corner of 12th Street and Clairmount Avenue? Or was it a deliberated and planned uprising carried out by activists in reaction to systematic racism or oppression? It depends, of course, on whom you ask.

"It's a complex question," answered Carl Taylor, a professor of sociology at Michigan State University, an African American who was seventeen years old at the time of the uprising and grew up on Hazelwood Street between 12th and 14th Streets, near its epicenter. "And the debate gets very sensitive depending on who you talk to.

"Sociologically, we define a riot as a sudden upsurge of collective violence directed at property or persons of authority," he said. "For me, I'm torn as a scholar. I felt it as a riot, but as I got into college and the Black Power movement began to manifest itself as definition and culturally, with the change of hair, etcetera, people began to refer to it as an insurrection, revolution, and rebellion. Rebellion, as defined in sociological terms, is really rare. It's an entire social and political order that is overturned usually by violence and reconstructed by principles and new leaders. There is where it becomes sensitive even in the black community."

Jack Schneider, an assistant professor of education at the College of the Holy Cross, cited the following excerpt from the 1968 Kerner Commission report when I asked him whether he called Detroit 1967 a rebellion or a riot: "What the rioters appeared to be seeking was fuller participation in the social order and the material benefits enjoyed by the majority of American citizens. Rather than rejecting the American system, they were anxious to obtain a place for themselves in it."

Schneider, in a piece published by the *Huffington Post* in December 2014, referred to more recent uprisings this way:

> "The tree of liberty must be refreshed from time to time with the blood of patriots and tyrants." So observed a sanguine Thomas Jefferson in 1787, responding to news of a violent uprising in Massachusetts.
>
> But who ranks as a patriot? And what counts as tyranny? As it turns out, it depends on skin color. Just look in a history textbook.
>
> If whites are involved, uprisings tend to be framed as rebellions. Flip through the index of any social studies text, and you'll find several of them: Bacon's Rebellion, Shays's Rebellion, Dorr's Rebellion. The list goes on.
>
> When blacks are involved, however, an uprising isn't a rebellion; it's a riot. Harlem, Watts, Chicago. Or, more recently, Ferguson.
>
> The point here is not that a riot and a rebellion are one and the same. They aren't. A rebellion is inherently meaningful. It connotes resistance to authority or control. A riot, by contrast, disturbs an otherwise peaceful society—it is an expression of power and energy rather than of simmering resentment and honest anger. After a riot, everyone goes home and sobers up.

Detroit Conditions in 1967

Only days after the uprising, the *Detroit Free Press* and the Urban League of Detroit and Southeastern Michigan commissioned a survey of 437 people who lived in the 12th Street and Grand River Avenue area and along Kercheval Street and East Warren Avenue—the western and eastern epicenters. When asked what they thought the reasons were for the uprising, the following percentages of respondents offered these reasons:

57% Police brutality

55% Overcrowded living conditions

54% Poor housing

45% Lack of jobs

44% Poverty

44%   Dirty neighborhoods

43%   Anger with local businesspeople

40%   Too much drinking

39%   Broken political promises

39%   Failure of parents to control children

Early Analyses Used "Riot" as Descriptor

In the *Detroit Free Press*'s first day of reporting, Monday, July 24, the paper used phrases such as "Detroit's first major racial disturbance in 20 years" and in its subheadline declared, "Looter Killed; 724 Held as Riot Spreads." In the same issue, the associate editor John A. Hamilton wrote a story that described several firsthand accounts of action along 12th Street, Linwood Street, and Dexter Avenue. In "Tears of Fear and Grief: The Meaning of Detroit's Riot," Hamilton used "riot" four times. The story does, however, use "rebellion" once: "Another young spokesman, who identified himself by an African name that I couldn't catch, called the rioting a 'form of rebellion.' He declared: 'The black folks are down so long that we feel we have to do something.' He accused city officials of ignoring Negroes."

Charles Colding, a Northern High School student who organized a boycott against school officials in April 1966, told of seeing a black person bayoneted. Colding conveyed to Hamilton that he witnessed the person bleed for twenty minutes "before aid came."

Colding described the events this way: "If it were a real revolution, then I might be for it. But this rioting doesn't do anybody any good. This is ridiculous."

The *Detroit Free Press* editorial board in its "Sift Ashes for Reasons behind Ghetto Outbreak," published on July 27, 1967, declared,

> One thing the riots were not. They were not a massive Negro uprising against white people. There was little hatred in the Sunday outbreak. There were Negro and white looters and snipers fought by Negro and white policemen and soldiers. It wasn't basically race against race. This needs to be emphasized because some terms used to describe what happened—Negro riots, ghetto uprising, Negro rebellion—don't really describe what occurred in Detroit.

Published on Saturdays, the *Michigan Chronicle*, the state's largest black-owned newspaper, used the term "riot" and compared the event to a public spectacle, labeling it a "Roman Holiday" in its front-page reporting on July 29, titled, "It Could Have Been Stopped: Did Police Just Write Off 12th?"

Councilman Nicholas Hood, the city's only black elected local governmental official, lived on the west side about three miles from the epicenter. He called police officials early Sunday morning on the first day of the incident. Reported in the *Benton Harbor News-Palladium* on September 12, Hood described the events this way: "The rioting had been going on for three hours. Before six o'clock I could hardly drive my car down 12th Street."

The Kerner Commission stated in its 1968 landmark two-hundred-thousand-word report on civil unrest throughout the nation, which included Watts in Los Angeles; Newark, New Jersey; and Detroit, "Negroes may 'come to support not only riots, but . . . rebellion' unless multi-billion-dollar measures are taken quickly to heal racial bitterness and riot ravages in city slums."

Hubert G. Locke, an African American city native who at the time was an administrative assistant to the Detroit commissioner of police and an adjunct professor at Wayne State University's Center for Urban Studies, routinely referred to the civil disorder as a "riot" and does not use the word "rebellion" in his 1969 book *The Detroit Riot of 1967*. He writes in its preface, "This book is necessarily, therefore, one man's opinion, subject to all the biases and limitations that such an effort obviously implies. It reflects, however, a deeply held conviction: that Detroit, and every other city in America is in a race with time—and thus far losing the battle."

Detroit Residents in the Epicenter Reflect Nearly Fifty Years Later

The events of 1967, in retrospect, are viewed differently among blacks and whites.

On July 19, 2007, forty years after the 1967 events, the *Detroit News* published a poll. Nearly half of the blacks said that the 1967 unrest should be called a rebellion. When asked whether the use of the word "riot" affects how people see events in a negative way, 49 percent of white respondents agreed, but only 31 percent of black respondents agreed.

When asked whether "rebellion" is a better word and whether it affects how people see events in a positive way, 49 percent of black respondents agreed, but only 22 percent of white respondents agreed.

I posed the question on my social media account. The responses varied. The retired public schoolteacher Brenda Perryman, an African American who lived in the 12th Street and Clairmount Avenue area in 1967, calls it a riot. Here is her recollection:

I was on 12th at 1 a.m. that morning . . . just riding, and that night was hot and tight. People were hanging out all over. My boyfriend even said, "If a riot ever started, it would start here." Then at 7 a.m., my mother's friend (who lived on 12th Street) called our home and said that he couldn't take me back to Eastern Michigan University because there was a riot on 12th, and he was blocked in his driveway and couldn't get out. So my boyfriend and I went back to 12th and the story begins. . . . It was a riot. The intentions of others were echoed. This was their chance to get goods without being harassed by police. I stood among the rioters, . . . talked to them and more. My brother was missing from Sunday until Friday that week. My mother was a nurse at Ford Hospital where one day there was a sniper on the roof of one of the buildings. It didn't start with good intentions. . . . That Saturday night was hot, hot, hot and muggy. Our convertible top was down. It was a riot.

William Warren, an African American, agrees. "A rebellion has a purpose, cause or reason. This was an opportunity to loot. I stood in the middle of it watching people loot and burn on Dexter and Tyler. There was no one calling for justice. This was a riot of opportunity."

Marsha Battle Philpot, a Detroit-based African American poet and historian, made the following observation: "I usually start, out of habit, saying riot, then correct myself and say rebellion. I have also referred to it as an insurgency, and, most recently in a poem I read at the symphony, a mutiny."

Francis Grunow, an urban planner and preservationist who is white, ponders the question and suggests that both terms are accurate.

That's a great question. Is it possible it was both? I've always struggled with the "what" of 1967, and the semantics. It is viewed differently by different people for different reasons. If it was a rebellion, or a riot, it has certainly also been an excuse for many people who moved out. As terrible and profound as these events were, I can't help but compare them to the traumas experienced by other cities, such as London or Tokyo or Berlin after WWII, which rebuilt and sought healing afterwards.

Steve Neavling, an independent journalist and publisher of *Motor City Muckraker* who is also white, describes the incident as a rebellion. "When a group of people are systematically discriminated against and their local government and police turn on them, they have no choice but to fight back. It's a fight for freedom."

Deborah Whitelow, an African American schoolteacher, calls it a riot: "A rebellion is an organized group who are rebelling against the government, and a riot is a group of people who are being disruptive against a government. This was certainly not organized because who would destroy their own neighborhood?"

Conclusion

Fifty years have come and gone, and the vigorous debate continues over what to call the Detroit urban uprising in July 1967. There still is not a consensus on either side of Eight Mile, Telegraph, and Alter Roads. The answer, figuratively speaking, is not black or white but rather a shade of gray.

The Problem Was the Police

Melba Joyce Boyd

The police. It's always the police. If you were black and living in pre–Coleman Young Detroit, you never called the police for help because they only made matters worse. Besides, the neighborhoods where I grew up had the lowest crime rates in the city. We left our doors unlocked, and in the summer, sometimes we slept outside for the fun of it.

When I was in kindergarten, Officer Wilson, who was white, visited our classroom to teach us how to safely cross the street. He brought puppets to amuse us, to capture our attention while teaching us about safety—how to cross the street, not to take candy from strangers, and so on. He also appeared before and after school, conducting traffic on Fort Street and Visger Road, the corner where Boynton Elementary School was located. We were five years old, trusting of adults and heroic myths about the police. After Officer Wilson's visits, many of the boys in the class would say they wanted to be a policeman or a fireman when they grew up.

Ten years later, our innocence and that illusion was shattered when some other cops slapped those same kids upside the head for "reckless eyeballing" during an unfortunate encounter with the Big Four. These were acts of intimidation to precondition young black men to fear the police and to fear the power of whiteness. This systemic repression was a precursor to much more dangerous and horrific encounters. I often wondered what Officer Wilson would do about these interactions, when those same cute, little, brown kindergarteners he used to protect were being abused by his fellow officers.

Almost everyone had a story that reverberated as warnings, like the time my stepfather, Siegel Clore II, flagged down a patrol car after another motorist rear-ended his new, red Plymouth Fury station wagon at a stoplight on Schaefer Road. What should have been a simple matter of issuing a traffic ticket at the scene of the accident transformed into an ugly abuse of power. As my father was explaining what had obviously transpired, one of the cops turned to the white motorist and said, "Go on. We'll handle this." The second cop grabbed my father from behind and cuffed him. What ensued was shocking but not unusual.

In the dark of night, the second cop held Siegel from behind, while his partner brutally beat him. However, my stepfather realized an opportunity to counter the assault when the cop's head came too close after landing a blow. He caught the cop's ear between his teeth, bore down, and bit off the earlobe, then spat it into the street. The maimed cop screamed in pain and scrambled to retrieve the bloody scrap from the asphalt.

The other cop shoved my father into the back of the police car and drove his partner to the hospital and my father to the police station. He was not locked in a cell; instead, they chained him to a chair in the basement of the precinct, where any cop who had the urge used him as a punching bag.

At the time, my father was a strong, healthy man of forty-seven years, and he survived the attack and the aftermath at the police station. But subsequently, he was arraigned and charged with resisting arrest and assaulting a police officer. He was found guilty of these charges, but his sentence was suspended after the judge saw photos of my father, bruised and swollen. Or perhaps the judge concluded that sending a college-educated, tax-paying citizen with no criminal record to prison was senseless; or perhaps he thought locking up a decorated World War II veteran, who had a Bronze Star and a Purple Heart, might be unpatriotic. Unfortunately, he didn't think that perhaps the right thing to do would be to charge the police officers with assault and battery and get them off the police force and the streets of Detroit.

But it was 1965, and there was no Michigan Civil Rights Commission or Detroit Police Commission or Detroit Coalition Against Police Brutality to investigate instances that violated a citizen's constitutional rights, as was the case for many others. Ron Scott recounted a horrifying encounter with Detroit police to Kim Hunter for his article "1967: Detroiters Remember the Rebellion." Ron said, "We did not feel the civil rights movement had a particular focus on the issues that we faced. In Detroit that was the police. Seven years before the disturbance Mayor Miriani had a crackdown in the Black community. I was 12 years old and a cop put a shotgun in my face and told me not to breathe." In 1968, Scott joined the Detroit chapter of the Black Panther Party and the League of Revolutionary Workers and, in the subsequent decades, led the struggle through his organization, the Detroit Coalition Against Police Brutality.

So when the news reported that there was a disturbance after a confrontation between the police and some Negroes at a blind pig (an after-hours establishment) on 12th Street, I was not surprised. Neither were most of the black people in Detroit. It was a cumulative response to police brutality—the straw that broke the camel's black back—and people were sick of it, sick of the police.

Ed Vaughn, who was known in the community because of Vaughn's Bookstore and who subsequently served in the Coleman Young administration and as a state representative, also blamed the Detroit Police Department in his comments to Kim Hunter. "The undercurrent of discontent was always there. We [the grassroots community leaders] were trying to tell them [the white power structure] that the police department was an army of occupation. People were being beaten, even killed." The Algiers Motel incident, one of the most shocking examples of police murders, happened during the 1967 rebellion.

Karl Gregory, a community activist and a professor at Wayne State at the time, described his encounter with the National Guard in July 1967 during an oral history session with the Detroit Historical Society. It occurred on the east side of Detroit when he was patrolling the streets with Alvin Harrison, trying to get people to return to their homes during the civil eruption.

> We continued until late that evening during a curfew. The National Guard stopped us. There was a young white guardsman who dismounted from his vehicle, approached, and told me, "Pull your window down." I was driving. [He] pointed his gun at me. I was concerned, but I wasn't afraid then. His hand was shaking . . . on the trigger. And I said, "Look, I'm a college professor. I am just trying to get the people off the street." And he looked like he was trying to determine whether or not I was a rioter (or what have you), and a sergeant came by and said something like, "Cool it." But this guardsman [the kid] was more afraid of me than I was of him. I don't know how many black persons, if any, that youth had been in contact with before in his entire life.

My family didn't live near the site of any of the civil eruptions, so I watched it on the television. In 1965, it was the Los Angeles community of Watts that exploded and was broadcast on the national news. LA was far away, and at the time, Detroit was regarded as a "model city." Despite declining jobs in the automobile plants, unemployment was low; therefore, the Detroit politicians were taken by surprise when anger and despair added their city to the growing list of racially war-torn cities.

Vietnam was the war we were concerned about at the time, because my oldest brother was in the Marine Corps and stationed in Vietnam. Our familial anxiety came from Darnell's military situation, and we watched the news religiously as if we might catch a glimpse of him on the screen or hear a report about his unit. Suddenly, we were watching imagery of the Vietnam War juxtaposed with similar scenes of conflict on 12th Street, which became even more bizarre when President Lyndon Johnson sent federal troops and tanks to Detroit and the two settings merged within the surreal world of television.

Poet Dudley Randall, who lived on the west side of Detroit and not far from the site of the rebellion, revealed his personal response in a letter to Broadside Press poet Etheridge Knight.

> I've owed you a letter for a long time. Partly my delay was because of this publishing project [*For Malcolm: Poems on the Life and Death of Malcolm X*]. There's so much clerical work that I don't have time for writing. And partly it was because of the recent events, when I too stayed by the radio & television, & read current newspapers & magazines. There was no harm done to me or my family, although there were a few anxious nights when there were rumors that they would get the "rich black folks." I never thought it was a crime to have a job.
>
> I don't know how this will turn out. The uprisings have focused attention on the ghettos. I hope that efforts will be made to eradicate the roots of the problem. On the other hand, many whites have been polarized to advocate repression, blind & brutal. I hope the sensible ones prevail. All little people like you and me can do is to support the sensible ones. And write sincerely what we feel. One wants to write with assurance that he knows all the answers, but one can write out of uncertainty and it'll be more sincere.

Despite Randall's initial reactions of uncertainty, in the aftermath of the rebellion, the opening of his article "The Second Black Arts Convention in Detroit" for *Negro Digest* in November 1967 was more reflective and definitive: "Weeks before the rebellion erupted in the 'city of motors,' the simmering mood of disgust and outrage which characterized the mood of many black people was in open evidence in the city." Randall's poem "Sniper," printed in *More to Remember*, was even more direct. In three succinct lines, he makes a personal statement about armed resistance:

Somewhere
On a rooftop
You fight for me.

"I could write forever about the sixties, which really didn't get rolling until well into the much-neglected seventies," said Detroit native and writer Al Young. His memories about 1967, recounted to this author, are linked to long-distance phone-call conversations with his family after the rebellion broke out.

By the summer of 1967, I had lived in California for close to seven years. I was working at the undergraduate library at Stanford University when the Detroit riots broke out. I called home immediately to get some kind of first-hand account. My sharp-eyed Uncle James, veteran of World War II in the European theater, Italy, set me straight.

"Ooh, Al," he said, "I haven't seen anything like this since the war. Great big old army tanks rolling down 12th Street! I didn't think I'd ever see anything like this. Look like that's what it takes to quiet this thing down. I mean, they've been burning down everything, everywhere. White folks doing it, too. But, you know, we the ones they write about and put on TV."

When my mother got on the phone, I asked her about specific businesses on 12th Street. I remembered asking, "Mother, did they trash the barbershop?" "That's one of the few places they didn't burn down. They must've liked old Jones' Barbershop," she said. "How about Buddy's?" "I think they spared them, too, but I can't say for sure. I mean, they are pitching a boogie! I was even worried about them coming up in our house until I saw those tanks. We're trying to keep off the streets."

Uncle James was renting a room from Mother, and I knew they both packed guns—and could shoot. Mississippi country people. Even my senior-vintage grandmother packed heat. I was probably the only non–gun advocate in the family, and here I was way off in California. My Aunt Doris had already told me, "You mean, you're out there in devilish California without a gun? Child, you better go get you a gun. May Jesus guide and protect you."

Frank Rashid, an English professor at Marygrove College, grew up on Lothrop Street and still lives in the city. His family is an interesting American ethnic mixture of Lebanese, German, and Irish who never moved out of their Detroit neighborhood, near the family business. His father was a merchant and owned a couple of businesses, including a market at 7525

Linwood that used to be an A&P grocery store. He explained in a Detroit Historical Society oral history interview his encounter with the uprising.

> We were going somewhere on Sunday morning. And we drove down from our house on Lothrop; we turned down 14th and then turned left on the Boulevard, and as we crossed 12th Street, we looked down and we saw, actually, that famous image of 12th Street completely covered with smoke and crowds of people—and we knew something was going on. We got a call from one of the customers that the store was being looted.

> There were all kinds of people milling about. The store, which had nearly ground-level to ceiling-level windows, was completely broken into. We went over there; the folks scattered when they saw us. We decided, again foolishly, that we would clean up the store. And we had four or five of our neighbors and customers helping us and, in a way, protecting us. All of them were African American.

> And so we started to sweep up the debris and all the stuff that was taken off the shelves, and we'd put it in baskets and boxes—which of course made it easier to take out later. . . . My dad was not going to leave; he was going to stay in the store. And these other three men were helping us, sort of watching out for us, because the traffic [people] was moving down Linwood from the north to the south, and there were catcalls, and there was some—it felt tense. We heard that a man who ran a shoe-repair shop down the street had been killed. As it turned out, that wasn't exactly true—he did die a few days later. But he was one of the few white victims in the riot.

> But we did hear about it, and I started to get scared, and one of the men who was watching us said, "You better tell your dad it's time to leave—we can't hold this off too much longer."

> So I said to Dad, "You know, you've been around for fifty-six years; I've only been around for sixteen. I'd like to hang around a little longer." And that convinced him finally that maybe we should leave. So we—I mean, my dad had a thing about locking the door, even though the windows were wide open—and these four guys surrounded us, walked around the three of us as we walked across the street, so that we'd be okay. And really at considerable risk, I think, they did this.

Some black businesses were also broken into and destroyed by fire. Karl Gregory's recollections of the rebellion also revealed dire, personal losses. His father had a tailor shop, which flourished in Detroit's Black Bottom. When Karl was a kid, he worked in his father's shop after school and on weekends. But when the federal government made plans to build Interstate 75 through the city, it was determined that bulldozing a black neighborhood was the best route for the highway. Their family business at 5739 Hastings Street was destroyed, and the business relocated on the corner of 12th and Delaware Streets. Despite "SOUL" painted on the shop window, which might have deterred looters, their business was destroyed by fire. Acts of arson may have been intended for white businesses (the establishment); but fire does not read, and the physics of combustion and natural forces are not politically informed.

Considering the instability of the area and the ongoing police repression, simmering frustration and resentment against "the establishment" and its "army of occupation," the area was primed for an explosion. Black poets and playwrights of the 1960s were already advocating an activist aesthetic, and the civil unrest motivated their purpose and contoured themes and subjects in their works. In Detroit, the '67 rebellion infused didactic poetic verse and plays. The Artist Workshop and the Concept East Theatre were engines of cultural production and expression. Racial unity and revolutionary zeal enthused and excited audiences.

After viewing a television news report, Detroit poet Wardell Montgomery wrote a different response, "Christmas in July," published in *Teenage Widow and Her Friends*.

> While we were out looting like it was a game
> One of our neighbors set our home a-flame.
>
> Looking at the burning cinders smoldering on the ground
> A reporter asked if my house burnt up; I said no; it burnt down.
>
> Mama is in jail because of her looting
> Papa is dead because of the shooting.
>
> I think we should have waited until December to buy
> Instead of looting and shooting and having Christmas in July.
>
> Somebody had to suffer so why shouldn't it be me
> Anybody want to trade a daddy for a bike, clothes
> And a color TV?

There were consequences in the aftermath. While a battle ensued between some citizens and police, the National Guard, and the US Army, the unbridled actions of dissenters caught up in a frenzy of looting and the fury of arson projected an image of rioting that dominated the narrative of television reporters. Sadly, innocent people suffered, many were unjustly incarcerated in horrible detention centers, and most tragically, forty-three citizens were killed.

Other methods of control over black communities in the United States resulted in an increase in the drafting of young black men into the military, while the neighborhoods were overwhelmed by heroin, the ill effects of drug dealing, and persons afflicted by addiction to this deadly and crippling drug. While the black community was contending with this internal crisis, the police did little to combat the devastation of this criminal activity. In fact, rumors suggested that some police protected and/or were paid off by these drug dealers. Indeed, the Tenth Precinct, on Detroit's west side, was nicknamed "The Dope House." To add injury to insult, John Nichols, the Detroit police chief, commandeered STRESS (Stop the Robberies, Enjoy Safe Streets), an undercover entrapment strategy. STRESS did not curtail drug-dealing activities but rather emerged as another form of police terrorism.

In *Working Detroit*, Steve Babson reported the consequences of yet another repressive police tactic.

> The 1970s began with Detroit's police killing more civilians than any other police force in the nation—seven civilian deaths for every 1,000 police officers on the force in 1971; Houston was second with a rate of five per 1,000. The 100-man "STRESS" unit formed that year added 22 more civilians to the death toll—21 of them black—while conducting over 500 provocative and frequently illegal raids in black neighborhood. Far from stopping crime, STRESS added to the growing violence.

Despite disturbing findings in research and reports that attempted to address the inequities responsible for the civil uprising, the politics of policing the black community did not experience any real change until after the 1973 election, when the city's first black mayor, Coleman Alexander Young, defeated his opponent, police chief John Nichols. Young's campaign declaration was, "The first thing I will do as mayor is fire the police chief and disband STRESS." Young's election was a definitive response of the people to decades of police repression and to its most recent series of STRESS shootings, when John Percy Boyd, Hayward Brown, and Mark Bethune, three young black men, were fired on by a STRESS unit and they shot back.

Murder at the Algiers Motel

Danielle L. McGuire

He said it felt like a routine day.

Even the sweltering humidity was normal for late July. Roll call began at noon Monday in the Thirteenth Precinct, and the Detroit police officers split into two groups. The sergeant ordered one group to stay in the Thirteenth and sent the other to the "Bloody" Tenth, home to 12th Street, a bustling business and pleasure district that was notoriously violent once night fell. David Senak, a twenty-three-year-old vice cop who normally worked the late-night cleanup crew, or the "whore car," climbed into scout car 13-6. William Croft got behind the wheel and Patrolman David Van Loo, a thirty-three-year-old from the Youth Bureau, rode up front. All were armed with twelve-gauge shotguns, perhaps the first sign that there was nothing routine about this day.

Senak probably still smelled like smoke from the fires the night before, though he washed the soot off his body when he got off duty at two that morning. His uniform was in tatters, his pants shredded on one side and his shirt torn. He barely slept, he said, still shaken from the scenes of mayhem and rebellious, even gleeful, looting that started Sunday just before dawn at 12th Street and Clairmount Avenue, where police raided a well-known after-hours drinking establishment inside the Economy Printing building.

It was a by-the-books bust: an undercover African American cop gained entry to the illegal bar, known as a "blind pig," around 3:30 a.m., bought a beer, and waited. Ten minutes later, four officers charged up the stairs to the second-floor hall, broke down the door with a sledgehammer, and secured the exits. "We heard these noises," said Bernice Jones in the *Free Press* on August 6. "'Pow, pow, pow!' We thought it was gunshots. Then we heard glass breaking. Then somebody shouted, 'It's a raid!'" Bodies collided, tables and chairs flipped, and the eighty-five black revelers, there to celebrate the return of two soldiers from Vietnam, hit the floor. Police had no way of knowing there were so many people inside and suddenly realized they were outnumbered. They arrested everyone present and called for backup.

The presence of police cruisers outside the popular 12th Street building drew a large crowd of onlookers: after-hours bar hoppers, gamblers, drifters, and early-morning laborers heading to work. At first jovial and friendly, the crowd's temper changed as witnesses said police roughed up the arrestees, beating and hitting them with gun butts and nightsticks, twisting their arms and dragging screaming women down the stairs and outside into the street. William Scott III, the son of the owner of the party spot, started shouting obscenities and urged the two hundred spectators to act. "Are we going to let these peckerwood motherfuckers come down here any time they want and mess us around?" he yelled, then grabbed a bottle off the ground and hurled it toward the cops. "Get your goddamn sticks and bottles and start hurtin' baby." As the last squad car pulled away about an hour after the raid began, a bottle crashed through the back window.

Within moments, the throng of angry bystanders surged down 12th Street throwing bottles, breaking windows, and looting. The first fire engulfed a shoe store at 12th and Blaine Streets, part of a three-story building that was home to eighteen apartments and five other stores. By the middle of the day, unrestrained rioting and looting seemed to spread alongside the fires billowing through nearby neighborhoods. The flames swallowed whole blocks of storefronts, flats, brick bungalows, and manor homes subdivided into apartments. What started as a routine takedown quickly became a deadly and destructive five-day riot that left forty-three dead, thousands injured, and tens of millions of dollars in property damage. As the *Free Press* put it on August 6, 1967, the raid on the blind pig was "the most expensive pinch in history."

— —

No one knew what the second day would bring. An early-morning report in the *Detroit Free Press* stated that looting was "almost city-wide." Barbara Stanton, a poetic journalist, reported on the same July 25 front page that thousands of people were "grabbing and running in a sometimes senseless, sometimes calculated snatch at the good things in life." Either way, Senak and his brothers in blue were determined to stop the looters' brazen defiance of law and order. And that morning they were told they could do so by "whatever means necessary." As Sidney Fine noted in *Violence in the Model City*, even Michigan Governor George Romney suggested that looters were fair targets. "Fleeing felons," he told the press gaggle in the wee hours of July 24, "are subject to being shot at."

Senak, Croft, and Van Loo began their Monday-afternoon patrol on Second Avenue and Euclid Street, a few blocks from where the trouble started the day before and one block west of Detroit's main artery, Woodward Avenue, which divides the city between east and west. Senak and his partners worked to contain the area, "chasing people away from buildings and stuff," Senak said.

It was about 1:00 p.m. when Senak spotted Joseph Chandler, a thirty-four-year-old African American man, climbing out of a hole in the window of Food Time Market with a bag of groceries. Croft slammed the brakes. Senak and Van Loo jumped out of the scout car with their shotguns and gave chase. Chandler saw the cops and perhaps heard their order to halt. Instead, he dropped his bag and broke into a run. He cut across the street and sped into an alley. Senak and Van Loo leveled their shotguns and fired. "I fired two times, I guess, and my partner fired three times at him. The man didn't slow up at all," Senak later told the novelist John Hersey for his 1968 book *The Algiers Motel Incident*. "Gad, I couldn't, I still can't believe it."

— —

Senak and Van Loo raced toward Chandler, who was eight yards away when he cut into a backyard and flung himself over an ivy-covered, five-foot-high fence. Van Loo and Senak shot Chandler as he disappeared behind it. "We hit the man with I think four shots," Senak said, incredulously. "And we hit him three times in the legs. . . . This man must have been in top physical shape. We were shooting double-o buckshot. Man didn't flinch."

Croft had finally gotten the scout car to the alley, but he was too late. Chandler was gone. The three police officers, initially believing they missed their target, piled back into the car, drove two blocks back to Food Time Market, and started making arrests.

Chandler, however, had not gone far. Had Senak and Van Loo simply glanced over the fence, they would have seen him stumble and fall. Maybe they looked and forgot to mention it. Perhaps they saw Chandler hoist himself up and limp across the alley toward Philadelphia Avenue, where he collapsed and tried to crawl under a car. Crumpled and bleeding, Chandler begged a passing white woman, Mrs. Alline Sims, to call his wife, who was a block away at home, waiting for him to return with the pack of cigarettes she requested. Instead Sims dialed the police, who arrived minutes later. Two patrolmen, undoubtedly Senak's colleagues in the Thirteenth

Precinct, conveyed Chandler to Henry Ford Hospital, where thirty minutes after his first foray into the riot zone, he was pronounced dead of a massive hemorrhage in the right lung and a gunshot wound that tore through his liver.

— —

Chandler's death was one of seventeen "riot-related" fatalities that day—the largest daily tally during what became known as America's worst civil disturbance. In the July 23, 1972, *Free Press*, a rookie cop remembered July 24, 1967, as a day of confusion. His colleagues, he said, were "piling in cars and patrolling up and down and up and down, . . . a bunch of them just doing what they wanted to." And Michigan's nearly all-white, scraggly force of National Guardsmen, who arrived the night before, added to the chaos. Poorly trained, out of shape, and unfamiliar with the city or its people, the young guardsmen were wholly unprepared for what they encountered. "Take these kids out of a small town up in the sticks of Michigan," Ray Girardin, the Detroit police commissioner, later told the Kerner Commission, "and bring them into a city, straight to a congested area with all the tension and excitement going on, they did not know how to act." They fired at nearly anything and everything, dispensing an estimated 155,000 rounds of ammunition in five days. According to the *Detroit News* on August 24, one newly arrived guardsman bragged, "I'm gonna shoot anything that moves and that is black." That same day, the *Free Press* quoted another saying, "I'm going to say halt and then bang, bang, bang!" "No, that's not the way to do it," his friend said. "You say bang, bang, bang, halt."

— —

Jimmy Breslin, a syndicated columnist in town to cover the explosion of violence, was aghast at the chaos, especially among police and soldiers. He reported in the July 25 *Detroit News* that guardsmen fired on one another, each thinking the other was a sniper; that Detroit police called for backup after seeing a sniper on a rooftop, then realized the "sniper" was a state policeman. They shot out streetlights to avoid detection. But when officers stationed a block away heard the gunshots and shattered glass, they believed it was from a sniper. "Detroit," Breslin said, "is an asylum."

Things got worse as the week wore on. What began as an outburst of long-simmering anger and resentment by African Americans against racial discrimination and police violence began to feel more like a state-sanctioned police riot against African Americans. On July 29, the *Ann Arbor*

News quoted one officer saying, "Those black son-of-a-bitches. I'm going to get me a couple of them before this is over."

David Senak got Joseph Chandler on July 24. The next night, after another "routine day," as he told Hersey, patrolling the rubble-strewn streets and arresting looters—or those who he said looked like looters—he got a few more.

— —

In the early-morning hours of July 26, 1967, a flurry of Detroit police officers, National Guardsmen, and state police officers, led by Senak and two of his colleagues, raided the Algiers Motel after hearing reports of heavy "sniper fire" nearby. The Algiers, a once-stately manor house in the Virginia Park neighborhood of central Detroit, was a relatively seedy place, what Hersey described as a "transient" hotel, with a reputation among police as a site for narcotics and prostitution. But that night, because of the uprising and citywide curfew, many people sought refuge at the Algiers, including two white runaways from Ohio, a returning Vietnam veteran, and the friends and members of the Dramatics, a doo-wop group who performed songs like "Inky Dinky Wang Dang Do" at the Swinging Time Revue, headlined by Martha Reeves and the Vandellas, downtown at the Fox Theater.

According to one witness quoted in the *Detroit News* on August 2, it was a "night of horror and murder." Just past midnight, police and soldiers tore through the motel's tattered halls and run-down rooms with shotguns and rifles. They ransacked closets and drawers, turned over beds and tables, shot into walls and chairs, and brutalized motel guests in a desperate and vicious effort to find the "sniper." At some point during this initial raid, David Senak and Patrolman Robert Paille encountered Fred Temple, a teen on the phone with his girlfriend. Senak and Paille barged into the room, startling Temple, who dropped the phone. According to Senak, quoted in *Violence in the Model City*, he and Paille fired "almost simultaneously" at Temple, who crumpled to the ground in a pool of blood.

— —

When Senak and Paille failed to find any weapons, Senak ordered all the guests against the wall in the first-floor lobby. One of the young black men at the hotel that night, seventeen-year-old Carl Cooper, rushed down the stairs and came face-to-face with a phalanx of heavily armed police and guardsmen. A witness, quoted in a report by Detective Inspector Albert

Schwaller, heard Cooper say, "Man, take me to jail—I don't have any weapon," just before hearing the gunshot that tore through his chest.

Police herded the other guests, a group of young black men and two white women, past Cooper's bloody corpse, into the gray and beige magnolia-papered lobby, and told them to face the east wall with their hands over their heads. Even though two young men were already dead, the lineup was the beginning of what Hersey called the "death game."

The details of exactly what happened next are complicated and convoluted—clear memories forever lost to the chaos of the moment, the tricks of time, and the disparate recollections of the survivors traumatized by violence and terror. But this is the gist of what we know: three Detroit policemen, David Senak, Ronald August, and Robert Paille, and a private guard, Melvin Dismukes, took charge of the brutal interrogation. They wanted to know who had the gun, who was the sniper, and who was doing the shooting.

When the young men and women who were lined up against the wall denied shooting or having any weapons, the officers mercilessly beat them, leaving gashes and knots on the victims' heads and backs. According to another witness interviewed by Schwaller, a police officer "struck [a] Negro boy so hard that it staggered [him] and almost sent him down to his knees." A military policeman, part of the contingent of federal paratroopers and National Guardsmen sent to help restore order in Detroit, who arrived at the Algiers in the midst of the raid, is cited by Fine as seeing a Detroit patrolman "stick a shotgun between the legs of one male and threaten to 'blow his testicles off.'" Senak and his colleagues raged against the two white women working as prostitutes at the Algiers, Karen Malloy and Juli Hysell, calling them "white niggers" and "nigger lovers." Both women testified that police ripped off their dresses, pushed their faces against the wall, and smashed guns into the their temples and the small of their backs. Roderick Davis, the stocky Dramatics singer who sported a stylish conk and moustache, told Hersey that Senak sneered, "Why you got to fuck them? What's wrong with us?" Another witness told Schwaller that he heard one of the cops say, "We're going to get rid of all you pimps and whores."

Then, the "death game" really began. The police pulled the unarmed men one by one into different rooms and interrogated them at gunpoint. Davis told Schwaller that Senak took him into a room, forced him to lie down, and then shot into the floor. "I'll kill you if you move," Senak said as he left the room and returned to the lobby.

"Want to shoot a nigger?" Senak asked Warrant Officer Theodore Thomas, as he grabbed the diminutive, baby-faced nineteen-year-old Michael Clark out of the line, pulled him into the same room, pushed him down, and fired at the ceiling. Senak told Thomas to stay with Davis and Clark and keep quiet. Then Senak returned to the lobby and, according to others, handed twenty-eight-year-old DPD officer Ronald August a shotgun. "You shoot one," he ordered.

"Now comes the tragic part," August wrote five days after the Algiers assault in a statement now held in the Detroit Police Department's "Algiers Motel" file. With help from Norman Lippitt, the lead attorney from the Detroit Police Officers Association (DPOA), August described the circumstances under which he shot and killed nineteen-year-old Aubrey Pollard. In that final "official" statement, which Lippitt likely typed up, August said that Pollard lunged at him and tried to take his gun and that he had no choice but to defend himself by fatally shooting the black teenager. But the self-serving justification was not in August's original written or oral statements. His first confession, after some sleepless nights, was to his sergeant, whom he pulled aside to quietly say he shot a young man at the Algiers Motel. He mentioned nothing about self-defense. That part came later.

When the FBI began an investigation of the police for violating the civil rights of the youth they killed, even J. Edgar Hoover had to admit, in a private memo at least, that their official statements were "for the most part untrue and were undoubtedly furnished in an effort to cover their activities and the true series of events."

— —

The surviving witnesses' testimony contradicted August's claim of self-defense. After hearing the thud of Aubrey Pollard's body on the floor and seeing Patrolman August flee out the front door, where he vomited near a tree, police ordered the remaining survivors, terrified and spread-eagle against the blood-spattered lobby wall, to leave. The white girls were bruised and nearly naked; their torn clothes lay in a heap on the floor. Davis recounted to Hersey that a cop said, "Start walking with your hands over your head. If you look back, we'll kill you."

As Roderick Davis, Michael Clark, and the others staggered toward the French doors that opened to the Algiers's back porch, they passed Carl Cooper's prostrate body, a reminder that for some there was no escape from the terror that night.

The young survivors from the Algiers crossed through the alley to Woodward Avenue. National Guardsmen on patrol at the Great Lakes Mutual Life Insurance Building across the street, who had no knowledge of the horrors nearby, held up their shotguns and demanded that the group get down on the ground and submit to a search. "What you been doing?" a guardsman shouted. "Why you walking home?" When Roderick Davis tried to tell them what happened, the guardsman said, "Too bad. Keep walking. You niggers are always starting some kind of trouble."

A mere thirty minutes after police burst through the Algiers's back door in a crazed search for snipers, Clara Gilmore, the African American motel clerk, called the morgue and asked them to collect the three bodies that were abandoned and discarded as casualties of the riot. The person working the phones at the morgue notified the police. When Detroit homicide detectives Edward Hay and Lyle Thayer arrived at the Algiers an hour or so later, they reported that three young black men had "apparently" been "shot to death in an exchange of gunfire." The *Detroit News* briefly mentioned the deaths the next morning—the result, it said, of a "gunfight." "Sniping" from "the roof and windows on all floors of the Algiers," the *News* reported on July 26, kept the "police and guardsmen pinned down for several minutes before the firing stopped." But witnesses told nearly anyone who would listen that there was no shootout. The police, they said, committed murder.

– –

Two intrepid reporters from the *Detroit Free Press*, Barbara Stanton and Kurt Luedtke, weary but wired from the nonstop riot coverage, also thought something was unusual. "Three deaths on one night," as Luedtke put it to this author, just felt wrong. They visited the crime scene and wondered, if there was a shootout as the homicide detectives described, why had no weapons been recovered? And if the police and army were pinned down by gunfire, how were there so few bullet holes in and around the motel? Luedtke and Stanton began their own investigation, going so far as to have the bodies independently autopsied. Their findings and subsequent riot reporting earned the *Detroit Free Press* a Pulitzer Prize. More importantly, their steady investigatory skills and courage to ask hard questions, during what was unquestionably an emotionally charged and devastating week that made it all too easy to assign blame and move on, helped push the city prosecutor to charge the police with murder and compelled Congressman John Conyers to request an FBI investigation as insurance against a complete whitewash.

It was a *Free Press* article that riled up twenty-nine-year-old Kenneth G. "Red" McIntyre, a towering red-headed assistant US attorney who had just returned to Detroit from four harrowing years spent investigating voter fraud and racial terror in Mississippi and Alabama. Reading about "three dead kids, cops kinda iffy about what happened," he told this author, "so incensed me that I called Washington and I said, 'We've got to do something and I'd love to be part of it.'" He got his investigation and ultimately led a major federal civil rights trial that helped expose systemic racism and injustice in the North.

Red McIntyre's hunger for justice was matched only by the passion and dedication of John Hersey, who came to Detroit in the waning days of the summer of 1967 to report on the most destructive urban uprising in US history. Everywhere he went, he said, "the Algiers Motel kept insisting upon attention." The case, he said, had "all the mythic themes of racial strife: . . . the arm of the law taking the law into its own hands; interracial sex; the subtle poison of racist thinking by 'decent' men who deny they are racists; . . . ambiguous justice in the court; and the devastation in both black and white human lives that follows in the wake of violence as surely as ruinous and indiscriminate flood after torrents."

Hersey interviewed nearly everyone involved in the case and then cobbled together the transcripts into a book. He hoped it would help change hearts and open minds when it was published in 1968. In a tragic twist noted by Sidney Fine, however, it served to close off one avenue toward justice, when Norman Lippitt of the DPOA argued that the publication of *The Algiers Motel Incident*, by Alfred Knopf, was too inflammatory and made a fair hearing for the police impossible. He was thrilled to be granted a change of venue to the nearly all-white town of Mason, Michigan, the Ingham County seat where three decades earlier the Black Legion, a Ku Klux Klan offshoot, terrorized Malcolm X's family. By then, Hersey had gone back to Yale, where he worked as a professor.

Heroic efforts by the local and federal prosecutors to expose the cops' false statements, to probe Detroit's history of discrimination and inequality, and to contextualize the summer uprising in a past littered by economic and racial inequality did little to change the white jurists' hearts and minds. Both major trials—the 1968 state murder trial in Mason and the 1970 federal civil rights trial led by Red McIntyre, in Flint—ended in acquittals. Fred Temple's mother, who watched the proceedings with increasing hopelessness, told Hersey that the jury's decision was the "latest phase of a step-by-step whitewash of a police slaying." Senator Coleman

Young, who went on to become Detroit's first African American mayor, told the *Free Press* on July 26, 1970, that the acquittals "demonstrate once again that law and order is a one-way street; there is no law and order where black people are involved, especially when they are involved with the police."

Distrust of Detroit's judicial system ran so deep, in fact, that local civil rights and Black Power activists decided to call a "People's Tribunal." Held at the Central United Church of Christ, beneath a stunning eighteen-foot mural of a black Madonna and child painted months before the uprising, the People's Tribunal brought together hundreds of Detroit's most militant activists for a mock trial on August 30, 1967. Among the black lawyers and activists presiding over the case, all of whom went on to become well-known civil rights and Black Power leaders, was the steely Rosa Parks, midwife to the 1955 Montgomery, Alabama, bus boycott. Parks's decades-long experience documenting and investigating racialized and sexualized violence in the deep South and in Detroit made her a symbolic link between the southern freedom struggle and the burgeoning Black Power movement in the North. Her presence also reminded everyone that police violence and abusive state power was not only a southern malady but an American disease that threatened the very essence of democracy, justice, and the meanings of citizenship.

-- --

Justice was but one of many casualties that week with ramifications that echo to this day. "I lost a son. I *lost* a son," Aubrey Pollard Sr. told John Hersey. There is a magnitude in the simplicity of his statement. But Pollard Sr.'s losses, like many others, compounded over time. His marriage fell apart, and he became separated from his other children. They lost daily interactions with their father. Mr. Pollard's oldest son, a soldier serving in Vietnam when the police raided the Algiers Motel, returned from the war to identify his brother at the morgue. The sight of his baby brother in a coffin triggered a nervous breakdown. He recovered slowly at a mental health institution in California. But parts of him were gone forever. Mrs. Pollard tried to carry on the best she could, but her life, like so many scarred by violence, was forever changed. In a 1967 interview with Hersey, she focused on her deceased son's artistic talent, mentioning repeatedly that Aubrey won a prize in elementary school for one of his paintings. There is the lost opportunity and wasted talent, an emptiness where the future once cast spells and planted dreams. The families of Carl Cooper and Fred Temple suffered similar fates. What happens to a dream destroyed? To lives torn apart by violence?

David Senak, Ronald August, and Robert Paille kept their lives but lost their jobs and their hopes for a fulfilling future as policemen. What they did that night at the Algiers tormented some of them for a lifetime. Worse, their acquittals haunted Detroit for decades, as unpunished police violence against black civilians soared in the years after the Algiers, wreaking havoc on the city and its people still reeling from the July 1967 cataclysm.

In that single week, forty-three people, including Joseph Chandler and the young men at the Algiers Motel, died. Seven thousand individuals, mainly young African American men, were arrested, and nearly twenty thousand armed police officers, National Guardsmen, and paratroopers patrolled the streets. As hundreds of businesses smoldered and citizens' hopes lay shattered amid the broken glass, the slow and steady march of tanks mounted with machine guns imposed order with frightening clarity.

While police harassment served as the spark that ignited the 1967 riot, there were myriad causes and consequences significantly more dangerous. The story of the Algiers Motel murders captures, in its tragic horror, the often-hidden infrastructure of northern racism and white supremacy. From rabid residential segregation and job discrimination to racialized and sexualized violence to economic and educational disparities and the everyday injustices and biased sentencing in the judicial system, racial inequality and segregation in the "Model City" were every bit as virulent as they were in the South. Maybe they were even worse.

-- --

Detroit still suffers from these past sins. Violence (in all its forms) echoes. Its toll multiplies, mutates, and reemerges in ways that are not always immediately visible but are undoubtedly clear. The origins of the 1967 riot and its aftermaths have much in common: poverty, lack of decent jobs, crumbling infrastructure, poor educational opportunities, aggressive policing, unequal application of justice, and municipal corruption. In 2016, as police violence, mass incarceration, and racial and economic inequality continue to plague urban communities throughout the United States, as young people surge through the streets declaring #BlackLivesMatter, and as racial tensions simmer and seethe in cities like Chicago, Ferguson, Cleveland, New York, and Baltimore, understanding the causes and consequences of the Algiers Motel murders and the history of the 1967 Detroit riot holds the promise for reconciliation and future change.

The Storytellers

GETTING TO THE HEART
OF THE MATTER

Timothy Kiska

In July 1967, Detroit's broadcast and print newsrooms were even less racially integrated than the 139 square miles of America's fifth-most-populous city. Five days of widespread violence were about to transform both the city— reduced by 2015 to our eighteenth most populous—and its journalistic culture. Major difference: the newsroom transformation was, by anyone's measure, progress.

The *Detroit News* and its broadcast properties WWJ-TV and WWJ radio drew a stark case in point.

The *News* had been a force in the community for almost a century. Its founder and various heirs and heiresses helped shape modern Detroit. Belle Isle is a public park because the *News* agitated for it. The Detroit Institute of Arts and Cranbrook, the 319-acre suburban educational, arts, and science institution, exist because of either the *News*'s editorial leverage or its owners' philanthropy. The *News* could make mayors sweat. Only months into office in 1930, Mayor Charles Bowles faced a recall campaign. Bowles was allotted two hundred words to defend himself on the ballot. He chose these twenty-two: "What the recall shall decide is whether the people or the *Detroit News* and the *Detroit Free Press* shall govern this city." The people sided with the newspapers, 57 percent to 43 percent.

The *News*'s community impact continued for generations. A tech-savvy Will Scripps, the son of the *News* founder James E. Scripps, became interested in radio. As a result, WWJ was among the first commercial radio stations in the country, and the *News* pioneered cross-promotion. A 1922 archival photo shows five thousand Detroiters, eager for World Series results but not yet having bought their first radio, gathered in Grand Circus Park. The broadcast was amplified from speakers placed beneath a banner reading, "World's Series Play-by-Play at End of Each Inning after 2:00 p.m. from the Detroit News WWJ." The announcer was H. G. Salsinger, the newspaper's top sportswriter. A photo a few years later features the eight-member Detroit News Orchestra, staffed by Detroit Symphony Orchestra musicians moonlighting as WWJ's de facto house band.

In 1936, a Hollywood-style opening night introduced the public to WWJ's new headquarters across the street from the *News* on West Lafayette Boulevard. Everything about the place, inside and out, implied stability and class. The fourth-floor women's lounge boasted silver-metal wallpaper from Germany and a sand-colored carpet bordered by narrow bands of terra cotta and white. Draperies featured a large Easter-lily pattern, complementing furniture upholstered in white leather. The sophisticated ambience endured a generation later, when WWJ-TV debuted as Detroit's first television station on Channel 4. Its chief competitor, Channel 7 (WXYZ-TV), prospered in the 1950s when the local comedian Soupy Sales was taking pies in the face five days a week. Such a sense of the absurd did not fit on West Lafayette. The late Mort Zieve, a Channel 7 producer before founding an ad agency, told the author this anecdote: A Channel 4 producer complained to Zieve, "You guys take shit and turn it into money." Zieve replied, "Could be. But you take money, and turn it into shit."

The shared architecture of the *News* and its broadcast properties across the street mirrored the near-interchangeability in the public mind, exactly as ownership intended. By 1967, however, that image was beginning to look a little fusty to casual observers and more so to professional analysts.

Annual studies of the Detroit television market revealed changing attitudes about the *News* and its broadcast cousins. WJBK-TV (Channel 2) hired the research firm McHugh and Hoffman to monitor viewers' attitudes. The 1962 report noted, "The *News* is an old, powerful, and successful institution on the Detroit scene, and there is a minimum of animosity directed toward it. By and large, it is a well-liked paper, and these attitudes of respect and approval of the *News* carry over in modified forms to WWJ in people's feelings about it." And the 1963 report said, "WWJ is acknowledged as the prestige station of the community."

But McHugh and Hoffman found that the old-line station's image was becoming a problem. The world of broadcast news was maturing. President John F. Kennedy turned the medium to his advantage with his personality.

CBS and NBC had expanded their nightly newscasts from fifteen minutes to thirty minutes in 1963. The reliable stuffiness of WWJ-TV's persona was wearing thin with its audience. As McHugh and Hoffman researchers noted in 1964, "WWJ's reputation in the news area is not quite as solid as last year. . . . Some fatigue and irritation with news has set in as an aftermath of the Kennedy assassination." And four months before the civil disturbance, they said,

> It appears that while Channel 4 has a definite place in Detroit television news, its image is built on external influences, habit, past reputation, and apparently slipping personalities. Also, one of its major qualities, its seriousness and formality, is a characteristic that can hinder as well as help. While some viewers find that Channel 4's seriousness adds to its air of competence, others feel that this makes the program dull and uninteresting, especially in a "blue collar" market such as Detroit.

A fifty-year-old female viewer told McHugh and Hoffman interviewers, "I just watch Channel 4 out of habit. We don't like the newscasters or anything about them more than any other. We just always turn it on."

Something else had changed. The *News* had acquired serious and powerful competitors. The American Broadcasting Company, which owned Channel 7, had begun putting money into its news operation. The orders came from on high, from New York via Washington. US Senator John Pastore (D-Rhode Island), who chaired the US Senate Communications Subcommittee, suggested to ABC chairman Leonard Goldenson that the network and its five owned-and-operated stations should pay more attention to news, an unspoken reference to license renewal time. So Channel 7, which had done as little as five minutes of news a day in 1959, got into the news business. Channel 2 (WJKB), meanwhile, became a real contender. Its anchor team, fronted by Jac Le Goff, John Kelly, and the meteorologist Jerry Hodak, had begun chatting with one another during the newscasts, making the newscast more viewer friendly. On the print side of the ledger, the *Detroit Free Press*, under ownership of Knight Newspapers Inc., had been chipping away at the *News*'s circulation lead for more than a decade.

That is the way the media landscape looked before dawn on July 23, 1967, as Detroit police raided a blind pig at 12th Street and Clairmount Avenue. News editors across the country learned in the next few hours that in Detroit, "blind pig" meant an illegal after-hours drinking spot. As arrestees were taken downstairs and out onto 12th Street, the violence began.

An ABC News correspondent interviews black leaders, including State Senator Coleman Young (*center*) and Congressman John Conyers (*right*). Image courtesy of the *Detroit News*, from the Detroit Historical Society Collection.

Detroit news media knew about the violence almost from the beginning. Both newspapers maintained a desk on the third floor of 1300 Beaubien Street, Detroit police headquarters. WWJ-TV news director Jim Clark recalled being alerted by the *News* city desk in the early-morning hours. He immediately dispatched crews. The *Free Press* reporter on duty, Red Griffith, who had covered the police department for decades and had countless sources on the street, knew that the official reports were wrong. The situation was getting out of control.

The Kerner Commission's 1968 report noted that Detroit's first-day coverage of the disturbance was unlike that in other cities that turbulent summer. For an entire day, Detroit television and radio stations sat on the biggest story of post–World War II Detroit. Mayor Jerome P. Cavanagh was unusually comfortable among reporters and had made the former *Detroit Times* journalist Ray Girardin his police commissioner. On this day, Cavanagh, along with the cochair of the state's Civil Rights Commission, persuaded the city's TV and radio stations to stay silent, hoping to tame a budding rebellion. WKNR-AM news director Phil Nye, who ran one of the best radio news operations in town, recalled to this author how Cavanagh chased him down via telephone on an Oakland County golf course. As Nye recounted, "He asked me not to air it. . . . He said, 'You remember we had the little problem on Kercheval [referring to two days of disturbances on the city's east side in 1966, which were quickly quelled]? We think it's going to be the same way." The lawyer Damon Keith, who cochaired the state's Civil Rights Commission, also phoned the area newsrooms and asked them to go mute.

Meanwhile, the Detroit Tigers were playing a Sunday doubleheader against the New York Yankees at Tiger Stadium. The Tigers were two games out of first place. With 34,623 fans in the stands, as broadcaster Ray Lane recalled to the author, Tigers general manager Jim Campbell phoned. "My instructions were simple. 'You are not, I repeat not, under any circumstances, to refer to the smoke over the left-field fence." As the *New York Times* later related in its July 23 edition, "But the Tigers would win the second game, while smoke from a racial disturbance in the northwest section of the city drifted high behind the left-field roof of the stands." There had been a brief report on WXYZ radio at 9:00 a.m. about a disturbance. The first television station to break the news was a bit outside the Detroit media loop. CKLW-TV, in Windsor, went on the air at 2:00 p.m. Reporters at the station, which had a tiny newsroom, could see the smoke from the station's offices on Riverside Drive, which abutted the Detroit River. They could see the smoke but could not pin down what was happening. One reporter finally got some information from Girardin, an old drinking friend. So Channel 9 viewers saw Detroit enveloped in smoke. The station simply turned a camera and let viewers decide if something was wrong. Announcer Irv Morrison described events to his audience with simple facts, pointedly not using the word *riot*. Detroit's television stations weighed in early that evening.

The disturbance began just before 4:00 a.m., July 23. The next newspaper press runs were the editions of Monday, July 24. Newspaper readers could see a major difference in the way the *News* and the *Free Press* covered the story. At the *News*, as at most newspapers, the news and opinion departments are separate operations. Front-page editorials might appear once a decade, if that. But on this day, in the *News*'s first edition since the violence began, it showed exasperation with the people in the street: "These mobsters, arsonists and looters were not fighting a civil rights battle. The neighborhoods torn apart do not teem with the unemployed. Times are not desperate in Detroit for people who want and can work and the rioters who rampaged were not confined to the unemployed."

Rather than lecturing, the *Free Press* got closer to the story. William Serrin was among the reporters on the scene. He parked his cream-colored

1967 Pontiac GTO in an alley and got so close that one rioter threw a milk bottle and hit him in the head. The wound required stitches, but the GTO was eventually recovered in surprisingly good shape. According to reporter Tom De Lisle, someone called the *Free Press* city desk regarding one of the paper's photographers, Ira Rosenberg. "Do you have a guy out here, little guy in red tennis shoes? The mob has come after him three times, but he keeps getting away. He's not going to be so lucky forever. You better get him out of here." Many Detroit riot photos were shot from behind police lines. Many of Rosenberg's were shot from the rioters' point of view. The Pulitzer photography jury recommended Rosenberg's work for a prize. The judges were overruled by the Pulitzer governing body, which awarded the local reporting prize to the *Free Press* but gave the prize in photography to a *Jacksonville Journal* staffer.

The *Free Press* newsroom took careful note of calls from citizens, many trapped in riot areas, some almost hysterical and seeking any information they could get. Even copyboys staffed phones and asked questions. "Where are you calling from? What do you see?" Many notes made their way to the rewrite desk, where James C. Dewey was on the phone interviewing staff reporters positioned around the city. Dewey, a former United Press Latin America bureau chief, crafted the *Free Press* lead story on each of the five riot days. Those stories stand up today as models of tight, logical writing.

While the *News* hired a private plane for aerial shots of the disturbance, the *Free Press* went directly into the neighborhoods with an armored personnel carrier (APC). The medium-duty vehicle was almost seven feet tall and a little more than seventeen feet long. Chrysler Corporation made only thirty such vehicles, eventually shipping them to Mexico. The transmission was operated via push-buttons, similar to Dodge and Plymouth cars of the time. The company removed the vehicle's gun and loaned the newspaper what became a symbol of how far the *Free Press* would go to get the story. Reporters who rode in the APC wore helmets, and many bystanders—including personnel from the 82nd Airborne and Michigan National Guard—saluted as they drove past.

The three *Free Press* staffers in the accompanying photo—Gene Goltz, Ira Rosenberg, and Tom De Lisle—riding in what was known around the newsroom as "the tank," illustrate the kind of journalists the paper deployed.

Gene Goltz earned his tuition for the University of Missouri Journalism School by loading five-hundred-pound ice blocks at a nearby ice plant. His most notable facial feature was an oddly shaped nose, almost an abstract work of art. It got that way en route to a Pulitzer Prize. Goltz reported on

Detroit Free Press staff entered the conflict area in an armored personnel carrier loaned to the newspaper by the Chrysler Corporation. They included (*left to right*) copyboy Tom De Lisle, photographer Ira Rosenberg, and reporter Gene Goltz. Image courtesy of Timothy Kiska and the *Detroit Free Press*.

fiscal malfeasance in Pasadena, Texas, a Houston suburb. Quincy James, the city's police commissioner and a former heavyweight boxer in the US Navy and at the University of Houston, became unhappy about being called into a grand jury to testify as a result of a Goltz story. He punched Goltz on his way into court—first a right, then a left—breaking the reporter's nose. The doctor examining Goltz told him, "I can put it back the way it was. But to tell you the truth, that's no bargain." Harding Christ and the rest of the Pulitzer jury called Goltz's Pasadena stories "a classic case of a reporter pursuing the public's right to know."

Photographer Ira Rosenberg was dubbed "First Wave Rosie" during his days covering warfare on numerous beaches during World War II. General Douglas MacArthur signed a letter granting Rosenberg an all-access pass in the Pacific theater. Rosenberg was at Guantánamo Bay during the Cuban Missile Crisis. In 1964, he photographed the Beatles for the *New York Herald-Tribune* when they got off a plane in New York for the first time.

Tom De Lisle was twenty years old and about to start his junior year as a journalism major at the University of Detroit and working at the *Free Press* as a copyboy. His work during the riot earned him a promotion to reporter less than three months later. He later joined the staff of Detroit Mayor Roman Gribbs before starting a career as a comedy writer in Los Angeles.

The *News*, mired in its long-standing persona as the Gray Lady of Lafayette, was no match. Channel 4, across the street, was similarly timid. The WWJ-TV street reporter Dwayne X. Riley commented to this author about his broadcast competitors, "They were putting on more reports rather than waiting until news time. We had set times, when the people who were running things decided, 'Don't put on any more than necessary.' We were not to refer to it as a riot. It was a disturbance. Even after the fires and the shots being fired, it was still a disturbance." The *Free Press* gave that issue careful consideration, gingerly using the word "riot" on the first day out of an abundance of factual caution. Staff debated when a mere "disturbance" became the more incendiary "riot." By the second day, there was no question.

The massive *Free Press* coverage filled one hundred pages during the disturbance. Afterward, a reporting team was detached to examine each of the forty-three related deaths. Many Detroiters assumed all were rioters. The *Free Press* team found that many were simply in the wrong place at the wrong time. The paper brought in the reporter Philip Meyer, fresh from a year at Harvard studying research techniques under a Nieman Fellowship, to study what caused the disturbance. He directed a survey of 437 African Americans in the city, a study paid for by Henry Ford II and other private donors via donations to Detroit's Urban League chapter. Meyer's conclusion, published in *Return to 12th Street*, was, "The vast majority of black citizens in the riot area, including the riot participants, thought of burning and looting as crimes. They had simply been caught up in the pressure of the moment." Editorially, the paper pressured the Wayne County Prosecutor's Office to pursue three particularly suspicious homicides at the Algiers Motel. Private autopsies arranged by the *Free Press* were key to the effort's success.

Down the street, meanwhile, the *News* bricked up its pressroom windows looking out onto West Lafayette. The newspaper's stolid newsroom culture and its stolid architecture became a national story. On November 17, 1968, the *New York Times* ascribed the renovations to "a fear on the part of management that the paper might become a target of black extremists."

The uprising revealed another uncomfortable truth. A minor, quickly contained disturbance had occurred on Detroit's east side in 1966. Major

The sociologist and politician Daniel Patrick Moynihan joined an NBC News crew and three young men preparing for an interview. Image courtesy of the *Detroit News*, from the Detroit Historical Society Collection.

rioting occurred in Newark just a week before police raided the 12th Street blind pig. But the violence that engulfed Detroit in 1967 took many people, white and black, by absolute surprise. Detroit was considered, if not a model of racial harmony, then at least a city where great strides were being made. It was not supposed to happen here—hence the lead paragraph of that July 24 front-page *Detroit News* editorial: "It HAS happened here." In truth, few places belied the myth of Detroit racial harmony as much as the institutions telling the riot story: the city's newsrooms.

This was not only a local problem. "The journalism profession has been shockingly backward in seeking out, hiring, training and promoting Negroes," wrote the authors of the Kerner Commission report, which estimated that African Americans held 5 percent of editorial jobs. During the week of the riot, the bylines of two African American reporters, Susan Holmes and LaRue Heard, can be found often and prominently in the *Free Press* archives. Susan Holmes, later Susan Watson, later became the paper's city editor and then a columnist. Heard later attended the Columbia University Journalism School before dying in an auto accident at the age of twenty-four. Joe Strickland appears to have been the only African American to appear in a byline in America's largest afternoon newspaper, the *News*. He made major contributions to the investigation of the Algiers Motel incident, tracking down an eyewitness to the shootings in Hopkinsville, Kentucky. Channels 4's and 7's on-air news ranks were all white. In assessing the riot broadcasts, the *News* radio-TV critic Frank Judge noted two African American reporters that week: WXYZ-AM's Bob Bennett and Channel 2's Sylvia Wayne. Judge assumed Bennett and Wayne had it "easier" in the cauldron because of their race. (The *News* ran dispatches from Sandra West, a UPI reporter whom the *News* described as a "Negro" and who lived only a few blocks from the riot's epicenter.) A few weeks after the disturbance, WWJ-TV interviewed and hired Jerry Blocker. Blocker later told the author, "We didn't know how I was going to be accepted by blacks or whites. It was quite a gamble." The McHugh and Hoffman researchers found shortly thereafter that he was accepted just fine. A year later, the station hired WXYZ radio reporter Bennett. Channel 4 officials, who could read census statistics as well as anybody, had been contemplating hiring an African American reporter. The riot had forced their hand.

In fact, all Detroit news media, deeply embarrassed by the failure to foresee the biggest riot in American history, made moves toward diversity. In addition to Blocker and Bennett at Channel 4, Channel 7 hired Don Haney, who as a young man had dropped off audition recordings at Channel 4. He related to the author that he was told, "You're a damned fool for trying to get a job at a white station." Haney moved to Canada, learned the broadcast business, and was hired at Channel 7. Channel 4 introduced a show titled *Profiles in Black*. WJR-AM hired the *Michigan Chronicle* columnist Bill Black, who became the dean of the City Hall press corps, revered for both his integrity and scholarly devotion to detail. By 1975, Detroit had the first African American–*owned* television station in the country, WGPR-TV.

As the debate ramped up about how to interpret 1967's seismic summer, with the city yearning for open and frank discussion about what had happened, both newspapers were shut by a nine-month strike. City Hall set up a "Rumor Control Center" to squelch some of the bad information getting out in a news vacuum. Two flimsy ad hoc "strike papers" hit the streets, each featuring "crime blotter" columns. Suspects were identified as "street thugs" and members of "jackal packs." According to the files of Newspaper Guild Local 22, when the strike ended, the *News* launched its own crime column, which carried equally salacious entries such as, "The assailant was described as a Negro, about 27, 5 feet 8, 170 pounds, wearing a light gray shirt and dark pants. . . . Three young men, one armed with a revolver, held up Our Enterprises, 3914 Joy, near McQuade, on the near west side, at

5 p.m. yesterday. One was a Negro." Many African American readers boycotted the paper. Across the street, WWJ had agreed to air a five-part series on Detroit's problems, produced by the Interfaith Action Council. The program was pronounced not prime-time quality by the station's general manager after only two episodes. WWJ-TV offered alternative times, but *News* publisher Peter B. Clark had to meet with angry community members. The remaining three installments aired on WTVS-TV, the city's educational television station, which had a smaller audience.

The 1967 riot was cataclysmic for a weakened Channel 4 and, by extension, the *News*, where nearly fifty years of cross-branding turned out to be problematic. McHugh and Hoffman reported in 1968, "Channel 4 is suffering grave consequences for its failure to adequately cover the riot and inform its audience of the situation accurately and often. The result of this failure has been an almost whole defection of news viewers to Channels 2 and 7, which were judged far superior in their handling of the civil disturbances." That winter, McHugh and Hoffman researchers found that Channel 4 was doing well among the upper-middle-class, older, and white viewers, but the station "was not communicating to the rest of the population of Detroit—and this is the growing majority which is asking and needing to be recognized. These people—the prospering working and lower middle classes, the emerging younger generations, and the increasingly prideful Negro viewers—feel no closeness with nor affection for Channel 4, consigning it to second position in their viewing preferences." The mistrust continued for years. A 1974 McHugh and Hoffman study of African Americans in Detroit asked, "Which Detroit TV station do you think best presents the views and problems of the black community?" Only 6 percent mentioned Channel 4, behind Channel 2 (18 percent) and Channel 7 (16 percent). It took years for Channel 4 to right the ship.

Half a century after the riot, technological advances have changed everything. The news blackout on the first day of the disturbance can never be repeated. YouTube would be neck deep in cell-phone video by noon. Further, real strides have been made in diversity on the Detroit journalism scene.

But the impact of modern technology raises another fundamental, vital demarcation point. Coverage of events changed the media landscape in Detroit almost overnight. More important, the media's efforts changed the course of the narrative.

In 1967, the *Free Press* went out and procured a "tank." The paper arranged private autopsies that blew open the Algiers Motel story. It hired an expert with a bag of research techniques from Harvard to study community attitudes and put the arm on local millionaires to pay for it. An entire team of reporters was assigned, after the riot, to make sense of what happened.

Who in today's blogosphere has the resources and institutional clout to pull off something like that? Who will shine such a bright light where it is needed? And who will pay for it?

The Mayor's Shadow

Berl Falbaum

Berl Falbaum was interviewed by William Winkel, April 21, 2016, and his transcript was edited by Joel Stone, November 23, 2016, to fit this volume's physical limitations. The complete original transcript can be accessed via the Detroit Historical Society's electronic portal (detroithistorical.org).

I was born in Berlin in 1938. We escaped Nazi Germany in 1939 for Shanghai, China, where I spent the first ten years of my life. Following the war, we were allowed to come to the United States—first San Francisco and then Detroit.

We moved into what is now called Rosa Parks Boulevard—it was 12th Street at the time—and I was enrolled in the fourth grade. There's a history in Detroit of movement of Jews from Hastings, way down south in Detroit, to 12th Street, then Dexter, then Seven Mile and Shafer, then Oak Park. And at the time we moved into 12th Street, that neighborhood was already dramatically changing.

I had very good experiences. I always grew up in an interracial atmosphere, which, of course, is very positive in terms of your education and interrelationships. My dad was a tailor, and he worked in a variety of shops. My mother became a domestic to help out because we were extremely poor.

Growing up in the 1950s, there was a lot of tension in the schools between blacks and whites. There were confrontations on the streets. I understood it, as much as a fifteen-, sixteen-year-old could understand. Of course, I understood it better as I grew older.

I graduated from Central High School in 1957. Then I went to Wayne State University and graduated in the summer of 1961. I was already hired by the *Detroit News* as a reporter full-time before I finished, and so I finished at night. I started out where everybody starts out, doing a variety of beats. I went to the police beat, where you cover crime, and then went to general assignment and did a little of everything. In 1965, I was sent over to City Hall to cover politics. I was at City Hall in '67 when the riot broke out. Sunday, I was sitting on my porch when I heard on the radio about the riot, and I said to my wife, "I gotta go downtown and go to work." She said, "You're not leaving the family for a riot." I said, "Yes, I am."

Driving in, I didn't encounter any police or military yet. It was just broke out, so I didn't go directly to City Hall. I went to the main office, to the City Desk, to see what my assignment would be. By 1967, my job was to cover the mayor, so I just attached myself to the mayor. Wherever he went, I went. Whatever meetings and press conference happened, I'd cover. I covered the press conference between Mayor Cavanagh, Governor George Romney, Cyrus Vance, who was sent in by President Lyndon Johnson.

So I didn't really cover the riot itself—the violence and so forth. I did go by myself once back to tour it, and a fellow I knew who I covered as a community activist, Joe Williams, said it wasn't safe for me to be alone walking the streets. So I didn't cover the actual devastation. I covered the political side of it.

Romney felt that he's the governor of the state, and he perhaps should take the lead. Cavanagh's feeling was, "This is my city, and I'm the chief executive officer." And then you had political issues: Should you have the federal troops? Is it too early for them to come in? What are the politics of it? So the federal government, according to Cavanagh—and I tend to agree with him—was a little slow to react. Some of it may have been based on waiting for a good assessment of the situation, or some of it may have been politics. I'm sure it was a combination of both.

So there's tremendous friction about when to send in the troops and how quickly, and Cavanagh was of the opinion—send them right away. And that was the major disagreement. There were, of course, little ego issues between who conducts the press conference and who goes first and all that.

I had covered Cavanagh, by that time, for three or four years. Here was a mayor who was elected at thirty-three years old in 1961. He got national headlines. He was on the covers of major magazines for doing all the right things in Detroit: integrating the police department, being responsive to discrimination against blacks. He was doing everything right. He became president of the US Conference of Mayors and the National League of Cities, at the same time. He was a national figure. Matter of fact, people had already started talking to him about being a presidential candidate.

The uprising took a tremendous personal toll on Cavanagh. Basically, "I've done everything right," and he ended up having not just a riot but the worst riot in the country. I don't think I saw him at ease—and I don't mean at ease, sitting back and just relaxing—but just at ease, throughout those days. I don't think I ever saw a smile on his face for anything.

I remember him coming back to the office about one o'clock in the morning, and our bureau office—not just the *News* but the *Free Press*—was right down the hall. I was the only one there, so I walked into his office—he let me come in—and we sat down. It wasn't to do a story, just to talk. And I could feel the pain. You know, we had a drink—he had a little bar in the back—and I could feel the pain. I don't think I ever saw him smile for a long time after that.

After everything calmed down again, Cavanagh was instrumental, if not the lead character, in creating New Detroit. The first president was Joe Hudson, and the members were the heads of organizations. At his insistence, staff people couldn't come as surrogates; it had to be the top man.

The problem for Cavanagh was that his political strength had ebbed dramatically. First, there was the riot. Second, he challenged former governor G. Mennen "Soapy" Williams for the primary nomination for US Senate, which hurt him badly; the Democrats felt it was Soapy's turn—Cavanagh should wait. It angered the party, and he lost. He also experienced a highly public divorce. This all sapped him, and he did not run again in 1969.

I later covered Roman Gribbs, then went into Governor Bill Milliken's office as administrative aide to Lieutenant Governor James Brickley.

As the riot sapped the strength of Mayor Cavanagh, so it sapped the city's economic strength. Neither was the same after 1967.

The Taxi Driver

Kathleen Kurta

Kathleen Kurta was interviewed by Noah Levinson, June 30, 2015, and her transcript was edited by Joel Stone, April 10, 2016, to fit this volume's physical limitations. The complete original transcript can be accessed via the Detroit Historical Society's electronic portal (detroithistorical.org).

In July 1967, I had a summer job. I was seventeen, and that was the summer between my junior and senior years of high school. The job was behind the counter at Greenfield's Restaurant on Woodward near downtown Detroit. So that's where I was on that Sunday in July. And somehow the managers there got word that there was a riot breaking out in Detroit, and they began to send the employees home. What we saw eventually was just masses of people running in front of the restaurant. Some had bats, some just were waving their arms, but it was just a huge mob of people.

At the time, besides the regular restaurant manager, we also had a district manager who was visiting from Ohio—if you can think of Barney Fife, that's kind of how his personality was. So he got really excited, and he was hollering in the restaurant like Barney Fife, "Hit the dirt, hit the dirt." And we all were afraid, so we were behind the tables; some of us were behind the counters, some went back into the kitchen, but people were just laying low because they weren't sure what was going to be happening.

Those who could go home left. Very few had cars, but some were able to catch a bus and get out of the area. The bus I needed to catch to go home was the Grand River bus; and that—according to the reports—was the area that was mostly being affected, and they were not running buses on Grand River. So I was stuck—downtown. And what I learned later is, in the meantime, my mom and dad had come home from a picnic, and my dad wanted to come down and pick me up. He was having a conniption at home that I was not safe. He called the police, and the police had already at that time put a curfew in effect. And they said to my dad, "If you do go down and pick her up, and we find you on the street, you'll be arrested." And my dad was a wreck at home, and my mom later said he just paced back and forth, because he didn't know what to do. He didn't want me there—but he had no choice.

So the district manager at the restaurant—the one that was visiting from Ohio—said to me that I would have to spend the night in the YWCA. Eventually we went into his car, and we were going to drive around downtown Detroit looking for the Y. I didn't want to go to the Y. I was scared. I wanted to go home, but he wasn't going to drive me home. So as we drove around, when we really got to the downtown area where Hudson's and the other stores were, there was hardly a car on the street.

We were approached by a taxicab, and the taxicab was driven by an African American cabbie. And he came up, kind of put his car next to us when the light changed, rolled down his window, and asked if we needed help. He said that he noticed the Ohio license plates on the car, wanted to know if we were lost, and asked if he could give us directions. So the district manager told him that he had this young girl in his car, they were looking for the Y, because she couldn't get home and she needed to stay someplace.

So the taxi driver said to the manager, "I would be willing to take her home." Well, then I kind of inwardly panicked over that one, because they were all talking about this being a race riot, and a seventeen-year-old white girl going in a taxicab with a black man at that point was not cool. But I wanted to go home. So I took a chance and got out of the car. I went in the cab with the driver. He told me to sit in the front seat rather than in the back seat. And as I did that, the district manager just drove away, and there I was. I had no chance to change my mind if I wanted to change my mind.

So he asked me where I lived. I gave him my address. I told him the cross streets and all of that and that I had usually gone up Grand River to go home, and he thought from the reports that he had heard on the radio that if he went up Michigan Avenue instead of Grand River, we might be able to get to my house. So we were going to head in that direction. The other thing he told me, you know, he looked right at me in the front seat, and he said, "If I tell you to get on the floor, get on the floor." I wasn't sure why at that point. I later learned, again, that if a black man was seen with a young, teenage white girl in the car, this would not be good for either of us.

Actually he was a wonderful man. As we drove up Michigan Avenue, he shared about his family, and what he told me was that he was not able to go home either. He lived on West Grand Boulevard, and West Grand Boulevard was up in flames and smoke as well; and so he had no way of communicating with his wife to see if she and his family were safe, to see if his house was safe. So he asked me about my family, and we had a wonderful conversation on the way home, just about life and things that were important to him, things that were important to me.

It was interesting because I learned that this gentleman was as scared as I was. Older, married, kids working already, you know, versus my seventeen years—but he was just as afraid as I was and afraid for his family. So he eventually got me home, parked the car in front of the house, came around, opened the door, let me out of the car, and literally walked me up to the front porch, where my dad was just standing by the door. He gave me to my dad, and my dad was so excited—he had tears in his eyes—he was happy, he thanked the guy, offered to pay him whatever he could pay him that he got me home safely, invited him in for something to eat, invited him in for a drink. But he didn't take any of that. He accepted no money, he declined to drink, he declined any kind of food. But what he did ask my dad was, "Please say a prayer that my family is okay." And so obviously my dad was a praying man anyways, and so he did, and we did pray for him. As I look back, I wish I knew his name, I wish—he told me his name, but I don't recall what it was—I wish even through this project, I wish there was a way that that man, if he's still alive, would come forward with his story.

I learned a lot from that man: that people are people, and it didn't make any difference what your background was, what your color was. Now I do social work, and it's the same thing. I meet with people of all different cultures and backgrounds and religions. And that man taught me well, that taxi driver taught me well.

ORAL HISTORY EXCERPTS

The oral history excerpts that accompany these photographs were generated by the Detroit Historical Society's Detroit '67 oral history project team. They have been edited for brevity. Full transcripts are part of the Detroit Historical Society Collection.

Detroit police officers stand by and observe the unrest. Donated by Henri Umbaji King, from the Detroit Historical Society Collection.

A Detroit police officer stands outside the looted Cancellation Shoes store at Harper Avenue and Van Dyke Street. Photograph by Tom Venaleck, *Detroit Free Press*. Donated by the City of Detroit Department of Information—Photography Department, from the Detroit Historical Society Collection.

"So what you had, you had a window full of shoes. All the shoes were left shoes, okay? You never put in a left and a right, because you put in a left and a right, then they have a pair of shoes. So they're only left shoes.

"[One morning after the looting], this guy comes in—and I'm behind the counter, there's no business, and Uncle Harry is doing something upstairs. The guy comes in, 'Man what's wrong with you? I want to know what's wrong with you?' So I said, 'What do you mean what's wrong with me? There's nothing wrong with me.' And he says, 'I came in here yesterday, I bought a pair of shoes, you only gave me the left!' So I said, 'Would you say that again?' He said, 'You only gave me the left shoe, where's my right shoe?!' I said loudly, 'I only sold you a left shoe?' So Uncle Harry turns around with fire in his face, I mean he is really angry. And, the guy looks at Uncle Harry, he looks at me and [clap] he's gone. He gets right out of there.

"So Uncle Harry says to me, 'Alan, follow him.' So I said, 'Follow him?! I'm eighteen years old; I'm not a detective! I'm not following this guy.' He says, 'Follow him. Just go see where he goes.' So I went outside, and I watched where he went. I went down like a block, and he walked across the street into an apartment building. I came back, I told Uncle Harry, and he called the police. They might have found a lot of left shoes."

—Alan Feldman

"When you're mad, you don't think. I don't even want to say what I heard from one of my friends that was looting. He actually looted and only got one shoe. Why would you take one shoe? I said, 'Why were you there?' 'I was with the rest of them, and look what I got—a shoe!' That's pitiful. I guess it's just when everybody sees everybody else out there, followers and not leaders were out there. I'll never forget that shoe—that's all he got was a shoe!"

—Shirley Davis

Firefighters, subjected to rock throwing and sniper fire while trying to save property, were joined by armed troops and police units for protection. Donated by Henri Umbaji King, from the Detroit Historical Society Collection.

An exhausted Detroit firefighter rested during a quiet moment. Photograph by Captain Joseph A. Mancinelli, Detroit Fire Department. Donated by the City of Detroit Department of Information—Photography Department, from the Detroit Historical Society Collection.

"I was 16 years old in 1967, living in a wonderful, close-knit neighborhood on the west side. My father was a lieutenant in the Detroit Fire Department. On Sunday morning, he received a call that he was to report to the fire station immediately. . . . We didn't actually see him until the following Friday.

"He came home exhausted and broken. His voice cracked as he told us about the rows and rows of houses that they tried to save and couldn't. He said people were coming up to them begging, pleading, and crying for them to try and save their houses and businesses, but there just wasn't the manpower or equipment to do the job. He also said he had to order his men to hide under the rigs many times as they were getting shot at. It broke his heart to see what was happening to his city.

"The only time my father smiled while relaying these stories was when he talked about the people who were neighbors to the firehouse. He said he had never seen so much food prepared and brought to them during those days. Firemen and police officers were being fed by the community with donated food, all day every day during the riot. My father said it was the best food he ever ate."   —Karen Zaleski

Firefighters attended the funeral of a fallen comrade. During the unrest, two fire-men were killed, John Ashby and Carl Smith. Detroit police officer Jerome Olshove was the only law enforcement officer to die. Photograph by Captain Joseph A. Mancinelli, Detroit Fire Department. Donated by the City of Detroit Department of Information—Photography Department, from the Detroit Historical Society Collection.

"In 1967 I was a second-year internal medicine resident at Detroit Receiving Hospital, which was the main teaching hospital of the Wayne State University Medical School. Receiving Hospital at that time was in the downtown area near Greektown. It was right across the street from the main police station.

"I was off on the weekend that the riots started. [I] called Receiving and said, 'You need any help?' And they said, 'Absolutely. But don't drive your car. It's hard to drive through some of this. It might not be that safe.' 'How am I gonna get there?' 'Try and see if the police will bring you.' I called the police, and they suggested that I call a black cab company. Now you have to understand that I didn't know there was such a thing as a white cab company and a black cab company.

"The cab driver was a really wonderful African American gentleman, and as we're driving, I could see him looking at me, and he was starting to get nervous.

And he said, 'Doctor, it wouldn't hurt your feelings, would it, if I asked you to scrunch down in the backseat?' Those were his exact words. And I said, 'No, no problem.' He was afraid we might be a target. And we're driving down the Chrysler, and it's dawning on me that things are happening. You can hear a lot of gunshot noise, you can see fires already, and that was just Sunday afternoon. When we got to the exit, there was a roadblock set up by the police. They wanted to know who we were, and I said, 'Doctor, going to the hospital.' They let us through.

"I had the foresight to realize that I might not be leaving for a while, so I had packed a small suitcase with shaving equipment and extra underwear and some

Detroit's doctors and nurses worked around the clock to provide care to over 1,100 injured citizens. The Detroit Police Department officially cited 657 injuries; 476 were to law enforcement and firefighters. They were treated at all area hospitals, primarily Detroit General, Henry Ford, and Receiving. Donated by the City of Detroit Department of Information—Photography Department, from the Detroit Historical Society Collection.

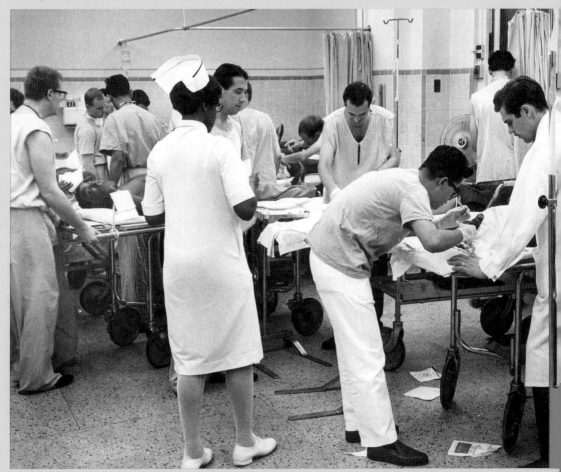

shirts and so on. And it turned out to be a good thing that I did that because I was stuck there for almost seven days.

"Basically, by the time the week went on, almost every patient in the hospital was a prisoner. [There] were traumas—knife and gun or people hit on the head with different things—but the medical patients that I was involved with would be people like diabetics, who would run out of insulin and they couldn't get to the drugstore because everything was closed. We also had injured police and injured firemen, who were being shot at by snipers.

So by the third or fourth day, when I would make my rounds going patient to patient to see how things were, I was going around with four soldiers, dressed in full uniform—82nd Airborne—full battle dress, carbine on their back, helmet. That's how I made rounds every day for the last three or four days of that week."

—Dr. Carl Lauter

A man walked down Euclid Avenue near 12th Street to inspect the destruction. Donated by Henri Umbaji King, from the Detroit Historical Society Collection.

A week after the uprising, girls in Sunday dresses seemed more interested in their popsicles than in the damage around them. Image courtesy of the *Detroit News*, from the Detroit Historical Society Collection.

Part IV

Out of the Ashes

In the immediate aftermath of rioting, local churches stepped up to provide food and water in affected neighborhoods. Supporters of black self-determination formed Operation Get-Down and Inner-City Sub-Center to provide long-term supplemental education, food, housing, recreation, and health-care options. These efforts were supported with money generated by the black community, as well as grants from the United Way and other philanthropic foundations. Additionally, faith-based organizations fostered a number of proactive initiatives, including the Inter-Faith Emergency Council and the Interreligious Foundation for Community Development.

One of the results of the uprising was that the Detroit Police Department began using helicopters for surveillance. During the World Series in 1968, the DPD leased one from Bell Aircraft Corporation, and officials were impressed. Police Commissioner Johannes Spreen convinced the Common Council of the helicopters' worth, and the city paid $50,000 each for two.

About this same time, elm trees across North America were being devastated by a beetle-borne fungus known as Dutch elm disease. Detroit streets had been planted largely with elm trees in the early 1900s, and the trees had established a dominant canopy over many neighborhoods. In an attempt to kill the beetles, municipal teams with truck-mounted industrial sprayers went down every street in the city, throwing insecticide 150 feet in the air. The procedure had only a small effect on tree mortality, and the beautiful elms were mostly gone by 1970.

In the black community, the two events were eyed with suspicion. The police commissioner gets two helicopters to better keep an eye on illegal activity, but pilots cannot see through the trees. Soon afterward, the entire city gets sprayed, and all the trees die. Coincidence?

Not everyone believed that tale, of course, but such was the suspicion of City Hall then that the story persists to this day. Suspicions about other aspects of the official record remain similarly alive and include body counts, arrest reports, behavior by government assets, and response to the Kerner Commission report.

Within the white community, distrust of the state of the city was quantifiable. Thirty thousand folks left in the year following the uprising. Some pulled up stakes while the uprising was in progress, taking what could be loaded into a truck and heading for the suburbs, never to return, no matter the cost.

Declining values panicked many property owners. Since then, tens of thousands of residents, black and white, have departed the city, attracted by suburban amenities and stability. Elements of economics, racism, and cultural pride drove many refugees to sell and move. Despite all of this, a stalwart faction remains, fighting valiantly for the city they love. Additionally, creative and curious people from around the world—historically drawn to Detroit—add to the melting pot today.

What the Children Said

Steven Balkin

The following selection of thoughts was collected by an elementary school teacher in the autumn of 1967. As he substituted in a number of predominantly black elementary schools, he got feedback from fifth- and sixth-graders in various parts of the city. While these selections have been edited for brevity, the spelling and punctuation have been left intact. It is notable, in these small voices, the expressions of excitement or fear. It is also pretty clear that, in many cases, these small voices reflect the big voices of people that they admired.

"I thought the riot was very uncalled for. The black man said that the white man wasn't doing him right. But to me, white man and black man is the same. The only difference is the skin. If a black man going with a white woman and a white man see him, he will want to kill him. But God make all man and women the same. To me there was no need for blood to be spilled. White man and black man should love one another because that the way God wanted it to be. The world should not have so much hate in it."

"Some of us were lucky that we didn't get burned out of our homes. Some of my friends thought it was fun. I thought it was terrible. There were snipers all over where I live. They wasn't doing nothing but clowning and acting like crazy fools."

"I think the riot was a good thing because it put some people in their place. I think all men are equal, one no better than the other. But it started when two white policemen killed a black cab driver. I'm glad they burned some of the stores down because the people who owned them talked to other people like they were dogs and cats and even worse."

"I was out in the riot and I think it was fun because I got a bike, a radio and a tape recorder. We call ourselves Black Power. Black Power is the name."

"The riot was just no good for Detroit. The people was just hurting their selfs. They was just ignorant thats all."

"I liked the riot. It was fun. We had to stay out of school very long. My sister went on Chene and got some coats, sweaters, shirts, pants and shoes."

"A lot of people were breaking into peoples stores and was stealing the peoples food and their clothes and their television sets and a hole lot of other things. They were starting fires and when the fire men came to put the fires out, the people would throw things at them and call them all kinds of names."

"I thought the riot was terrible except for when they looted the bike shop. On the windows and door were painted Soul Brother. In the streets they wrote Black Power."

"I think the white people didn't want to pay the negro for what they work for. The white people want to keep the money for theirselves."

Detroit's children were firsthand witnesses to the chaos. These student drawings accompanied their stories and illustrate what they experienced. Donated by Stephen Balkin, from the Detroit Historical Society Collection.

"I saw guards in the neighborhoods. They were breaking windows and burning houses down. My father and a man downstairs got their guns and started shooting at the people in the alley. We were on the floor. I were scared so much. This white man was shooting at this color man."

A soldier and a young man chatted on Westminster Street. Donated by Dr. Carol Chadwick Burleson, from the Detroit Historical Society Collection.

"I saw army mens killing teenagers and stabbing teenagers. Once I was going to the store and this police jumped out of the car and shot this boy. The only reason he shot the boy, because the boy was backing into the store. And the police told me to go home because they was going to kill everyone walking the street, but I wasn't afraid of anything."

"I didn't like the riot because them white niggers tried to beat up the black people. The black people beat the nigger up. The dam niggers can't do a dam thing to us negros 'cause we will beat their ass like we did before. If I see a white boy while a riot is going on, I am going to beat their ass."

"There was one man who had a store and the people was ready to break in his store. So he open the store and said 'you can take all you want as long as you don't burn my store down.' So they burn it down anyway. I feel sorry for that man."

"The riot was very good because my father and I looted 4 color T.V.s, 2 bottles of beer, 7.5 dollars at the drug store, and a washing machine—just for the fun of it. My cousin got him a couple of bikes and I got 9 cartons of pop. My brother got so much I just couldn't believe it. My nephew got about 32 rugs and a bottle of Johnny Walker. The next night of the riot we went beating up 62 white mother fuckers."

"I wasn't living in Detroit when the riot was here but I know lots about it. The riot in Detroit was about freedom. The negros want freedom but the whites don't want to give it to them. But one of these days, we are going to get it. We may steal and we may lie but we got just as much right to freedom as they got. These little white people walk around here with their nose up as high as they can get it and we walk around here with no clothes. The white people just laugh and say look at these black people."

"I was so scared that my teeth were clattering. Plenty of people were killed. The hospitals were jammed. People were driving down streets taking pot-shots. The riot began on my sisters birthday. She was very mad."

"I think the riot was the worst thing that ever happened to Detroit. They just did it to be doing something. They knew they couldn't get away with stealing so they created something so they could steal and burn things. I myself did not stay in the house. I went to my girlfriends back porch. We played records, danced and spent the day having fun, not paying much attention to the riot."

And the Beat Goes On

CONTINUED CONFRONTATION

Joel Stone

Nearly every analysis of the July uprising cites the tense relationship between the Detroit Police Department and the black community as the major cause of the conflict. The issue was exacerbated in subsequent months as law enforcement found itself at odds with elements within city government and with both the black and white citizens. Events that played out during the remaining years of the decade further challenged reform, exhibiting an entrenched and intractable culture within the DPD.

Police in communities throughout southeastern Michigan were increasingly at odds with public perception and municipal budgets. Crime rates continued to climb, and blame generally fell to the men with badges. Residents in all neighborhoods lamented the rash of robberies and holdups, further accelerating white flight to the suburbs and promoting vigilantism. Gun sales and recruitment of volunteer police officers grew rapidly in white communities such as Dearborn and Bloomfield Township. New black gun clubs, such as the Medgar Evers Rifle Club and the urban Fox and Wolf Hunt Club, while not significant threats to public safety, reflected the feeling that legitimate law enforcement was not getting the job done.

Despite the rise in crime, force sizes remained static. In fact, in 1968 the Detroit department was about 7 percent below its designated strength of forty-seven hundred officers. At the same time, municipal leaders resisted calls for increased wages and pensions for police departments. "Blue flu"— informal sick-out strikes—represented a widespread passive reaction by various units to denials of increased compensation. The effect was to further reduce the number of officers on the streets and reflected a severe erosion of morale within these departments. Despite the DPD being the third-highest-paid force in the nation, patrol officers in Detroit said they felt alienated.

Most mayors were vocal supporters of their troops, but some were forced to compromise their praise with measured criticism. Mayor Jerome Cavanagh admitted deficiencies within the DPD and addressed them by replacing top commanders and encouraging the promotion and recruitment of minority staff. While openly critical of the performance of some elements of the force, he was careful to support the professional and measured reaction of uniformed men in their day-to-day duties. Detroit was a tough town in which to be a cop, and it was too easy for critical citizens and the media to lump properly responsive officers together with overzealous ones.

— —

Suspicions within the black community regarding the police were further reinforced by a number of incidents over the next two years. By September 1967, it appeared that officers involved in the Algiers Motel incident would be exonerated. Two policemen faced a three-day pretrial hearing in Judge Robert DeMascio's court; only one was bound over for trial.

Reaction within the black community was predictably fierce. Rev. Albert Cleage, quoted in John Hersey's *The Algiers Motel Incident*, noted, "the type of justice we receive in Recorder's Courts is the same kind that is meted out in Mississippi." Two graduate students, Dan Aldridge and Lonnie Peek, attended all of the pretrial hearings and were frustrated that Assistant Prosecutor Avery Weiswasse failed to call significant witnesses; among many police officers was but one nonuniformed witness to the shootings. Aldridge and Peek were justifiably suspicious of the possibility of conviction, with Aldridge stating to a *Michigan Chronicle* reporter for the September 2 front page, "It was a game. They were playing a game."

At a meeting of the City Wide Citizen Action Committee (CCAC), a black activist organization, it was suggested that the community hold its own "tribunal." With direction from the attorney Milton Henry and Carl Slaughter of the *Inner-City Voice* newspaper, Aldridge and Peek began gathering the necessary depositions and evidence to present at the mock trial. The event was scheduled to take place at the Dexter Theater on Wednesday evening, August 30. The theater had previously hosted a rally by the black radical H. Rap Brown. But pressure was brought to bear on the manager, John Ashby, and the tribunal was moved to the Central United Church of Christ.

Three white patrolmen and a black private security guard were charged, in absentia, with first-degree murder. Kenneth Cockrel served as judge. Jurors included Rosa Parks and the novelist John Killens, and the mock trial was covered by journalists from Sweden and France. By the time the proceeding began, the church was packed. Many witnesses were called, and the testimony was damning. Of course, no police officers were present, and while the verdict was clear, no sentences were published. In fact, the *Detroit News* placed a short story in the fourth section near the comics, and the *Free Press* seems to have missed it entirely. The *Michigan Chronicle* had it on the front page.

Back in the real legal world, judges, prosecutors, and lawyers bandied the case against the single accused officer through Recorder's Court, Circuit Court, the Court of Appeals, and the Michigan Supreme Court. As the trial went forward, counsel for the accused petitioned successfully to move the trial out of Detroit to Mason, Michigan, the small town where Malcolm X's father had been murdered. The officer was eventually cleared of the charges by an all-white jury. Later, federal conspiracy charges were brought against the same four men tried in the mock trial. The proceeding was again moved out of Detroit, and another all-white jury found all four innocent. Civil cases filed against the city by the families of two of the dead men were settled out of court for $62,500 each, the last one in 1976.

-- --

In early April 1968, following the assassination of Martin Luther King Jr., riots and demonstrations erupted in cities across the United States, leaving over two dozen dead. Michigan Governor George Romney instituted a state of emergency the day after the murder, placing thousands of National Guard troops in black neighborhoods around the state and instituting a nighttime curfew. The *Michigan Chronicle* (the *Free Press* and *News* were on strike for much of the year) described Detroit police headquarters as an armed citadel.

Detroit fared better than most large cities. An estimated thirty-seven hundred blacks were involved in numerous protests in both the city and suburbs. Only one Detroiter and one Highland Park resident were killed, the former evidently while looting. Over four days, 1,092 people were arrested—602 for curfew violations and 60 during an all-white demonstration in northwestern Detroit by the Interfaith Action Council. By comparison, Washington, DC, saw eight people killed and five thousand arrested by a force of over eleven thousand troops. The Democratic governor of

Delaware maintained a military presence in black neighborhoods of Wilmington until mid-November. Both Mayor Cavanagh and Governor Romney complimented the overall behavior exhibited by police and military personnel, crediting them for Detroit's tempered response compared with other cities. On April 20, the *Michigan Chronicle* headlined an article, "How Did Detroit Keep Its Cool?" It noted that no officials thanked the African American community or its leaders for their restraint in the face of the government's lockdown.

Notably, of the protests that took place in Detroit, the highest profile incidents were at public schools. Many students staged impromptu walkouts. Cooley and Southwestern High Schools recorded interracial fights and vandalism. An outdoor march at Loren M. Post Middle School brought police with riot sticks who "manhandled" students and adults alike. As a result, the Detroit Public Schools system closed thirty middle and upper schools. An internal investigation on the Post incident, as reported in the *Michigan Chronicle* of April 13, 1968, described police tactics as "a mild over-reaction by some, and extreme over-reaction by a few." Mayor Cavanagh defended the department to the *Michigan Chronicle* on April 13 but commented, "Our police are not automatically white-washed. We know there are problems, and we are working constantly to correct them."

Another incident during the curfew occurred when three men were arrested coming from a memorial service for King. Myron Wahls, president of the black Wolverine Bar Association and later a judge, Raymond Sewell, and Dr. Sims were detained, according to the *Michigan Chronicle* on April 20, "due solely to their race and color." Officers were verbally abusive and held a gun to Sewell's neck. When Judge George Crockett ordered police to release the men, officers refused to act on the judge's order. An infuriated Crockett took more direct action eleven months later.

— —

A month after King's assassination, an effort was made to continue his plans for a "Poor People's March" on Washington, DC, in May. Dr. Ralph Abernathy, who had taken up the mantle of chairman of the Southern Christian Leadership Conference (SCLC) from King, requested that people from around the nation join him in peaceful protest in the capital. Several thousand answered the call. Traditional southerners, represented by Senator John McClelland (D-AR) and quoted in the *Detroit American* on May 10, imagined the rally turning into "an orgy of rioting and violence" at the behest of black militants, and six thousand troops were called in to maintain order. They outnumbered the protesters on the Mall, a reaction to the chaos following King's murder.

In Detroit, plans were quickly developed for a supportive march down Woodward Avenue and a rally at Cobo Hall, Detroit's new convention center. People traveling by caravan to Washington, DC, from Chicago and other western locations were offered food and lodging if they wished to join the event. About six hundred accepted the invitation, joining two hundred Detroiters heading to the capital. Students were encouraged to stay in school.

The march was scheduled to begin at 2:00 p.m. at Blessed Sacrament Cathedral, the home of the Roman Catholic Archdiocese of Detroit. Marchers hoped that Rev. King's brother, A. D. King, would join them, but after a two-hour wait without his appearance, attendees linked arms fifteen abreast and began the four-mile walk down Woodward. On May 14, the *Detroit American* reported that Mayor Cavanagh told four thousand people at the rally along Jefferson Avenue near Cobo Hall, "The citizens of the community endorse the objective of your drive. No one can doubt the importance of what you are doing. Your aims are beyond dispute. Your method is beyond reproach: the peaceful petition of our government for a redress of grievances."

"Only" one incident marked the parade. Accounts differ significantly. The *Detroit American*, a daily newspaper that was popular while the major outlets were on strike, reported that as the crowd headed toward the convention center, police attempted to move a stalled car that was part of the group. When people "started to mill around," police moved in with nightsticks "to prevent a serious disturbance from developing." Nothing more of the incident was recorded in that edition.

The *Michigan Chronicle* told a different story. Its May 18 headline shouted, "Local Police Blackjack Poor Marchers at Cobo Hall." As police began to move toward the stalled car, the Alabama pastor Charles Billups, an associate of King at the SCLC, intervened and requested a little time from the officers to allow the automobile to be restarted. Members of the march surrounded the car to prevent it from being towed. In reaction, fifteen to twenty members of the mounted police unit were ordered to confront the marchers, strategically deploying their horses to force the crowd off the street and into Cobo Hall, trampling and clubbing as they went. Meanwhile, in the convention center's lobby, officers in riot gear saw a mob fleeing before the mounted police and decided to keep them out of the building. Even as city officials and civil rights monitors pleaded for calmer tactics, helmeted DPD assets at the doors of the hall used clubs against the defenseless throng trapped between them and the horses. Twenty-six adults and youths were hospitalized, one seriously. An internal inquiry by the DPD called a few of the officers to account, but despite pressure from advocacy groups, no charges were filed; two men were penalized, stripped of a few days of vacation.

— —

Early on a Thursday morning in late July 1968, a year after the initial up-rising, Detroit nearly experienced another conflagration. The story was reported in the August 3 issue of *Detroit Scope* magazine, a tabloid-format "strike rag" under the editorial direction of newsman Lou Gordon. Some-time after midnight, a group of youths began breaking windows and looting along 12th Street. As the activity spread, two cars and seven buildings were set ablaze.

The DPD's reaction was immediate and sure. In marked contrast to the year before—but curiously similar to the successful "Kercheval Incident" response in 1966—the police announced a tactical alert at 2:30 a.m. and moved in with measured force. By 2:45 a.m., Police Commissioner Johannes Spreen, Deputy Superintendent Charles Gentry, and Sergeant Harold Liggett were on the scene, walking the street with bullhorns, encourag-ing residents to return to their homes. The crowd dispersed, Detroit Fire Department crews contained the damage, and the whole thing was over by dawn. The publication did not report arrests or casualties.

— —

On October 10, the Detroit Tigers packed Tiger Stadium for the final game of the 1968 World Series. Many residents and politicians felt that the team had given the city something to cheer about, a genuine morale boost after the events the previous summer. It should be noted that following the vic-tory, downtown Detroit went wild, rife with vandalism, looting, robbery, and physical violence. Most of the city's police were staged in the area near the ballpark, about a mile from the city center. In what was termed a "cel-ebration" by the *Free Press* on October 11, store windows were smashed and looted, an entire parking garage full of cars was vandalized, at least twenty-five people were arrested, an unknown number were robbed, several were stabbed, and at least two were shot to death. The measured reaction of the DPD—perhaps because the crowd was overwhelmingly white or perhaps to avoid unfavorable publicity—stands in contrast to its prompt and forceful response to other such events that same year.

– –

In late October, the Cobo complex was again the scene of a melee. It was Tuesday, October 29, a few days before the presidential election, and American Independent Party candidate George Wallace, former governor of Alabama, was speaking to supporters at a rally in Cobo Arena adjoining the convention hall. Protesters clashed with the crowd, and when forced from the arena, they taunted police. The results were predictable.

Wallace was the third man in a three-way race for the White House. Republican Richard Nixon, former vice president under Dwight Eisenhower, was running a close race against Democratic candidate Hubert H. Humphrey, the sitting vice president under Lyndon Johnson. An outspoken supporter of segregation, Wallace was popular in southern states and with transplanted southerners in the North, particularly those in large unions. He gained the support of United Auto Workers locals in Chicago, Flint, and Detroit, as well as steelworkers in Pennsylvania, Ohio, and Indiana. The *Detroit Free Press* writer James J. Kilpatrick opined on October 2 that "The Wallace Thing" was a gut-level connection with hardworking white voters marginalized by government, although analysts generally agreed that race was Wallace's primary strategic issue.

Because of Wallace's divisiveness, his rallies generally drew mixed-race groups protesting his stance on integration and fair housing rules. Prior to arriving in Detroit, he had been heckled at events in Grand Rapids, Kalamazoo, and Lansing with cries of "If you like Hitler, you'll love Wallace." Earlier in October, demonstrators clashed with Wallace supporters and club-wielding police in New York City, Newark, Buffalo, and Cleveland.

Confrontation in Detroit started with a fistfight between men of opposing views; the Wallace man sprayed his opponent with a mace-like substance. Later, private security guards in Cobo Arena attempted to remove a man who had been tossing spitballs into the crowd. When the activist refused to leave, he was bodily removed by police and members of the huge Wallace crowd. People in both camps began to throw folding chairs at each other, with the protesters having the advantage due to their less desirable seats in the upper arena. More mace-like sprays were used to force protesters outside. Before they left, though, the *Free Press* reported the next day that Wallace harangued them from the podium with "If you get a good haircut, that's all that's wrong with you. It would be a load off your mind." His ten thousand supporters sent up an ovation that shook the rafters.

According to some reports, well over a thousand protesters waited outside until the rally was over. Detroit police officers and Wayne County sheriff's deputies attempted to keep them away from people leaving the event, gradually forming a line abreast and forcing the anti-Wallace group up Washington Boulevard. Retreating to the veranda of the nearby Pontchartrain Hotel, the more aggressive protesters began shouting insults and pelting the police officers with stones. Officers hesitated a moment, then charged across the street and onto the veranda. With clubs swinging, the police forced the unruly elements off the porch, some falling six feet to the sidewalk below. Afterward, law enforcement regrouped and chased the scattering mob through downtown streets.

Seven people were arrested; five were held on charges of inciting a riot or resisting a police officer. They included a fourteen-year-old boy and his father, as well as a woman charged with spitting at an officer. Judge Crockett released the father and son but remanded them for trial on the charges. A police officer was temporarily injured by an aerosol spray, and one young college student from Birmingham was treated and released from Providence Hospital for a broken thumb and abrasions. Despite community protests, the city defended its police officers. After all officers were cleared of wrongdoing, the *Free Press* of March 7, 1969, quoted Commissioner Spreen praising them for doing a "top-notch job" of preventing an even larger disorder.

– –

As if to bookend this series of actions, the next clash occurred a few days later at the Veterans Memorial Building, situated immediately east of Cobo Arena. This venue was a popular location for parties and dances, with a beautiful view of the Detroit River. Indeed, what occurred was not the result of an organized protest but a clear example of the strained relations between police and the public.

On this Friday night, two dances were taking place on separate floors of the building. In the main ballroom on the first floor, the union wives' association of the Detroit Police Officers Association (DPOA) was hosting its annual ball. Upstairs on the sixth floor was a youth dance sponsored by Ebenezer AME Church. According to seventeen-year-old Derrick Tabor, the son of a Ferndale church pastor, cited in a November 3 *Free Press* story, white men entered the lavatories and verbally insulted the youths there. Later these same men, showing evidence of intoxication, "elbowed" youths

View of Detroit's skyline about 1966, with scenes of confrontation. On the riverfront far to the left is Cobo Hall. Cobo Arena is the round building adjoining it. To the right of the arena is the Veterans Memorial Building. The Pontchartrain Hotel is the dark, medium-tall building across Jefferson Avenue, between the arena and the Veterans Memorial Building. From the Detroit Historical Society Collection.

in the stairwell as they were exiting the dance about 12:30 a.m. and following them toward their cars. Two black youths were physically thrown out of the building.

According to news reports, one youth retaliated to the taunting by shoving one of the men down a couple of stairs. At this point, fifteen to twenty men poured out of the building. One drew a pistol and fired it, presumably in the air. Another claimed to identify himself as a police officer. Tabor testified that several of the men—he said they never identified themselves as police officers—began kicking and beating him, subsequently dragging him into bushes for continued beating. He noted that at least two other young men got the same treatment. Other officers approached a Ford Cougar with two church youths inside and began kicking the fenders. One staggering man climbed onto the roof of the vehicle and began jumping on it. The younger people scattered as they could.

Although not reported, uniformed officers must have arrived to resolve the fracas; the car was impounded as evidence. A police cruiser later picked up James Evans III stumbling along the street several blocks away. Dazed and cut, he was taken to Detroit General Hospital for treatment.

The Sunday edition of the *Detroit Free Press* reported that Commissioner Spreen immediately appointed Inspector James Bannon to work with Detective William Owens of the DPD's Citizens Complaint Bureau and administrative aide Marvin Brown, "a Negro." By late Saturday, a dozen witnesses had been questioned. The DPOA publicly agreed to cooperate in the investigation but expressed disappointment that the administration and upper brass seemed willing to bow to the black community at the expense of their officers. State Senator Coleman Young organized a press event at the Evanses' home to call for a Justice Department investigation. It was attended by members of the Catholic, Protestant, and Jewish communities, DPD community relations people, and various civil rights organizations.

Nine officers were suspended during the investigation, and five were forwarded for review. One patrolman was fired for violating department rules. Two sergeants had their ranks reduced to patrolman (a move Cavanagh later rescinded for one officer), and the fourth forfeited about six months' pay and benefits. The final officer was found to be innocent. The city paid for damage to the Cougar.

Municipal police departments and badge organizations tried many approaches to improving community relations, from town halls to immersive training. In early March 1969, Commissioner Spreen went on local television and identified the cure to Detroit's woes. In a presentation titled "Love and Crime," described in the *Free Press* on March 12, he suggested that "people make the scene together" to unify communities. "If you do your thing well within the bounds of the law and within the bounds of propriety, . . . that is love. If you care about your fellow citizens no matter what their hue, . . . that is love." Quintessential sixties.

— —

On a Saturday night a few weeks later, the New Bethel Baptist Church was active late. Located on Linwood Street in one of the riot's hardest hit neighborhoods, the three-story building was a beacon in the black religious community. Rev. C. L. Franklin had built a powerful following that numbered in the thousands. This evening, the church was rented out for a meeting of the Republic of New Africa, a self-professed black separatist organization that had attracted radicals from across the country: California to New Jersey.

Men in all-black paramilitary uniforms and carrying long guns stood as sentinels near the entrances.

Sometime after 11:30 p.m., a police cruiser carrying two officers stopped to ask the men about their firearms. From this point, witness testimony varies widely. When exiting the car—accounts differed as to whether their guns were drawn—they were met by a hail of bullets. The rookie officer Michael Czapski was shot seven times and died before reaching Henry Ford Hospital, a short distance away. His partner, Richard Worobec, also seriously wounded, was able to radio for support. Additional units responded from four precincts and reported heavy fire from the church as they arrived; those who were in the church decried this claim. Within a short time, numbers favored the police, and about fifty officers stormed the church. They found a large crowd, most of whom were unarmed and not overtly aggressive. All 142 people were arrested, taken to police headquarters, subjected to nitrate tests for gun powder, fingerprinted, and held without counsel or outside communication.

Word of the battle spread quickly, and by six the next morning, George Crockett, presiding judge of Recorder's Court, established a pop-up bench at police headquarters and began releasing people. Wayne County Prosecutor William Cahalan vehemently objected but was eventually forced to admit that most detainees had been held illegally for hours without probable cause. By the afternoon, all but two prisoners had been released. Three of the original detainees were later charged in the death of Patrolman Czapski; none were from Detroit.

There was widespread criticism of Crockett's highly unusual and disruptive actions. Editorials and barbershop grand juries questioned his competence and abuse of his position. He was assigned a twenty-four-hour security detail and a secure telephone line. However, he was strongly supported by the New Detroit Committee and elements of the local legal establishment. Crockett's background in constitutional law was widely recognized, and his actions brought to light long-standing practices in the legal process that violated basic tenets and rights. Speaking to the *Free Press* on March 31 about the police, he vowed, "They aren't going to get away with it as long as I'm around." The men arrested for shooting Czapski and Worobec were tried—not in Crockett's court—and eventually exonerated by juries. The affair further polarized Detroit's white and black communities.

– –

Through the close of the decade, relations between the police and the black community remained toxic. Criticism from the white community became louder, too. With the incoming administration of Mayor Roman Gribbs and his appointment of John Nichols as police commissioner, the high-profile STRESS (Stop the Robberies, Enjoy Safe Streets) unit attempted to combat rampant crime and a heroin epidemic that ravaged southeastern Michigan. Without significantly positive results, the unit's emphasis on undercover decoys and strong-arm tactics further antagonized the black community. Activists, both white and black, called for the DPOA to be dissolved.

It was not until the installation of Coleman A. Young as mayor over Nichols in 1974 that the police department underwent drastic changes. STRESS was disbanded, "ministations" opened in neighborhoods across the city (a concept initiated by Gribbs), and the proportion of black officers reached more than 50 percent by the mid-1990s. Unfortunately, a spike in drug and gang violence, as well as corruption within the DPD, did little to improve the public's opinion of law enforcement.

First Time I've Ever Seen Justice

Rev. Daniel W. Aldridge Jr.

Dan Aldridge was interviewed by William Winkel, June 22, 2016, and his transcript was edited by Joel Stone, November 29, 2016, to fit this volume's physical limitations. The complete original transcript can be accessed via the Detroit Historical Society's electronic portal (detroithistorical.org).

I was born in Harlem, New York, in 1942, and we moved to Queens when I was young. Growing up, I was very much aware of the civil rights movement because my aunt Dorothy Hite was president of the National Council of Negro Women. She was a ghostwriter for Marcus Garvey and the assistant to Mary McCleod Bethune. She was one of the best friends of Eleanor Roosevelt, who used to come by and take her out to lunch. Just imagine how different, how much has changed. Eleanor Roosevelt would drive her own car to Harlem, park out in front of the YWCA, go in and get my aunt, and they would go out to lunch as girlfriends.

I was aware of that. I was aware of the black nationalist movement because all these movements were in the city. If you were a kid and you went to the barbershop and got a haircut, you heard all this stuff buzzing around. You may not have known what to make of it, but you were cognizant of something going on.

I first came to Detroit in 1965 for a job at Chrysler. To me, Detroit was a dynamic place. I used to like to go down to Washington Boulevard and just walk. They had so many nice, lovely stores. I used to like to eat, on occasion, at the Statler Hilton. There was a lot of jazz here. I fell in love with the jazz music. I found the city very easy to get around in terms of transportation. Detroit was really a dynamic, energetic city.

I also liked Wayne State University and met a lot of nice people. I met Kenny Cockrel there, and I met Lonnie Peek there. I met Elliott Hall and became friends with Frank Joyce, who led People Against Racism and worked for the UAW [United Automobile Workers]. I got involved with Rev. Cleage's church, which evolved into the Shrine of the Black Madonna. I had a lot of very good friends there who were very much interested in the community and helping people out and talking about black nationalism and reading books, everything. Frank Vaughan had just opened up a bookstore on Monterey and Dexter. I liked Detroit very, very much.

My consciousness was more in terms about what was happening nationally and what was happening in the South. I was influenced by Stokely Carmichael's call for Black Power. My sense of Black Power was not Black Power against the white people, though that's how many white people heard it. It was really about self-determination and having control over your community and the institutions in your community. I was attracted to that. I had read all of Marcus Garvey's stuff, W. E. B. Du Bois, Lerone Bennett, John Frankman, Frederick Douglass, Langston Hughes, and Richard Wright.

Nearing graduation, I was hired on the campus by Chrysler Corporation as a personnel manager trainee to work in Highland Park at the main office. I worked there, and then I moved around. It helped me learn Detroit. I worked at Mack Avenue Stamping Plant, which is now called Chrysler North. I worked at Huber Avenue Foundry, at Mack Avenue Engine, at Highland Park Assembly Plant. I did small stints, three- or four-month stints, at those different places.

I was very involved in what I would call the black nationalist movement. People talked about something happening, but I didn't sense anything. I wasn't attuned to it. We read books; we talked a lot about the movement; we talked about the kinds of things we would do to help ourselves, to help the community. We talked about racism, but nobody ever talked about violence. That doesn't mean somebody didn't say something every now and then, but it was not a predominant part of any conversation. We talked about the history of black nationalism, the history of African American culture, sometimes European philosophy.

I got to know Lonnie Peek and Herb Boyd. Lonnie Peek and I were practically inseparable at one point. Herb Boyd was at my house every single day. Now, Lonnie was my friend. Herb and I were both friends, and I would say we were intellectual soul mates. We read books, compared stuff, dreamed stuff, talked about the bigger stuff. I was also friends with Jim Ingram and most of the people in the movement, and a lot of our activity was centered around the Shrine of the Black Madonna.

— —

When things broke out in July 1967, I was in Newark, New Jersey, at the Black Power conference that weekend. Someone in the hotel stopped me and said, "Aren't you from Detroit?" I said, "Yeah." "You gotta get outta here." I said, "Why?" "Haven't you heard about the riots in Detroit?" I said, "No," and went back to my own room and turned on the television. Everybody thought of themselves as a revolutionary, and so how could you be in Newark when the revolution was going on in Detroit?

I think I came back that Sunday night. I flew in, and the young white fellas had commandeered I-94. They were just riding up and down with rebel flags, waving a machete, like that. I was picked up from the airport by Dorothy Duberry—we later married—and came the back way into Detroit. I got a chance to see what was going on.

I was shocked, stunned. Community was burning and on fire. There were people looting, none of which we were a part of. I can say I was scared. I didn't know what was going to happen. I didn't know what to do. We observed the curfew because we thought that we would be targets. During the daytime, we went around trying to discourage young people from looting, trying to tell them, "This is not what it's about." I tend to not see the rebellion as positively as others do because I think that there's no real benefit when you tear up and burn up the place where you live, the places where you shop. That was not good and has not been remedied to this day.

— —

I first heard what was going on at the Algiers Motel through Dorothy. One of the boys that got killed, Carl Cooper, was her cousin. Carl's mother, Margaret, called and said, "My son has been killed by the police at the Algiers Motel. I need some help." So I called Lonnie Peek and Kenny Cockrel, and we went over and met with the family. I got Kenny because he was in law school, and he knew, in my mind, how to take proper notes. So we went down; we interviewed the family members of the boys who got killed and tried to interview witnesses. We also knew some of the boys in the Algiers Motel with Carl Cooper—Aubrey Pollard and Fred Temple. We got involved then, trying to put together a case saying that the police had murdered these boys.

Basically, the mock trial was my idea—well, sort of. What happened, during that time, Rap Brown came to town and spoke at the Dexter Theater on top of the roof. We complained that these boys had been killed by the police, so Rap says to me, "Hey, man, why don't you have a tribunal? Educate the community." The theater was owned by the great Detroit harpist Dorothy Ashby and her husband, the playwright John Ashby. After the crowd that Rap drew, they won't let us have that place. So I said, "Let's go to the Rev. Cleage and ask if we can put on the mock trial at his church." Rev. Cleage said yes.

The driving force was that the police were not doing anything. We had been to the hearings, and we had been thoroughly shamed by the police. The whole front section of the courthouse was nothing but police in uniform—thoroughly intimidating. Plus, with me, they would do things like this [*draws finger across throat*], make the sign of wanting to kill you. They had some record of having done this, so, you know, it was taken seriously. We were young. They were not going to make us back down at all. Our job was to hold the tribunal and to expose them. We wanted to bring out the total truth because we thought that the truth did not come out in the first trial. We wanted to bring out all the facts and the truth about what actually happened. That was our primary motivation.

William Serrin, who later became head of the *Free Press*, said, "Dan, if you do this, give us unrestricted access. We'll make it a big story." That's another reason I wanted to do it, because I was promised that the *Free Press* would make it a big story. We let the *Free Press* in, *Michigan Chronicle, Detroit News*. *Free Press* had full staff there to cover the story.

When we later saw the newspaper, the story wasn't there. I was so angry that I charged down to *Free Press* and got in Bill's face. He told me, "Dan, the editors would not let us put it out there. I got the full story, had my full staff, and the editors said that they were going to squash the story; and they did. There was nothing I could do about it." He told me he was awfully embarrassed. I was very upset by that.

The other thing I recall regarded John Hershey, who wrote the book *The Algiers Motel Incident*. I was writing an article on the tribunal for the *Michigan Chronicle*. Hershey came by Dorothy's office and stole my manuscript and published it in the book as his own. If you read that chapter, I think it's called "Fuel for the Fire Next Time," you'll see for yourself it says, "And Dan Aldridge said . . ." It's nothing of his in that entire chapter but me.

I went to Random House in New York and complained. They claimed they didn't know anything about it. Random House offered me three books as compensation, but I refused to accept it.

At the end of the tribunal, I would say that people felt good and people felt joy. There was celebration. There was ecstasy because they heard the truth. The church was packed. Not only was the church packed; it was packed in the street, the sidewalk outside of the church. So the community felt proud that something like that went on. They were also proud that I didn't take any cheap shots and that there were white people involved. I hired good attorneys on both sides and said, "Let's just hear the evidence." First time I've ever seen justice. Just listening to the facts, that's all.

A Call to Action

THE CHANGING FACE OF INNER-CITY ACTIVISM

Joel Stone

As described in earlier chapters, social activism has been a part in Detroit's African American community for a long time. As the city's black population increased in the twentieth century, the form and substance of that activism was refined and amplified. The crisis in July 1967 caused a significant shift in these activities, a shift largely attributable to anger and resentment fomented by the July unrest.

The 1960s were a pivotal time for organizations promoting the welfare and civil rights of people living in the United States. Highly visible opposition to Jim Crow laws in the South drove the racial debate, but socially conscious citizens also elevated issues related to women's rights, the Vietnam War, exploitation of farm and factory workers, abuse of the environment, government control of media, morality and religion, and a youth subculture that embraced drugs and alternative lifestyles.

Detroiters were involved in most of these movements. Not surprisingly, blacks in Detroit focused particularly on the issues of civil rights and workers' rights. Various organizations—together and separately—sought to improve access to housing, employment, education, health care, and safe streets. Following the July uprising, the focus remained on these basic rights, but the voices for change became louder and more strident. In the words of the Detroit journalist Betty DeRamus, writing for the *Negro Digest* in November 1967, "In the days of endless dialogue and search that have followed the Detroit riot, the mantle of leadership has been resting more and more on the shoulders of what had been virtually an underground movement, the motley group of people who call themselves 'black nationalists.' For several years, Detroit had been considered the center of black nationalism, overshadowing even New York, but the ferment of its fiery activists had drawn little public note. Now it is inescapable."

It is this transition of leadership that makes the years after 1967 notable. Established black civil rights organizations such as the National Association for the Advancement of Colored People (NAACP) and the Detroit Urban League (DUL) saw their influence usurped by numerous newly hatched progressive groups. The leaders of the new initiatives espoused an agenda that was both aggressive and militant. While they did not reflect the attitudes of all Detroit blacks, their message struck a chord for many citizens looking for a new direction and fresh rhetoric. The excitement and energy generated by the young upstarts perhaps best embodies what many considered a revolution.

Before discussing the panoply of organizational activity that took place following the insurrection of July, it would serve to provide context with a brief discussion of the institutions and associations that were in place when rioting began. At the beginning of the twentieth century, there arose a number of labor and social rights organizations, some specifically aimed at blacks. Out of these came two powerhouses. The NAACP, founded in 1909, opened a Detroit branch in 1912. By the 1920s, Detroit's NAACP branch was the largest in the country, and it remains so at this writing. The Urban League, officially formed in New York City in 1910, had a Detroit office by 1916. Both were advocacy groups for the welfare of blacks, working through legal channels to improve cooperation from government and business interests. Other national organizations had a presence in Detroit, including the legal watchdog the American Civil Liberties Union (ACLU); the conservative, economically focused Congress on Racial Equality (CORE); and the radical, though short-lived, Student Nonviolent Coordinating Committee, whose leader, Stokely Carmichael, was proselytizing in Detroit in 1966. Additionally, the Northern Student Movement and Adult Community Movement for Equality (ACME) had local adherents, but they were comparatively few.

On a local level, Detroiters became increasingly active following World War II. The Trade Union Leadership Council (TULC) was formed in the late 1950s under the leadership of Horace Sheffield, Buddy Battles, and Jack Edwards. This integrated group was intent on coordinating union activity and within a few years had several thousand local members. At almost the same time, the People's Community Civic League was incorporated to support the black residents with educational scholarships, as well as with emergency financial and food assistance. In 1959, the Detroit Board of Education formed the Citizen Advisory Committee on Equal Education Opportunities, to address racial inequalities within the school system. The committee was composed of prominent educators and leaders from the black community, including Arthur Johnson and Damon Keith.

Mayor Louis Miriani created the Citizens Advisory Committee as a forum to address issues between the community and the Detroit Police Department in 1960 but gave it no enforcement power. The following year, the department formed the Internal Community Relations Bureau, which much of the community regarded skeptically. The Michigan Civil Rights Commission was formed in 1964 with enforcement powers, but these were exercised infrequently.

The year 1963 marked the launch of three groups whose leaders were important to the postrebellion period. The first was UHURU, the moniker being a Swahili word for "freedom." This politically driven group had Wayne State University (WSU) students at its core. Among its members were Luke Tripp, brothers Milton and Richard Henry, James and Grace Lee Boggs, Gwendolyn Kemp, John Watson, Kenneth Cockrel, and General Gordon Baker. A similar organization was the Association of Black Students, a WSU club formed later by Lonnie Peek. The radical approach of these two groups was akin to the Group on Advanced Leadership (GOAL), led by Rev. Albert Cleage and the Henrys, which also formed about this time. Less militant was the Detroit Council for Human Rights (DCHR), formed by Rev. C. L. Franklin in May, a group that had broad support from TULC, CORE, UAW, and Cleage's supporters. The aggressive rhetoric of these three organizations resulted in a schism with the NAACP, DUL, and more conservative churches.

The Citizens Committee on Equal Opportunity, formed in 1964, represented the more established power structure and was led by the Episcopal bishop Richard Emerich, attorney Hubert Locke, UAW president Walter Reuther, and corporate leaders, and it worked with the NAACP behind the scenes on employment, housing, and police relations. The following year, the Boggses formed their Marxist-based Organization for Black Power, and Lorenzo "Rennie" Freeman organized the West Central Organization (WCO), described variously as the most effective and vocal of the political groups addressing housing, urban renewal, and social support.

The year 1965 was when the poet Dudley Randall founded the pioneering Broadside Press and Dr. Charles Wright opened his International

"Black Power" painted across a store window indicated African American ownership and was intended to prevent vandalism and looting. Image courtesy of the *Detroit News*, from the Detroit Historical Society Collection.

Afro-American Museum. Edward Vaughn's Book Store on Dexter started offering progressive black literature in 1963—the only store in Detroit to do so. At this time, media for the African American community was limited to the conservative *Michigan Chronicle*, some limited-run publications such as Cleage's *Illustrated News*, WJLB-AM, and WCHB-AM. Cleage's Central United Church of Christ hosted a Black Arts Conference in 1966 and 1967, with the help of the artist Glanton Dowdell.

In the matter of educational inequity, it was students who took the initiative. In April 1966, the black student body of Northern High School

Rev. Albert Cleage, pastor of the Central United Church of Christ, spoke during the Grass Roots rally at Detroit's City-County Building on August 9, 1967. Image courtesy of the *Detroit News*, from the Detroit Historical Society Collection.

staged a walkout. Karl Gregory, a professor of economics at WSU, recalled in a 2015 Detroit Historical Society interview that Northern was "a troubled school on the verge of becoming a not-too-subtle institution of incarceration pretending to be a school." According to several accounts, relations between the administration and students were antagonistic. A police officer patrolled the hallways. Teacher turnover was higher than normal, and academics suffered. Gradually, the building itself was allowed to deteriorate, a situation—the students noted—that was not allowed in the all-white schools. "It was a place of declining learning requiring a change agent to turn it around," said Gregory. "The students became the change agent."

On April 23, the majority of students at Northern walked out. Naturally, the Detroit School Board, City Hall, the media, and even some parents condemned the action, assuming it to be a protest without a goal. However, the Northern students formed the Detroit Freedom School. With the help of Gregory, Frank Joyce, Father David Gracie, and dozens of volunteer teachers, a curriculum was created and classroom space arranged, mostly at Gracie's St. Matthews & St. Joseph Episcopal Church, incidentally within a block of the high school. The success of the Freedom School impressed the school board. A new principal and assistant principal were brought to Northern, as were new teachers, and some infrastructure issues were addressed.

The foregoing narrative illustrates the growth and increasingly radical activism prior to the explosion on 12th Street in 1967. Although only a few of these organizations survived beyond the uprising, they were instrumental in forming relationships and tactical approaches for councils and alliances that developed afterward. One approach that appears to have been leveraged to a greater degree than before was a more focused attack; radical groups became more militant and increasingly concentrated on a single issue or arena. As the preceding narrative was roughly chronological, the following one looks at each of the major issues and the organizations that developed to address them.

Improving police relations was at the top of everyone's list. There was constant friction between the Detroit Police Department (DPD) and the mayor's office, residents across the city were unhappy with the skyrocketing street crime, and black residents were openly antagonistic toward the police. The Detroit Police Officers Association, the officers' bargaining unit, resisted calls to increase the number of black officers. Despite that effort, the number of African Americans on the force grew gradually, and that cadre formed the Guardians to look out for the black patrol officers' interests. Within certain precincts, Citizen-Police Community Organizations were formed. In addition, two citizen groups were created following further violence. After the fiasco that developed out of the Poor People's March in May 1968, the Ad-Hoc Action Group–Citizens of Detroit was organized by a young student named Sheila Murphy. The mostly white membership took on the role of police watchdog, both at public rallies and at police precincts. A few months later, following the racial incident at the Veterans Memorial Building, the Detroit Task Force for Justice was created.

This mostly black organization was led by the Ferndale pastor Willis Tabor, whose son was beaten during the fracas, and supported by US Representative John Conyers, Michigan State Senator Coleman Young, Mary Jane Hock, and the attorney Kenneth Cockrel, among others.

Issues in the education system were not being entirely ignored, and efforts were made to understand them. Wayne State University partnered with the US Department of Health, Education, and Welfare to create the Developmental Career Guidance Project in the Detroit Public Schools system in 1964. The study's report, written by Thelma J. Scott in 1973 for the American Institute for Research in the Behavioral Sciences in San Diego, showed that placing emphasis on self-worth, parental involvement, and future promise improved student potential in poor schools. As with many reports, broad implementation was not sufficiently addressed; however, a number of social organizations within the community created educational programs with these edicts in mind.

During this period, Rev. Robert L. Potts worked with the city to form the Youth Opportunity Council, promoting career-path direction. Rev. Cleage created the Inner City Parents Council (ICPC) to elevate dialogue on education issues. In keeping with the pastor's increasing affinity for self-determination, ICPC agitated in favor of black schools for black children, a turnabout from Cleage's earlier calls for immediate integration. It was a theme that carried over into his other initiatives.

One such council was the Federation for Self-Determination (FSD), which came together under Cleage, Gregory, Freeman, and Don Roberts. It was born after the CCAC, attempting to work with the postuprising New Detroit Committee on funding, became disillusioned and dissolved itself. Although short-lived, the FSD had an economic focus and served as a think tank and open forum for the many voices encouraging blacks to be less dependent on white institutions for income, information, education, housing, and culture. Workings of the federation laid the groundwork for several other successful initiatives. The most influential of these was the Inner City Business Improvement Forum (ICBIF), founded in 1970 and successful in supporting black-owned business and housing for over two decades. In the words of Gregory, ICBIF was "a wellspring of ripples that gave rise to waves, some of which became bigger as they spread. Some vanished." At its peak, ICBIF had a staff of twenty.

One of the waves was the First Independence National Bank, which opened its doors on May 17, 1970. Known today as First Independence Bank, this institution opened the way for loans and access to capital not generally available to blacks from other Detroit banks. A small-business consulting service was created to help with strategic planning and management for new businesses. In addition, at least two Small Business Investment Companies (SBIC) were formed: Independence Capital Formation and Pooled Resources Invested in Minority Enterprises (PRIME). The bank, the SMICs, and ICBIF received financial support from New Detroit, the Ford Foundation, and other prominent businesses and leaders.

Another wave was known as Accord Inc., which assumed responsibility for housing programs. This group was headed by Gregory, and board members included Cleage, Don Parsons and Steve Miller of Bank of the Commonwealth, the businessmen Edgar Braselton and Fred Matthaei, the architect Howard Sims, the attorney Alan E. Schwartz, and Coleman Young. Their business plan involved purchasing apartment buildings from absentee white landlords, who were selling in a panic, and putting them in the hands of community members. The buildings were to be operated as tenant cooperatives, with renters gaining equity with their investment. Unfortunately, a downturn in the economy caused both inflation and interest rates to rise, and private capital dried up. Accord went bankrupt.

Three other organizations were formed at this time to actively promote economic self-sufficiency in the black community, all on the city's lower east side. Only recently closed, the Inner-City Sub-Center (ICSC) had been a fixture in the city since its founding in 1969. The center provided programs for the community that included youth entrepreneurship, after-school education and athletic teams, a food co-op, programming for seniors, and emergency food and clothing distribution. According to Michigan State University professor Richard Thomas, in "The Black Community Building Process in Post–Urban Disorder Detroit, 1967–1997," impetus for ICSC came from the Association for Black Studies at WSU, with financial support over the years from numerous community funds and churches. In 1986, the organization served over ten thousand people. According to its 2009 presentation material, ICSC promoted positive African American values, pride, and respect while raising the level of black consciousness, awareness, and understanding throughout the community.

Similarly, in 1971, Operation Get-Down (OGD) was incorporated, growing out of a leadership program at St. Mark's United Methodist Church, led by Barry Hankerson, Bernard Parker Jr., and Frances Messinger. OGD services were akin to those of ICSC but also included health care, particularly sickle-cell and prenatal education. In Thomas's words, "Both organizations were founded by young radical blacks motivated by the spirit of Malcolm

X," and both "used white resources to develop some of their most important community-based programs. Yet, neither organization compromised its commitment to the philosophy of black self-help as a community strategy." OGD still serves Detroit residents at this writing.

The third organization had a comparable philosophy but did not enjoy the longevity. The activists Frank Ditto and Dan Frank created the East Side Voice of Independent Detroit in 1968, with its publication *Ghetto Speaks*. The organization at various times offered everything from editorials to community patrols (the journalist Lou Gordon called them storm troopers) to job counseling. Along with Dan Aldridge and Richard Slater, Ditto ran an alternative school and continually confronted public school administrators. Ditto was briefly a member of the New Detroit Committee, with Max Fisher's blessing.

Perhaps most indicative of the self-determination movement is the birth of Albert Cleage's Pan-African Orthodox Church. Cleage rebranded his Dexter Avenue church as the Shrine of the Black Madonna, and it became the spiritual home for black activists, black nationalists, black separationists, and Black Power militants. Cleage also took the African name Jaramogi Abebe Agyeman. A number of other religious organizations were born of the July 1967 events, operating to draw many diverse cultures and beliefs together. On a national scale, the Interreligious Foundation of Community Organizations (IFCO) was also founded in 1967. This group sponsored a Black Economic Development Conference (BEDC) event in Detroit, April 1969.

Locally, the Interfaith Action Council (an outgrowth of the postriot Interfaith Emergency Council) began in 1968 to encourage dialogue between Jews, Christians, and Muslims, particularly with regard to racism and the inequities in black neighborhoods. This organization had only modest success, partially due to incompatible degrees of progressivism but largely attributable to a lack of funding. Another group, called Alliance, provided an ecumenical forum within the black religious community. Launched just prior to the uprising, the Churches on the East Side for Social Action (CESSA), sponsored by twenty-six churches near Kercheval Avenue, offered prenatal health care, child care, and a food bank.

The final three issues on which African Americans in Detroit attempted to increase their control—employment and labor, politics, and media—are closely intertwined. Most of the businesses and organizations described in this section espoused the gospel of Black Power and relied on Marxist and Maoist rhetoric to guide their actions. Because many of the same people operated across factions, there was symbiotic support: labor action fostered political action; political action needed a voice; and media—in a variety of voices—spread the message of the workers and politicians.

Unemployment in the black community contributed to the disturbances of 1967. Thomas Klug has pointed out previously in this text that the employment picture in Detroit through the early 1960s was pretty good. Middecade, overall unemployment stood at about 2.5 percent in the region and at 3.4 percent in Detroit's black neighborhoods. However, by July 1967, the overall number had jumped to 6.2 percent, and speculation puts joblessness in the poorer neighborhoods at 30 percent, particularly among young black men. The Career Development Center, under the guidance of Alvin Bush and Irma Craft, offered business-skills training and job placement to youths and adults on the near west side. Bush proudly announced in the August 3, 1968, issue of *Detroit Scope* magazine that "not one cent of government money is involved." In 1968, the Volunteer Placement Corps was organized under the aegis of the New Detroit Committee to counsel and assist black students to get into college or appropriate job-training programs.

The more vocal element of the jobs struggle was in the labor movement and largely within the automobile plants dotting the city. Blacks held a majority of the factory-floor positions but very few managerial or skilled-trades spots. As the companies strove to cut costs, workers struggled with mandatory overtime, production-line speed-ups, poor environmental conditions, defective equipment, antagonistic management, and subpar compensation. Injuries and dismemberment were common. Deaths occurred too frequently. Appeals to the union, the United Automobile Workers (UAW), fell on deaf ears; according to Dan Georgakas and Marvin Surkin, in *Detroit: I Do Mind Dying*, while about 30 percent of the union's members were black, the executives, staff, and stewards were overwhelmingly white.

Early organization with a black voice began about 1957 with formation of the TULC at Local 600, Ford's River Rouge Plant. The voice of militants within the union spread and after 1967 became louder. The following year, workers as Chrysler Corporation's largest assembly plant, locally known as Dodge Main, organized the Dodge Revolutionary Union Movement (DRUM) under the leadership of General Gordon Baker, Ron March, Glanton Dowdell, and Rufus Griffin. Wildcat strikes had high participation and drew concessions from both Chrysler and the UAW. DRUM leveraged the *Inner-City Voice* newspaper to organize blacks in factories across the city. The "RUM" philosophy and strategy spread to other industries, including health care, the *Detroit News*, and United Parcel Service. Drawing all these militant labor groups together resulted in formation of the League of Revolutionary Black Workers (LRBW) in 1969.

The LRBW's leadership, as for its predecessor, included Baker and March, as well as Kenneth Cockrel, Mike Hamlin, Luke Tripp, John Watson, John Williams, and Chuck Wooten. With the new—though familiar—blood came a greater diversity of agendas and opinions about the future of the organization. The LRBW was eventually stricken with philosophical divisions; should it concentrate on in-plant organizing or expand into a nationwide support network for workers? One group of dissenters formed the short-lived Black Worker's Congress in 1970, and further fracturing led to dissolution of the LRBW organization the following year. The gap was briefly filled by the Marxist-Leninist Motor City Labor League until 1976. During the LRBW's history, the organization made modest inroads on the shop floor and improved the lot of workers. It also grew from a basic grassroots labor cadre into a legal and respected—or feared—bargaining unit, creatively controlling its militant, antiestablishment message and opening communication channels within the black workforce for the future.

Politics in Detroit's black community after 1967 saw an increase in radical rhetoric. Television and newspapers showed images of angry youths with clenched fists in uniforms, in suits, and in traditional African garb. Even conservative ministers and politician were seen in conversation with the militants. The Black Panther Party, famously formed in California in 1966, had a Detroit office on 16th Street by the spring of 1968. Ahmad Rahman, a Panther himself, in a piece called "Marching Blind," cited Ron Scott and Eric Bell as the principal organizers, along with Aretha Hankins, Jackie Spicer, and William Chambers. Familiar names such as Mike Hamlin, Frank Ditto, and Dan Aldridge were involved also. The group was as militaristic as it was militant. Rahman noted that the organization "drew on an African American subculture of crime long predating the Panthers," resulting in a clandestine core that had little respect for law or law enforcement. This effectively divided the organization into two factions: one above ground, the other operating as urban guerrillas. The "legitimate" wing did community service, offered citizens protection, and distributed a radical newspaper. The other wing robbed drug houses, harassed their enemies, and prepared arsenals for the battle they knew was coming.

The battle arrived in October 1970 at Panther headquarters, as Panthers stood on the sidewalk selling papers. Patrol officers confronted them, and a Panther shot the black patrolman Glenn Smith. A hundred police officers converged on the building, and a nine-hour siege ensued, with both sides exchanging gunfire. In a matter of time, thousands of neighborhood residents arrived and surrounded the police line. During a cease-fire, the fifteen Panthers eventually surrendered. In court, the lawyers Elliott Hall and Ernest Goodman got all the murder charges dismissed. Three men were convicted of felonious assault. Afterward, the Black Panther Party in Detroit faded quickly, the victim, in the eyes of Rahman, of increased infiltration by law enforcement and the inability of its leaders to mount an effective counterintelligence offensive.

Equally radical, but far more sophisticated, was the Provisional Government of the Republic of New Africa (RNA). An outgrowth of the Malcolm X Society and founded by Detroit brothers Milton and Richard Henry (later Gaidi Abiodun Obadele and Abubakari Obadele, respectively), this organization was born in 1968. Demands were put forth that included an independent "state" in the US Southeast, millions of dollars in reparations to the descendants of former slaves, and support to make the country's black population self-sufficient. This platform was similar to the tenets put forward by James Forman in his "Black Manifesto," presented at a Black Economic Development Conference (BEDC) in Detroit in April 1969. BEDC was a national, multidenominational group representing mostly white suburban congregations, and although the organization initially embraced this document, it distanced itself from Forman and by association the RNA.

The RNA expected the US government to reject all of its proposals and prepared for armed resistance by forming a paramilitary Black Legion, similar to the Black Panthers. This band was involved in the shooting of a Detroit police officer at the New Bethel Baptist Church, described earlier in this volume, while the RNA was celebrating its first anniversary. Continued altercations with law enforcement at all levels and the incarceration of some principal leaders took much momentum from the movement. However, the organization survived, with several thousand adherents into the twenty-first century.

While these organizations and their inflammatory rhetoric grabbed media attention, they did not represent the majority of blacks in the area. In October 1968, *Detroit Scope* magazine, a multiracial publication launched during a prolonged newspaper strike, stated, "One obstacle to peace is the habit the press has of giving the black militant more attention that his numbers warrant and playing up the threat of violence. It's no wonder that whites think Black Power is hostile."

In general, politics in the black voting precincts was similar to that in white precincts. As the community increased its presence in legislatures and on the bench, it grew more politically savvy. The Black Slate had proven effective in getting Cavanagh elected and continued to expand its influence. It was strong enough that a number of names were put forward to run for the open mayoral office in 1969. They included Conyers, the banker and state representative James Del Rio, Rev. Nicholas Hood of Plymouth Congregational Church, former councilman William Patrick Jr., Senator Coleman Young, and conservative Rev. Ray Shoulders. In the end, Richard Austin, who sat on the Wayne County Board of Auditors, narrowly lost to the former prosecutor and Wayne County sheriff Roman Gribbs. The outspoken activist Young won the mayoral job four years later.

In exploring attempts to spread control of the media's message to alternative voices, two factors must be considered: the contentious strike at Detroit's two main newspapers, which created opportunities, and energy and inventiveness vested in the community, which took advantage of changing landscapes. The strike against the *Detroit Free Press* and *Detroit News* began in the middle of November 1967, right before the profitable Christmas advertising season. The work stoppage lasted for 267 days into early August of the next year. Both readers and advertisers looked for alternatives. Two dailies—the *Pontiac Press* and *Macomb Daily*—and numerous community and ethnic weeklies saw a bump in readership and ad revenues. The biweekly, coupon-oriented *Shopping News* beefed up its news staff.

More pertinent to this discussion was the birth of several "strike papers" that offered an urban perspective. For conservative whites, there was the Hamtramck-based *Detroit American*, with a circulation of 170,000. The biracial editorial staff of the *Black and White Reporter* reached perhaps half that number of people but was able to attain a contract with UPI that gave it a broader news base. The *Detroit Daily Press* was short-lived. Offered in a tabloid format was *Detroit Scope* magazine, under the direction of the fiery Lou Gordon and Jim Ingram, offering outspoken editorials and reporting from both the progressive white and black perspectives.

Prior to the disturbance in July 1967, the *Detroit News* unwittingly brought together John Watson, Mike Hamlin, and Kenneth Cockrel, who all worked in the distribution department. All three were WSU students active in leftist politics. In September, Watson and Hamlin, along with Luke Tripp, led the founding of the *Inner-City Voice*, a small-format publication addressing issues such as police violence, labor union intransigence, education disparity, women's liberation, and intractable poverty. It was leveraged by other Marxist organizations such as DRUM and became the de facto voice of the black militant community.

A year later, Watson and his supporters managed to secure enough votes to assume managerial control of the WSU student newspaper, the *South End*. In *Detroit: I Do Mind Dying*, Georgakas and Surkin describe how Watson, along with Nick Medvecky, Tripp, and Hamlin, transformed it from a publication "run like a high-school paper" to a progressive paper "that belonged to the whole population"—or at least that part of the population with far-left attitudes. While WSU had a radical history—many in union leadership had attended the school—the editorial board was under constant fire from university administrators for the paper's content. Watson's tenure lasted only until the following spring, but through 1969, the *Inner-City Voice* and the *South End* provided Detroit's militant leftists, and particularly urban blacks, with a legitimate voice.

There were other alternative voices, most notably the *Fifth Estate*. The year 1965 saw the birth of this colorful tabloid published independently by WSU students led by Harvey Ovshinsky and Peter Werbe. Radical but far less militant, it was created to serve a broader audience on the left, covering arts and culture, the antiwar movement, homelessness, and issues facing women. It remains in publication as of this writing.

Revolutionary—not in stance but in cultural impact—were opportunities opening to the black community in the realm of television. In 1968, Detroit's public television station, WTVS, Channel 56, launched a show called *CPT*, ostensibly an acronym for "Colored People's Time." An all-black production team led by Gil Maddox and the host/producer Tony Brown created a weekly, magazine-format show carried on a modestly powered UHF station available only on better televisions with good antennas. Quality programming engaged the black community and drew it together. The name soon changed to *Detroit Black Journal*, which morphed into *American Black Journal*—still hosted today by Detroit Public Television (DPTV) and seen around the world. Gil Maddox later produced and hosted a show called *Profiles in Black* on the NBC affiliate in Detroit, WWJ-TV, Channel 4. Launched in 1969, it succeeded for a decade in showcasing black perspectives on mainstream television.

More important from an industry perspective, the Federal Communication Commission's approval of the license transfer of WGPR-TV to Rev. Dr. William V. Banks, nearly a decade after the 1967 unrest, marks the beginning of the first black-owned television station in the nation. A lawyer and entrepreneur, Banks and his team created or purchased programming for a mostly black audience yet carried such diverse local favorites as a black dance show called *The Scene*, a scary-movie slot hosted by "The Ghoul," and

Detroit Red Wings hockey games. The station is known today as WWJ-TV, now a CBS affiliate.

Reaction in the black community following the uprising was naturally broad and deep. The general public felt caught between the rioters, militants, and the police. Conservatives and moderates felt that active or armed resistance was destroying decades of progress. Young radicals saw an opportunity to advance a new agenda.

Black radicals—and they carried that appellation with pride—were much different from most of their white counterparts. White radicals focused on expanding social and artistic mores of society. Black radicals focused on controlling the economic factors that worked against their community, including banking, media, real estate, education, religion, and the factory floor.

The foregoing narrative, generally covering the major issues—police, education, business, community and religion, employment and labor, politics, media and culture—is in no manner a complete list of organizations or a fraction of the people involved in advancing the welfare of African Americans in Detroit after the looting waned. Hopefully it serves to illustrate the character of activism and protest before and after. There is no doubt that the most militant and vocal groups gained the most notoriety. Equally certain is that the moderate entities with broader and more practical agendas proved resilient and survived beyond the initial unrest.

On the *Detroit Black Journal*'s twentieth-anniversary show in 1989, the host, Tony Brown, stated, "We were angry. . . . The rebellion today, unfortunately, is not there. We don't rebel anymore." This is not to say, almost thirty years after Brown's statement, that black militancy doesn't survive. Events of the past few year have prompted a return to activism—even radicalism—in the black community. The issues are essentially the same, and before long, there may be a new chapter of this story to write.

Black Power, Black Rebellion

Betty DeRamus

This piece is reprinted from the *Negro Digest*, November 1967, by permission of the Johnson Publishing Company. Original spelling and punctuation have been retained.

"Slick" Campbell is an actor at Detroit's Concept-East Theater, a bushy-haired barrel of a black man who likes to strut on stage and trumpet a poem he composed entitled, "Let Freedom Ring." "Ka-ping, ka-ping," he mocks a rifle at its conclusion. Then, after a pause, comes the cruel irony: "Damn fool, don't you know that's freedom's ring?"

Campbell's verse, devastating in its directness, describes a state of mind that is mushrooming in his town, Detroit, where night snipers came to symbolize avenging assassins and in the explosion of their rage completed the birth of a breed of black man who is unafraid.

As a result, in the days of endless dialogue and search that have followed the Detroit riot, the mantle of leadership has been resting more and more on the shoulders of what had been virtually an underground movement, the motley group of people who call themselves "black nationalists." For several years, Detroit had been considered the center of black nationalism, overshadowing even New York, but the ferment of its fiery activists had drawn little public note. Now it is inescapable.

Heading the Citywide Citizens Action Committee (CCAC), formed in the riot's wake, for instance, is Rev. Albert Cleage, would-be politician, veteran organizer, a man whose angry fires scorch: "Black people are tired of hearing 'I had a dream.' America is a nightmare." The Rev. Mr. Cleage calls his church, Central United Church of Christ, "the black nationalist church." And the CCAC, which nominated officers at a rally attended by

FOCUS ON DETROIT:

The Post-Riot Black Establishment
A Burned City's New Opportunity
The Second Black Arts Convention

The cover of *Negro Digest* magazine in November 1967 highlighted events in Detroit. From the Detroit Historical Society Collection.

several hundred citizens, some community leaders and organization heads, now is known as the "new black establishment."

This "new establishment" proposes to negotiate with and "give orders" to the New Detroit Committee, composed mainly of leading white business-men, which is charged with planning the city's rebuilding. CCAC includes, according to militant attorney Milton Henry, "some moderates, some not so moderate, a few who are a little radical and others who are just plain out of sight."

This surge of community involvement by self-styled militants, while not unexpected—nationalists have built noisy, if short-lived, confrontations around every crisis from a poverty program cutback to a high school student boycott, occurring in the past five years—nevertheless has deep implications now for Detroit, where the nation's most destructive riot has triggered an identity crisis of mass proportions. Middle-class Negro leadership, which had boasted of its ability to freely enter the smoke-filled rooms of the white power structure, now is in a frantic race to reclaim its connection to the Negro, whose plight was its only real excuse for being. Meanwhile, this so-called Negro mass, seething with unlocked tensions, seems likely, out of the torment, to spawn its own leadership.

The fact that leadership from the outside cannot be superimposed on this mass, no matter how desirable this leadership may seem to outsiders, was well demonstrated during the riot. Young, "do rag" nationalists and others jeered and flung rocks at young and supposedly popular U.S. Rep. John Conyers Jr., nearly toppling his halo in the process. But, as Conyers himself later admitted, only someone with the violent connotations of a Malcolm X could have spoken with authority to the rioters. For the destruction in Detroit went beyond the point of self-hating Negroes lashing out at their own environment, a feeling which still can be channeled through promises of improvement. The naked thing that Conyers confronted was the release of pent-up rage, by some fairly middle-class as well as lower-class Negroes and even poor whites, that had been so long suppressed it was uncontrollable when it burst free.

A civil rights program supposedly is not built on rage, but in reason. Yet, for black nationalists, particularly black internationalist revolutionaries, who consider themselves part of the world-wide struggle by black people to end their oppression, anger is the prime mobilizer. And this is the Detroit dilemma. The struggle now for the still largely uncommitted mass is being waged between the established Negro leadership and the more militant forces. So far, aided by a greater facility for the "gut talk" of the people, since they often *are* the people, the militants are winning this battle, their cries for action, unity and change effectively capitalizing on the mood that lingers, with the cinders, in the city's ravaged communities. It is a mood that unmistakably calls for many meaningful responses to the explicitly expressed discontent.

Some nationalists, and the term often is elastic enough to include even an outspoken speaker, had begun to seize control of the riot when it was forming in the streets. Some "do rag" brothers, who are considered incipient nationalists, encouraged looting and arson, while a few internationalists are believed to have aided the mystery snipers. "A riot is not a revolution," explains Glanton Dowdell, co-chairman of the Rev. Mr. Cleage's CCAC and a man who says he "believes in" black nationalism. "But sometimes at its height, people geared to it find it necessary to intervene so people don't become mutilated; a disciplined revolutionary will not participate in or encourage a riot unless there is no other alternative."

In Detroit, maybe there wasn't. Author Louis Lomax, who journeyed here in the midst of the destruction, felt nationalist involvement in the riot had been crucial, charging in a front-page series in the *Detroit News* that door to door salesmen peddling "black power" had set the stage for the rebellion several weeks before its fires erupted. And it is a fact that the celebrated blind-pig whose raiding triggered the violence had also been a meeting place for minors under the tag, "The United Community League for Civic Action."

Nevertheless, most local observers now agree that the riot was largely spontaneous. But nationalists, understandably, are not surrendering without a struggle the rich philosophic gains that are theirs to be snatched from the holocaust. In the riot's midstream, Richard Henry, brother of Milton and a technical writer, issued a list of ultimatums to the city in the name of the Malcolm X Society, including amnesty for rioters, which he claimed would quell the disturbance. Predictably, the ultimatums were largely ignored. But a key weapon remains in the hands of nationalists—the drive for unity.

Unity, for the time being, is a goal of the entire Negro community . . . unity in demanding changes, unity in resisting any resulting increase in the forces of bigotry, unity in defining the real needs of Negroes and interpreting them to the white community. And this goal of community unity closely resembles the black nationalist goal. "Regardless of geographic boundaries, language differences, etc.," one told me, "we are one, part of a black nation, first and above all else." Detroit nationalists, also, are remarkably unified themselves. Separatists, who want country-states for Negroes, work with nationalists like Rev. Cleage, who believe Negroes must control their own communities, and the "do rag" nationalists who quote Malcolm X but imitate whites by "processing" their hair.

This new call for unity, which now finds many people thinking, temporarily or permanently, like nationalists, can be unsettling to both Negroes and whites. A white employee of a downtown office cornered a Negro co-worker, proud of his white collar and equally white diction, the other day and whispered worriedly: "Say, Eddie, what about this H. Rap Brown?" "Why ask me? I don't know as much about him as you do," was the offended Eddie's swift reply. Eddie, of course, was lying. H. Rap Brown drew an audience of 5,000 persons, many milling in the streets, when he spoke here recently at the Dexter theater, and Eddie was one of them.

The shift to the open airing of nationalist sentiment is even more evident in the pages of the formerly conservative Negro weekly, the *Michigan Chronicle*. Shortly after the riot, Rev. Cleage was given a column in the *Chronicle* and one of his first pieces was entitled "Unite or Perish." Avowed nationalist Henry Slayton also has begun writing for the *Chronicle*, one article headlining, "Black Power Can Build as Well as Destroy."

The fact is the nationalists' kind of talk is beginning to make sense to many Negroes, particularly youths, who are turning inward for solutions to their problems, including the new fear of genocide through Vietnam, which is gaining currency in the community. "The only people the white community respects are those who speak up," Nadine Brown, community-labor figure and newspaper columnist, who openly identifies herself as a nationalist, told a CCAC rally. And some of the people present had heard many other speakers, received many promises in this town where labor unions taught Negroes the meaning of militancy and organization and the auto industry built hopes in a growing middle class that society never quite fulfilled. Malcolm X had whipped some into a frenzy of bitterness but spurred no action. And then came Stokely Carmichael with his black power in a year when Congress reversed itself; the dream of integration died during Martin Luther King's march in Chicago; Africa, its customs and hair styles became palatable, and the momentum of the rights movement screeched to a halt.

Now there is something on the scene called black nationalism and it is a search, a state of mind, a hardening conviction that whatever went before was inadequate. The Detroit challenge is how the middle-class Negro is to keep the place that he has won while others find theirs. "There's lots of Negro prosperity here, but too many guys aren't getting a piece of the action," the *Chronicle*'s managing editor, Al Dunmore, told a *New York Times* reporter.

Yet Dunmore's words are tame alongside those of "Slick" Campbell. "Ka-ping, ka-ping," he fires at his audiences, who always sit silently, awaiting the inevitable fury. "Damn fool, don't you know that's freedom's ring!"

It Was a Good Time for Organizing

Mike Hamlin

Mike Hamlin was interviewed by William Winkel, December 22, 2015, and his transcript was edited by Joel Stone, November 28, 2016, to fit this volume's physical limitations. The complete original transcript can be accessed via the Detroit Historical Society's electronic portal (detroithistorical.org).

I returned from Korea in March of 1960 and got a job at the *Detroit News*. I had U of M credits and I had military, so they hired me. I started off as a jumper, which was assisting the distribution drivers. We'd take papers to stations and unload them, where the newsboys were, or we were the guy who drove around downtown and put papers in the boxes. Soon after I got hired by the *News*, they bought the *Detroit Times*; and all of us had seniority over the people from the *Times*, so I got to be a driver.

At the same time, I started going back to school at Wayne State, and that's when I got politically active. I met with Ken Cockrel and John Watson while at the *Detroit News*. I would drive Ken to law school on my way to work, and he would join me later when he'd come to work. Sometimes he'd ride with me when we delivered papers. And John was working there and going to school, too. Together, we engaged in repartee with all the other guys on the loading dock, testing their intellect and their analytical capacity. Ken was like a machine gun; if you heard him talk, he sounded like a machine gun. And John would bring it. They both were geniuses. I was very privileged to work with them. They were good friends.

John, who graduated from Cass Technical High School at seventeen years old, introduced me to Marxist analysis, and I introduced Ken; and we studied together. We analyzed the society and grew angrier and angrier. First of all, I had already seen enough outrages while I was in the army and overseas. Ken had been in the military, too, in the air force. John had not—he was too young.

But anyway, we were angry. We had gone through a flowering among the black artists, and there were key books that came out that affected us: James Baldwin's writings, Ralph Ellison's *Invisible Man*, Richard Wright, LeRoi Jones, etcetera. We were studying. We were rapping. We were pretty profuse debaters. And we also realized we had to do something. So we started working with some people. We worked with the Rev. Cleage and James and Grace Lee Boggs. In Detroit in the early '60s, there was a party founded by Cleage, the Boggses, and the Henry brothers called the Freedom Now Party. But you know, we emerged with a more militaristic approach.

— —

You know what drove '67? What drove Black Power? What drove the movement? The working-class black reached a point where he could not take it anymore. I told people many a time, then and since then, that during that period, I didn't care whether I lived or died, but I was going to live or die with some feeling of freedom. I understood our oppression. I understood our exploitation. I had not only seen it; I experienced it. And I saw the family, how they were abused, in the community, the neighborhood. We had worn a uniform. We had been good citizens. And the police brutality—they think it is bad now, they should have been here in the sixties; in Detroit, it was really bad. You know, we wanted a pound of flesh because of the humiliation. This rage was felt across the nation.

— —

The rebellion happened in July. By September, the cry for Black Power had activated us, and we joined the movement. It seemed like something we had been waiting for: the idea of self-defense. And so I began a correspondence with Jim Foreman, and I asked him if we could get Rap Brown to come to Detroit and speak for a fund-raiser. Rap was a fiery orator who was going around saying, "If America don't come around, we're gonna burn it down." And he was delivering that message all over the country. So Rap came, and we had him at a theater over on Dexter. It was an overflow crowd.

Prior to 1967, John Watson and I had begun to go through the process of starting a newspaper, based on a theoretical concept. John approached Peter Werbe, who was publishing the *Fifth Estate*, and asked him to show him how to produce a newspaper. The Rap Brown event raised money to launch the paper. We rented a place over on Warren, right behind

St. Paul's Church, and we started a newspaper called *Inner-City Voice*. And it was not difficult to attract people—poets, artists, dancers, actors—who hung around. But after the first edition, you know, John and I did most of the work.

About this time, General Baker had been fired from Dodge Main for protesting how black workers were abused at the plant. Now, remember, a lot of the older workers had come from the South, and they would tend to be deferential to whites. But these were young workers; this was a new generation, and they were talking. Ron March, an organizer, would come by about once a week, and soon I started joining him. Ron and General pulled together various witnesses. I interviewed them, wrote down the incidents that had taken place at a plant, and put it in the *Inner-City Voice*.

We would distribute the paper at Dodge Main and into the stores. It became a newsletter for DRUM (Dodge Revolutionary Union Movement), was hard-hitting, and spoke to what was going on in the plant. It had enormous impact—began to rouse these young workers. And you know, it was attacking not only the company but the union too—really hitting the union hard, and they felt it. But we were young, we were angry, and so neither the union nor the company wanted to mess with us. Plus we had about thirty lawyers supporting us.

We had an interesting relationship with the young lawyers. A lot of young lawyers came here to neighborhood legal services, and I did the orientation for them when they came to town. Ken Cockrel and his partner, Justin Ravitz, were big influences. When we struck Dodge Main, we had thirty lawyers willing to take depositions, to do whatever needed to be done.

The newsletter took off like wildfire, and then we started doing them in other plants—at Eldon Plant, at Cadillac, Ford. I also got involved with students. So many kids in these high schools had their own issues, and we helped them get organized. They had already struck, on their own, at Northern High School. So we incorporated them and gave them the support—a place to meet; they did a newsletter. The group was called the Black Student United Front. It was a good time for organizing. I personally was involved in helping organize the welfare workers organization and was involved in organizing the secretaries at Wayne State. We were involved in an attempt to organize Ford Hospital, but that failed.

We had all these components—organizing, education, publishing, negotiating, filmmaking—and we had to find a way to link them together. And we did. That was the League of Revolutionary Black Workers (LRBW). We had a central staff, an executive committee, and we had great success. But you know, ideology . . . We tried to downplay individual plaudits. In fact, we understood that enough in the beginning to state that. But it was undeveloped politically, and so people didn't take the educational process serious. Some of them thought the classes were boring. They wanted action.

We expanded as a result of our successes. Foreman came here because the Student Nonviolent Coordinating Committee had shut down—the students had got tired of taking whoopings. He had gone out to California and couldn't make it with the Panthers, so he opted to come here. Some people told me in advance, "You know, Foreman is the kind of guy who wants to control or destroy." He came here and lived with us for a year and a half. That didn't work too well. There were some very powerful egos around and brilliant people—John Watson, Kenny Cockrel, General, John Williams, Luke Tripp—these were all smart folks. We put it together, and immediately there were clashes of egos.

I had helped organize the Motor City Labor League (MCLL) and asked these young whites to come together and overcome some of their differences in forming this organization. I could see a lot of potential for it, and they agreed. I didn't want us to be isolated. We were having some internal shenanigans that caused me to worry—we planned dangerous things, and some people were becoming irresponsible.

I also organized Alliance, which was a group of religious figures—men and women—good people. And we got involved with the Black Workers Congress (BWC), which was an attempt to force the churches to face their history of exploitation, their role in slavery and Jim Crow, and all of the other evils of the country. And they responded—a lot of them.

When the BWC came about, we had all this growth, but the consciousness and the understanding did not keep up with the development. If you would ask me what brought about the demise of the League and the BWC, it was two things.

In an atmosphere like that, the police is not far away—that's number one. People's ideological weaknesses made them argue for being part of leadership. The problem with that is there are secrets that the organization has that you cannot share with everybody, and people are offended that you're withholding information from them. But people wanted to be part of the decision-making process and wanted to know everything that was going on. This is a dangerous game.

The other thing about it was that there's a class thing involved. I tried my best to establish a moral standard within the organization, because we were attracting people's kids—people's teenage kids, including teenage girls—on the one hand. On the other hand, we were attracting what Marxists called déclassé elements—lower-class folks—in some cases thugs, maybe people who were a little mentally unstable where it's not apparent. We didn't knowingly have any addicts, but I'm sure we had drunks. And they engaged in reckless behavior. One teenager was killed at a high school dance. One sixteen-year-old girl, who was a very high honor student, got pregnant. There were a couple of rapes that took place in the office. So those were things that brought about the disintegration of our organization.

— —

Now the particular splits. The split with John was over those issues, and John just walked away. I only saw him once after that, and he told me that the FBI had told him that he better get out of town. The split with Ken was because he wanted to go into electoral politics, and we always had a policy against that.

What I told the group that left with me—we had meetings—I said, "Look, guys, the movement has come to an end. You don't want to go where these other guys are going because they are going into rote Marxism and really heavy authoritarianism. What you need to do, and what I'm gonna do, is find something where I can help people and can feel like I'm helping mankind, even if I have to do it one at a time."

From then, I went back to school, got a master's degree in social work, and became a clinical social worker with troubled workers at Ford, GM, and Chrysler—mainly with Ford. I probably had face-to-face meetings with ten thousand autoworkers over a sixteen-year period. My job was to diagnose them, find a program that would rehab them, and get them back to work. The company had accepted the idea that it's better to rehab a good worker who has succumbed to alcohol or drugs than to hire somebody off the street. Overall, it has been a glorious life.

In the Uprising's Wake

REACTION IN THE
WHITE COMMUNITY

William Winkel

To stay or to go? The uprising left an indelible mark on the white community. Even before the embers cooled, the white community was faced with a litany of questions without easy answers. For many, the most pressing question was whether to stand and fight or to run and hide. For whites, both in the city and in the suburbs, this question was a difficult one, as the uprising shattered for many the hope they shared for the Model City.

For those—and there were many—who stayed, the next question would be, "What is there to fight for?" In the aftermath of July 1967, members of the white community fought for the city they believed in, often taking divergent positions. The battle over what the city would be after the uprising was contentious. Many who stayed did not actively fight, yet their presence spoke volumes. For others, the flight to greener pastures could not come soon enough. To them, the city's swan song was the tanks in the streets and smoke filling the sky. Before the National Guard retreated, thousands of Detroiters had their suitcases packed.

The reactions of the white community in the wake of the 1967 uprising reflected its confusion and disillusionment but also hope. As the events of July unfolded, decades of social, political, and racial tensions highlighted the partitions that divided Detroit: differences between whites, blacks and whites, and the city and suburbs ensured that a unified response remained out of reach. Furthermore, the uprising provided fresh conflicts that further split the white community.

The Great Spectrum Takes Shape

Dissent over the root causes of the uprising exemplifies the disunity of the white community. Elliot D. Luby and James Hedegard's "A Study of Civil Disorder in Detroit" sought to understand how the city's white and black communities interpreted what happened and reveals the spectrum of dissenting opinions among Detroiters. Luby of the Lafayette Clinic and Hedegard of Wayne State University Medical School were intimately familiar with this demographic.

The Luby and Hedegard study found that 23 percent of whites stated that "the riots were primarily the work of agitators, organizers, and criminals." In addition, 23 percent also said that the "rioters were motivated by jealousy, greed, [or] a desire to get something (not deserved)." In comparison, only 2 percent of black residents agreed with the former and 6 percent with the latter. Conversely, only 28 percent of whites responded by citing "rioters' frustrations, . . . feelings of depredations, or hopelessness," joining 35 percent of black respondents holding that opinion.

These sentiments were iterated by a follow-up question. When respondents were asked to decide the root cause of the uprising, three options were presented: people were being mistreated; criminals did it; or people wanted to take things. The top response among whites was "people wanted to take things" at 35 percent, followed by "criminals did it" at 30 percent. In unison with the previous question, 28 percent of whites chose "people were being mistreated" as the chief instigator. The black response rate was nearly the opposite: 17 percent to the first, 10 percent to the second, and 64 percent attributed it to mistreatment.

The inclination toward criminal undertones is not without consequence. This slant allows us to infer that members of the white community placed a great deal of blame at the feet of the black community. Also, despite the uprising taking place in largely black areas, many whites owned property in those areas (stores, apartments, houses, etc.) that was largely lost or crippled.

One question that aligned the vast majority of white respondents was "Do you sympathize with the people who took part in the rioting?" Eighty percent of whites said "no," 10 percent said "yes," and 10 percent responded with "somewhat." Blacks responded with slightly closer margins, 53 percent said "no," followed by 30 percent with "yes," and 17 percent answered "somewhat."

The divide over the root causes of the uprising was not isolated between blacks and whites in the city. Suburban whites stood equally divided over the root causes. A follow-up study by Donald Warren, "Suburban Isolation and Race Tension: The Detroit Case," compared the responses of black Detroiters with their suburban white counterparts. Warren's study exemplifies the white community's continued confusion over the issues that motivated the uprising.

Warren focused on nine suburban communities (Plymouth, Royal Oak, Livonia, Madison Heights, Dearborn, Southfield, Southgate, East Detroit [today Eastpointe], and Warren) and Detroit. When asked to rank ten possible causes, suburban whites remained unsure. The top response was "Black Nationalism" (16.0 percent), followed closely by "Poverty" (15.7 percent), then "Criminal Elements" (10 percent), "Lack of Jobs" (9.1 percent), "Failure of White Public Officials" (7 percent), "Powerlessness" (6.9 percent), "Poor Housing" (6.7 percent), "Too Much Welfare" (6.6 percent), "Teenagers" (4.7 percent), and "Police Brutality" (0.7 percent). Even though only 16 percent selected "Black Nationalism" as the chief cause of the uprising, six of the nine communities made it their top response, with two others placing it second. "Police Brutality" was the top response of Detroit blacks, compared to all nine suburbs ranking the issue last.

Actions Speak Louder than Words

The spectrum of reactions and responses inspired a wave of new activism. Many of those who decided to remain in Detroit chose to take an active role in shaping the city's future. The white community still constituted the largest racial bloc in the city. The goals of these organizations did not always align, nor did they share in a common vision for the city. A trait shared by many of the new activists was their youth. It was an activism that left a lasting impact on the city. Exemplifying the youth of Detroit's activists were Sheila Murphy and Donald Lobsinger, two very different individuals.

One of the youngest activists, twenty-year-old Murphy came to epitomize the members of the white community who chose "Police Brutality" as the root cause and those who were not frightened by "Black Nationalism." Additionally, Murphy embodied young, white, left-wing radical activism. Raised in Detroit to Irish American parents, her father worked as a distributor for the *Catholic Worker*, a pseudo-anarchist newspaper.

On May 20, 1968, Sheila Murphy founded the Ad-Hoc Action Group—Citizens of Detroit in response to the violent clash between the Detroit Police Department and members of the Poor People's Campaign who were finishing their march at Cobo Hall earlier on May 13. The events became

The logo and motto of the activist organization Ad-Hoc Action Group. Image courtesy of the Walter P. Reuther Library, Wayne State University.

well-known as Cobo Hall 1. Ad-Hoc's primary purpose was to function as a police watchdog group, earning the moniker "cop watchers." Its work included lobbying for civilian oversight, investigating reported abuses by police, and protesting and picketing to highlight grievances and to pressure government officials. Within a year, Ad-Hoc was the preeminent white radical organization in Detroit.

Ad-Hoc grew into a highly sophisticated operation. The group was headquartered at Newman Hall on Woodward Avenue in Detroit, a property owned by the Archdiocese of Detroit. Funding was procured through voluntary donations as well as fund-raising. No membership fees were assessed. Aside from donations, Ad-Hoc received substantial funding through the Archdiocese of Detroit and the patronage of John Cardinal Dearden, archbishop of Detroit. In terms of structure, the city was divided into sections, and members were organized based on where they lived. Their work was guided by the group's *Police Observation Manual*, and workshops trained new activists. Membership was also kept informed via a mailing list and the group's *Ad-Hoc Newsletter*, emblazoned with its logo: a clenched fist, inlayed with the peace symbol and the words "Peace" and "Power."

Ad-Hoc grew not only in sophistication but also in membership. The group ballooned to over 700 members. Detroiters represented 443 people, and their suburban cohorts numbered 257. An exposé by *Detroit Scope* magazine in its May 24, 1969, issue indicated that the membership was well regarded, noting, "Professors, doctors, retirees, housewives, teachers, clergymen, and engineers make up the backbone of the organization. It's this respectable image that makes Ad-Hoc a potent force." The membership of Ad-Hoc reflected the youth of its leader. The average age of the members was thirty-two.

In the *Detroit Scope* magazine profile, David Tankard, a Wayne State University professor, stated that the group was not antipolice, simply antiabuse: "Police are not always, in every instance, your friend." Tankard elaborated, "And in the same respect, the poor, the shabby dressed, those people different from you are not something to fear." As Detroit splintered and trust broke down across the city, this was a prominent pillar of Ad-Hoc's mentality.

Murphy and Ad-Hoc were quick to find allies in the city. Aside from recruiting middle-class whites to the group, Ad-Hoc forged strong bonds with black radicals. Partnerships with the young leaders of the Dodge Revolutionary Union Movement (DRUM), Kenneth Cockrel, Mike Hamlin, and John Watson—who also went on to found the League of Revolutionary

Black Workers (LRBW)—led to the creation of the Motor City Labor League (MCLL). The MCLL was designed to work as an umbrella group for left-wing organizations native to Detroit. One of the first projects of MCLL was the Conflict, Control, Change (CCC) book club. CCC was the brainchild of Mike Hamlin and facilitated by Joann Castle. Castle operated as a member of Ad-Hoc and identified as a white, young, radical, Catholic feminist.

According to James Geschwender in his *Class, Race, and Worker Insurgency*, CCC was tasked with educating white liberals and radicals and laying the "foundation for revolutionary thought," as well as "socializing the membership to a radical perspective." Membership surged, and CCC boasted seven hundred members. Due to the focus of the group, only 2 percent of the membership was black. The group concentrated primarily on black history and black issues. Lectures hosted by prominent black radicals such as James Foreman, Kenneth Cockrel, and John Watson were highly attended and enthusiastically welcomed. CCC not only explored black issues but also hosted feminist lectures and anti-Vietnam lectures from Jane Fonda and Tom Hayden.

As Ad-Hoc and Murphy represented the vanguard of the political left in Detroit, Donald Lobsinger stood as champion of the right. Lobsinger was the leader and spokesman for the group Breakthrough. Like Murphy, Lobsinger was relatively young, ideologically driven, and vivacious. Thirty-four years old in 1968, he was an army veteran who was stationed in West Germany and witnessed communist rule across the border. Also, like Murphy, he told this author that his Catholic faith drove his work fighting the "atheist Marxist Communists."

Breakthrough was founded in 1963 as an anticommunist, pro–Vietnam War organization. Breakthrough viewed the events of July 1967 through a Cold War lens, interpreting the events in Watts, Newark, and Detroit as communist-backed rebellions.

The rise of black militants and self-avowed Marxist-Leninists (like Kenneth Cockrel) in Detroit prompted Breakthrough to fresh activism. Following the uprising, the group placed a great deal of effort into thwarting the work of leftists in the city. Breakthrough did not lack adversaries. Ad-Hoc, Mayor Cavanagh, DRUM, the Black Panthers, and anyone else deemed to be in league with communists or communist sympathizers were judged as traitors.

Breakthrough rivaled Ad-Hoc in size and reach. Boasting over seven hundred members, the group sold out banquets, fund-raisers, and speeches.

Members of the activist group Breakthrough interrupted a demonstration at Kennedy Square. Donated by Donald Lobsinger, from the Detroit Historical Society Collection.

Members were kept informed through the group's newsletter, *Battle-Line*. Breakthrough's mission and motivation were exemplified by its logo and motto: a closed fist tearing through a Soviet flag and "America Forever, Communism Never."

Breakthrough employed a myriad of tactics in order to exert pressure on both public officials and rivals. It placed "Wanted" posters of Mayor Jerome Cavanagh and Governor George Romney across the city and physically disrupted rallies and demonstrations by other groups, such as Martin Luther King Jr.'s speech at Grosse Pointe High School in 1968 and an Angela Davis demonstration in 1971.

Following the uprising, a regional arms race took off. The police registered 10,416 handguns in 1967, compared to 13,145 in only the first six months of 1968. This number of handguns may not reflect the total number acquired. Ohio had far less stringent requirements, which ignited the trend of driving to Ohio for purchases. Sales of long guns (shotguns and rifles) shot up as well but were not officially recorded. With the mass purchase of weapons, ammunition sales also spiked.

Breakthrough was a staunch proponent of arming the white community. Driven by the expectation that the police would be overwhelmed in the next uprising, Lobsinger encouraged gun ownership and training. By sponsoring the Douglas MacArthur Hunt Club and partnering with the Detroit Police and Fireman's Association for Public Safety, the American Legion, and the Michigan Militia, Breakthrough demonstrated its resolve to see the white community stand firm in the face of another uprising. At meetings, the National Rifle Association was a regular fixture promoting various weapons. The purpose of this initiative was to keep whites who remained in Detroit from leaving as well. Alarmist whites in Detroit were not the only ones purchasing firearms and stockpiling provisions. It was a trend embraced by moderate and alarmist whites, blacks, and suburbanites.

— —

Not every Detroiter who fought did so with radical political or ideological agendas. Eleanor Josaitis represented those in the city who wanted to rebuild the city together peacefully. Along with Father William Cunningham, Josaitis founded Focus: HOPE in May 1968. Josaitis and Father Cunningham were older than the other activists across the city (Cunningham thirty-eight and Josaitis thirty-seven) but no less energetic. Focus: HOPE's intent was to aid in the redevelopment of the community across racial and ethnic barriers by focusing its efforts on community building, food assistance, and job training.

Breakthrough's emblem was an American fist breaking through the flag of the Soviet Union. Donated by Donald Lobsinger, from the Detroit Historical Society Collection.

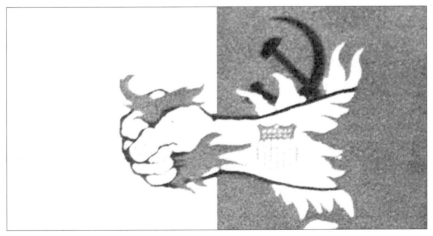

A group of Roman Catholic nuns and volunteers prepared packages of food to be distributed to neighbors. Looting and fires destroyed many local grocery stores. Photograph by Bud Johnson, *Detroit Free Press*. Donated by the City of Detroit Department of Information—Photography Department, from the Detroit Historical Society Collection.

The New Detroit Committee was founded in the closing days of the uprising on July 27 by white Detroit elites led by Joseph Hudson. The organization represented the elders of the white community. New Detroit, while overwhelmingly white, did have prominent black members as well, including Councilman William Patrick and a number who were considered radicals. With financial capital as the group's primary tool, it sought to encourage the revitalization of Detroit's economy, to aid social stability, and—according to its mission statement—to "identify and eliminate racial disparities in the region by building economic equity, social justice and racial understanding."

— —

Despite the work that was being undertaken, for many whites, the question was never "Should we stay?" but "When to go?" Since 1950, Detroit's white population was in steady decline. From a peak white population of 1,545,847 in 1950 to 1,182,970 in 1960, the white community began the great exodus, which was regarded as "white flight" long before 1967. Although the uprising did not create white flight, it certainly acted as a catalyst for further flight. In the years preceding the uprising, Detroit was losing an average of 22,000 people a year. The number more than doubled to 47,000 in 1967 and then nearly doubled again in 1968 to 80,000, followed by another 46,000 in 1969. No longer were whites 80 percent of the populace; by 1970, whites and blacks were at 55 percent and 44 percent, respectively.

Many people who left Detroit departed with neither the expectation nor the desire to see the city's problems and strife depart with them. In 1964, Detroit Public Schools began to utilize mass busing as a means to combat persistent de facto segregation. In 1962, 72 of Detroit's 271 schools remained all white, and eight stood as all black. By 1967, 15 of Detroit's public schools were all white, and the number of all-black schools grew to 16. The mass exodus of whites to the suburbs after the uprising tipped the scales. By 1970, Detroit's 11 all-white schools paled in comparison to the 30 all-black schools. From the onset, the busing initiative was controversial. The school board was charged with undermining neighborhood cohesion and stability. As with housing, Detroit schools were protected by rules. In order to attend a school, the student had to live within a neighborhood's boundaries. Not surprisingly, boundaries were redrawn as demographics changed.

After the uprising, the political climate shifted. The Board of Education sought to integrate the remaining schools by busing blacks and whites to new schools, but the initiative collapsed. The board's president, A. L. Zwerdling, recalled in Wilma Wood Henrickson's *Detroit Perspectives*, "All the trouble was because for the first time we devised a plan that not only moved black students into white schools, but also required white students to go to black schools." The pushback resulted in the formation of the Citizens Committee for Better Education and culminated in the recall of the four board members who supported the program: A. L. Zwerdling, Rev. Darneau Stewart, Dr. Remus Robinson, and Andrew Perdue.

In response, the National Association for the Advancement of Colored People (NAACP) sued; the federal judge Stephen Roth presided. The suit was over a proposed plan that would have placed Detroit students in the suburbs and vice versa. Opposition to busing built to a fever pitch. On August 30, 1971, ten Pontiac school buses were targeted by protesters and bombed. On September 27, 1971, Judge Roth agreed with the NAACP's claim that de jure segregation permeated throughout the city's public schools. Roth stated in his opinion in *Bradley v. Milliken* "that Detroit schools are segregated by law because of the 'actions and inactions' of local and state officials contrary to the US Constitution."

As a result, the Michigan State Board of Education, the NAACP, and the Detroit Board of Education were mandated to formulate and execute a plan that would rework the district in order to remove the systemic segregation inherent in the system. Specifically, Roth stated that "[proposals] must look beyond the limits of the Detroit school district for a solution to the problems of the Detroit Public Schools." The board recommended the consolidation of all of the school districts in Wayne, Oakland, and Macomb Counties and large-scale racial and ethnic population scattering.

Despite Detroit remaining a majority-white city, the suburbs were still a world apart. In the face of metropolitan Detroit's massive population increase, its minority population increased only from 3.6 percent to 3.7 percent. Furthermore, by 1970, blacks remained a scarcity in most major suburbs: Warren (population 180,000) had only five black families; Dearborn (population 100,000) had one black family. Grosse Pointe had two; Harper Woods, Hazel Park, and Birmingham each had one black family.

Gone were the days of federal support for these initiatives. The *Free Press* reported on December 11, 1970, that President Richard Nixon promised that "forced integration of the suburbs is not his policy." Gerald Ford came out against such programs; Housing and Urban Development Secretary George Romney, although originally favoring it, also ended up against it. Despite being upheld by two lower courts, the US Supreme Court struck down the busing plan in *Milliken v. Bradley*.

The decision set the tone for suburban-city relations for decades. This relationship later morphed into code for white-black relations. Despite all the work that was done in the wake of the uprising, much of the white community departed Detroit within the next two decades.

The number of whites in Detroit decreased every year until 2015. The divisions that permeated the white community hindered the collective response that the city needed. The whites who stayed represented hope for better days, although they were certainly not in agreement on how to accomplish that. Those who left represented the lost promise of the Model City.

Part V

The More Things Change . . .

In the half century following 1967, the city has had eight mayors. Jerome Cavanagh handed off the baton to Roman Gribbs for four years. Coleman Young, a political firebrand, became the first African American mayor of Detroit in 1974, holding the post for five four-year terms. Dennis Archer Sr., the first black president of the American Bar Association, took office in 1994 and was replaced by the hugely popular Kwame Kilpatrick in 2002. Council President Ken Cockerel Jr. stepped in during a City Hall crisis, until a 2009 election made Dave Bing the seventy-fourth mayor of Detroit. Mike Duggan took the oath of office in 2014. Of those named here, five are black and three are white.

Soon after the uprising, Detroit suffered the worst of rust-belt reputations. The oil embargo that began in 1973 put a damper on auto sales, particularly for the large, gas-guzzling vehicles made in the United States. After a decade of redesigns and layoffs, automobiles made by the "Big 3" were again competitive. Jobs and profits during the late 1980s and 1990s were plentiful, and the region rebounded. Additionally, the phenomenon of burning abandoned homes—mostly wood structures half a century old—on Devil's Night (the night before Halloween) was finally doused through a campaign of civilian patrols that rebranded the evening Angel's Night. It appeared as if Detroiters were taking back their city.

Economic and human factors conspired to set the city back again in the early years of the twenty-first century. A lending scheme fostered by Wall Street banks allowed almost anyone to attain a mortgage, drawing many Americans into homeownership for the first time. Predictably, borrowers in all classes purchased beyond their means, and when the real-estate bubble burst, the US economy crumbled. Ripples from the crisis spread around the world.

Big-ticket purchases were curtailed in all markets served by Detroit automakers. The Great Recession forced General Motors and Chrysler into bankruptcy; Ford barely escaped that fate. Unemployment in Michigan reached 14.2 percent in 2009. Within Detroit's city limits, the rate officially topped 29 percent; some people say it was actually closer to 50 percent. Many thousands were thrown out of their homes, losing everything.

During this period, Detroit government came under investigation for widespread corruption and institutional entitlement. Many city agencies were dysfunctional. The mayor, a councilperson, and numerous executives in both the city administration and the school system went to prison. This was followed by the largest municipal bankruptcy in American history. Much like the 1967 uprising, Detroit was not the only American city with problems; it was simply one of the worst affected.

As of this writing, General Motors, Ford, and Fiat Chrysler Automobiles are reporting record profits. Southeastern Michigan has also diversified its economy, attracting high-tech, biotech, and entertainment-related investments. For the first time in decades, large amounts of capital are pouring into construction and improvements. Yet the region's underclass, both black and white, remains marginalized. We know the causes. We have seen the results. Experience should direct our actions moving forward.

Detroit 1967 and Today

SPATIAL RACISM AND ONGOING CYCLES OF OPPRESSION

Peter J. Hammer

More than any other city, Detroit exemplifies the ongoing legacy of northern racism. Anyone who understands this country's history of structural racism knows that some form of civil unrest in the late 1960s was inevitable in Detroit. Sadly, these same racialized forces of oppression have operated largely unabated since 1967, further stamping "separate and unequal" onto the landscape of southeastern Michigan. Opportunity mapping by Jason Reece and Christy Rogers at the Kirwan Institute documents the contemporary segregation of race, wealth, and opportunity in metropolitan Detroit, defining the region in terms of its "spatial racism." Entire cities like Pontiac and Detroit are opportunity deserts, surrounded by seas of opportunity. In this segregated world, geography is destiny. The zip code that a child is born into is more important in determining that child's future education, occupational status, and life expectancy than individual aptitude. This is the complete inversion of the mythic American Dream.

What drives racial inequity? Spatial racism in Detroit is no more natural than apartheid was in South Africa. Yet like fish unaware of water, most Americans fail to see the inequity that surrounds them. Americans are often blind to the racism that defines basic aspects of life in most large cities. Seeing things for what they are is not always easy. We need new ways of seeing and understanding.

Just as deep understandings of interconnected ecosystems transformed environmental law and policy, systems-based thinking about interrelated networks of economics, power, and opportunity is transforming approaches to racial equity. Theories of structural racism examine the dynamic processes that produce and reproduce racial disparities over time. Understanding these processes requires understanding the coevolution of American belief systems and social institutions. How did the beliefs and institutions underlying slavery, Jim Crow segregation, and spatial racism produce and reproduce themselves over time, transitioning from one institutional form into another into the next? These new understandings require greater appreciation of the operation of complex social systems, with sensitivity to the interconnections among dynamics such as race, health, education, employment, transportation, and opportunity.

How can this framework help us understand the conditions that led to the rebellion in 1967 and that have continued in force to create the oppressive reality of spatial racism today? In housing, what has created spatialized notions of race and racialized notions of space, controlling where people can and cannot live in Detroit, and how have these oppressive patterns changed over time? In employment, how have racially and spatially segregated employment options created conditions of opportunity for some regional residents and conditions for endemic poverty for others? With these questions as a foundation, we can examine the downward economic sprawl that spatial racism has created for Detroit, calling into question the city's and the region's very social and financial viability. Symptomatic of this crisis is the unprecedented displacement of tens of thousands of long-term Detroit residents through tax foreclosures and water shutoffs. Sadly, these real-time tragedies are the predictable and inevitable outcomes of racialized policies at the local, regional, state, and federal levels that first led to the 1967 rebellion and have now trapped Detroit in the apartheid-like reality of spatial racism.

Housing

Spatial racism is the defining reality of southeastern Michigan. What can lead to such a total and complete segregation of race, wealth, and opportunity? To look for historical antecedents is to begin to understand the social production and reproduction of systems of oppression. It is first and foremost a story of the physical control of the movement of human beings. If people were gas molecules, they would be evenly dispersed throughout space. It takes effort, intentional and often physically violent effort, to keep people confined in predestined physical spaces.

Imagine a series of maps of Detroit outlining the predominant race (black and white) by census track from 1930 to 2000. In 1930, the African

American community was confined to a few segregated areas: Black Bottom, Paradise Valley, a small neighborhood in northwestern Detroit, and a small area near Wyoming Avenue and Eight Mile Road. The story of Dr. Ossian Sweet was an object lesson for any African American, no matter how well educated and cultured, of the consequences of breaking the color line. These segregated areas expanded slightly on the margins from 1930 to 1950 but were bursting at the seams in terms of density, with large increases in the African American population coming with the Great Migration. In 1950, the most densely populated area of the city ran right down Hastings Street in Paradise Valley; these levels of density were more consistent with high-rise multifamily residential housing, but there was no such housing in Detroit at the time. Imagine the political, legal, economic, social, and physically violent forces necessary to impose such segregation. By 1960, the color lines inside the city had already started to yield, as the demographic forces foreshadowing white flight and the reproduction of segregation and spatial racism at a regional level were already well under way. These patterns continued through the 1960s, '70s, and '80s.

Imagine another series of maps showing the predominant race (black and white) at the regional level from 1950 to 2010. Between 1900 and 1950, the tricounty area surrounding Detroit grew slowly, largely as a vestige of the growth of the city of Detroit. In 1950, with few exceptions, the African American population was contained largely in dense, segregated areas of Detroit, with the rest of the region being almost exclusively white. From 1950 onward, the region grew largely at the expense of, and in opposition to, the city of Detroit. Southeastern Michigan is one of the most fractured regions in the country, with more than 150 separate municipalities governed by state laws and home-rule laws that encourage extreme balkanization.

The physics of segregation combines the power of fractured home rule with the push and pull of the racially subsidized forces of urban sprawl—historically discriminatory home-mortgage lending, commercial redlining, state road policies, and the federal highway system—and the express racism of increasingly unsuccessful efforts to enforce the color line inside the boundaries of Detroit. The consequence is the social reproduction and enforcement of segregation (spatial racism) at the regional level, with black areas now associated with entire cities rather than specific neighborhoods. By the 1990s, Detroit was almost all black, while the remainders of the suburbs were almost all white. By 2000 and 2010, black flight was following white flight to some of the inner-ring suburbs, with renewed ripples of white flight flowing farther and farther into the region's hinterlands.

Little in this story is accidental. It is important to connect the dots. The same individuals who formed "neighborhood improvement societies" and used physical violence to maintain the color line inside the city now became the mayors, Common Council members, and chairpersons of the planning commissions of suburban cities and townships. This is perhaps best typified by the political careers of Orville Hubbard, the unapologetic racist mayor of Dearborn (1942–1978), and L. Brooks Patterson, the former prosecutor and current executive of Oakland County, who started his public life demagoguing the issue of school integration in the wake of judicial findings of intentional racial discrimination in the Pontiac and Detroit public school districts. Patterson infamously stated to the *New Yorker* columnist Paige Williams, "What we're going to do is turn Detroit into an Indian reservation, where we herd all the Indians into the city, build a fence around it, and then throw in the blankets and corn."

In Detroit, forms of intentional and structural racism tragically merged. Much of the story is mediated through segregated housing and unplanned urban sprawl. The regional population increased between 1950 and 1970, only to decrease between 1970 and 1980, remaining relatively stable with future slight declines between 1980 and 2010. During this same period, however, Erica Raleigh of Data Driven Detroit notes that the region built "an average of 10,000 more housing units in the tricounty area each year than households required." The implications for the housing market inside Detroit were as predictable as they are catastrophic. "Excess supply on the fringe causes successive filtering outward, leaving tens of thousands of vacant dwellings in the core."

This is the planned death of a major American city, with highly racialized consequences for its residents. Homeownership is part of the mythic American Dream. From a systems perspective, homeownership is the principal means for the accumulation and intergenerational transfer of wealth for the middle class. Homeownership in the collapsing housing market of Detroit held no such promise, even if one could overcome the barriers of redlining and predatory subprime lending. The entire city of Detroit, along with its housing, was rife for regional abandonment.

Employment

If the first part of the story is about housing and the physical control of where people could and could not live, the second part of the story is about the spatial and economic segregation of where people work. The best defense against poverty is a good job paying a living wage. Where there is no work, there is no opportunity. The location and availability of jobs in Detroit have shifted over time along with the changing racialized demographics, largely to the detriment of Detroit residents.

In an important sense, the auto industry first made and then unmade Detroit. Those who think about Detroit as the Motor City intuitively think about the metropolitan area and not the city of Detroit. Leading automobile headquarters, financial capital, manufacturing plants, and auto jobs have been flowing out of the city for over a century. Ford was the first to leave, moving its manufacturing facilities from Detroit to Highland Park (a city inside Detroit's borders) shortly after the company's founding. Ford has not built a car in the city since 1910. Ford's famous River Rouge plant is located in and pays taxes to neighboring Dearborn, not Detroit. Chrysler was second. In 1925, the same year Dr. Sweet was attacked, the newly reformed Chrysler Corporation moved its headquarters to Highland Park, then moved to the suburbs of Auburn Hills in 1992, with devastating consequences for Highland Park. In contrast, General Motors has been the most faithful, moving its headquarters from Flint to Detroit in 1923 and remaining in Detroit to the present day.

Far more important with regard to jobs is the location of manufacturing facilities. In the beginning, most auto plants were in Detroit. This also changed early. In a pattern that presaged contemporary forces of globalization, auto plants moved first from Detroit to the green fields of the emerging suburbs, then to southern right-to-work states, and increasingly overseas. According to Thomas Sugrue in *The Origins of the Urban Crisis*, "Between 1945 and 1957, the Big 3 auto companies built twenty-five new plants in metropolitan Detroit, all of them outside the city." As in any complex, interconnected system, the loss of manufacturing jobs had cascading negative effects on Detroit neighborhoods and the city itself. Loss of auto jobs led to the closure of businesses supplying the auto industry and those dependent on the spending of autoworkers. Sugrue states, "Cities like Detroit struggled to recoup the tax revenues that they lost when companies closed their doors." Finally, even the land itself was scarred and damaged. "The environmental impact of factory shutdowns was also grave. Redeveloping brownfields . . . became difficult because of the residue of decades of industrial waste left behind."

When systems collapse, they often do so at an accelerating rate. The downward spiral of Detroit's job loss is staggering. According to research by Gary Sands and Mark Skidmore published in *Detroit and the Property Tax*,

"In 1970, there were 735,000 jobs in Detroit. By 2000, there were 390,000 fewer jobs in the City." This is a loss of more than 50 percent in thirty years. From 2000 and 2012, Detroit's private-sector jobs declined an additional 30 percent to 180,300, with those losses having a disproportionate impact in the neighborhoods. Furthermore, there has been an increasingly stark segregation of wealth and opportunity *inside the city*. "By 2012," Sands and Skidmore comment, "the downtown core accounted for 48 percent of the jobs and 61 percent of payrolls." Not surprisingly, the dramatic lack of jobs is associated with some of the highest poverty rates anywhere in the country. Concentrations of poverty are also increasing. Since 2000, the number of "high-poverty census tracks" in Detroit more than tripled.

It is important to realize that while jobs left the city, they did not leave the region. As the Kirwan Institute's opportunity mapping reveals, southeastern Michigan and in particular Oakland County remain areas of rich opportunity. Spatial racism is not the story of the lack or opportunity; it is the story of the segregation of race, wealth, and opportunity. The shifting location of jobs further illustrates the point. Recall the spiraling number of Detroit jobs from 1970 to the present. These jobs did not just disappear. Sands and Skidmore note, "Many jobs were relocated to the suburbs, where employment increased from 1.2 million in 1970 to 2.3 million in 2000. Detroit's share of total metropolitan employment fell from 38 percent to 13 percent during this period." We also know that this trend will continue. Of the three hundred thousand new jobs projected for the region by 2040, only 2 percent will be in Detroit.

The employment story becomes even more complicated, illustrating again the racialization of space and the spatialization of race. The city of Detroit has become a jobs desert, with an island of opportunity in the downtown district. For Detroit residents, there is barely one job for every four people in the city. While there are many valiant exceptions, it is not unfair to say that anyone who has the means to leave the city has left the city. This suggests that many of Detroit's poor residents are literally trapped in their homes, a shrinking asset they cannot sell. Public transportation inside the city is deficient; public transportation at the regional level is virtually and intentionally nonexistent. One in five Detroit residents does not have access to a vehicle (let alone the capacity to own a car in the Motor City). If they own a car, they pay disproportionately high auto-insurance rates.

In this setting, an interesting regional jobs dance takes place in southeastern Michigan every weekday morning. Many of the 48 percent of Detroit's downtown jobs, accounting for 61 percent of Detroit's payrolls,

Campus Martius reflects the resurgence of downtown Detroit, with new buildings and a high occupancy rate in both residential and office spaces. 2012 photograph by Joel Stone, from the Detroit Historical Society Collection.

are very desirable jobs. There are many less desirable, low-skilled, service jobs scattered throughout the region. Every morning, despite tremendous challenges in transportation, 61 percent of employed Detroiters get up and leave the city to go to work. Whom do they pass on their way out? An astonishing 70 percent of the jobs in Detroit are held by commuters living in the suburbs. The vast majority of "good jobs" in Detroit are held by outsiders, while the majority of employed Detroiters are forced to leave the city for less desirable opportunities outside. This is yet another defining characteristic of spatial racism. As in the "Sundown Towns" of old, however, we know how the dance ends. Everyone is safely confined to segregated homes by the end of the day.

The Downward Spirals of Spatial Racism

What does spatial racism do to the abandoned city and the people left behind? The prospects for municipal success are far worse in 2017 than they were in 1967. Clear patterns emerge. The balkanized municipal space in southeastern Michigan corresponds to dysfunctional economic and political processes that lend themselves to manipulation to create and reinforce patterns of spatial racism. Urban sprawl, the overbuilt regional housing market, and segregated employment opportunities have undermined Detroit's real-estate market, property-tax revenues, and fiscal health. Even before the wave of predatory subprime lending and the effects of the Great Recession, Detroit's real-estate market was fragile and under stress. Today, there is no functioning property market in large areas of the city. Moreover, despite the fact that the national headquarters of one of the largest mortgage companies in the country is in downtown Detroit, almost no residential mortgage lending takes place in the city.

At a foundational level, the political, economic, and social fabric that is supposed to hold a city together is being torn apart. The municipal tax base has eroded, population has declined, and the real-estate market and corresponding property-tax revenue have collapsed. In response, for more than a decade, the state has made substantial reductions in its revenue sharing for cities and has exhibited no leadership in regional or race relations. Rather than addressing the complicated root causes of Detroit's regional financial distress, the state has imposed a regime of emergency management that displaces democratic and political rights in African American communities and dictates an austerity agenda that further ratifies the second-class economic status of urban residents.

We have traced ongoing cycles of oppression leading from slavery to Jim Crow to spatial racism. The fence that L. Brooks Patterson threatened has been built in the form of segregated opportunity, endemic poverty, an eroded tax base, unsustainable debt, and the lack of public transportation. His reference to the Native American experience is sadly prophetic. After being abandoned and left alone for decades, parts of Detroit have recently been targeted for development. The lessons of history are clear. When marginalized groups in America hold resources desired by powerful others, the marginal groups are displaced, and their resources are taken.

Perversely, the instrument of this physical displacement is the very poverty wrought by structural racism itself. Detroit suffers some of the highest poverty levels in the country. At the same time, Detroiters face some of the highest water rates in the country. Detroiters also face the highest property taxes in the state and some of the highest rates in the country. Moreover, the city made little effort to adjust property taxes in the wake of the Great Recession, leading to situations in which back taxes often exceed the market value of the home. It is expensive to live in a poor city.

It is no surprise that many impoverished citizens cannot pay their water bills or their property taxes. Rather than seeing the obvious and widespread

Despite the effort in neighborhoods to maintain properties and security, Detroit's once-vast housing stock, outside the city's core, is subject to vacancy, deterioration, and vandalism. Scrapping, crime, and arson have taken a toll that threatens nearly every sector of the city. 2015 photograph by Joel Stone, from the Detroit Historical Society Collection.

mismatch between bills and income as symptoms of deep structural problems, the city responded by shutting off water for tens of thousands of poor households, without any consideration of the public health consequences of the action. In addition, the city reversed a previous moratorium on tax foreclosures of occupied residences and started foreclosing on tens of thousands of homes. This not only produces devastating homelessness but actually increases the blight associated with vacant buildings and further depresses an already-moribund property market, likely reducing future property-tax revenues even further.

Data on the tragic human toll of these actions are hard to assess because the city is making no effort to collect or examine them. With conservative assumptions of the number of residents per household, well over one hundred thousand people have likely been affected by these decisions, constituting nearly 20 percent of the entire population. The water shutoffs have been condemned as a human-rights violation by the United Nations. Detroit's water shutoffs and tax foreclosures are creating a new class of American refugees and internally displaced persons. Sadly, as focus shifts from 1967 to 2017 to 2067, it is becoming clear that there is little room in Detroit's Future City for poor people of color.

The fiftieth anniversary of the 1967 rebellion has to be placed in the context of nearly five hundred years of slavery and failed race relations in America. In terms of spatial racism, Detroit is ground zero. Detroit is the Selma of our generation, and structural racism is the challenge of the new civil rights movement. These realities are clearly visible, if people want to open their eyes to see.

Hindsight

THE SHIFT IN MEDIA FRAMING

Casandra E. Ulbrich

Ask any native Detroiters old enough to remember about their reflections on the "Detroit riot" and you are likely to hear vivid memories of burning buildings, tanks in the streets, or neighbors protecting one another's homes. They will tell you about the smell of the smoke, the crackling of breaking glass, or the fear that comes from the unmistakable sound of gunfire in the distance.

But you are also likely to hear a refutation of the word *riot*. "It wasn't a *riot*," some will tell you. "It was a *rebellion*." And just like that, the images just described assume a completely different meaning. The actions of those who were involved are transformed, as are the actors themselves. The historical context is redefined, and societal responsibility suddenly becomes part of the discussion.

It was those very conversations that led this author to study how the media helped to frame and reframe this historic uprising over the years, as well as the implications of such shifts. By analyzing local media coverage for the thirty days following the uprising and comparing it to similar coverage of the uprising's fortieth anniversary in 2007, we see divergent frames emerge.

There is no doubt that words matter. How events, issues, and even people are described—which elements are highlighted and which are ignored—can impact how others view them. Called "framing," this rhetorical process helps define complex issues and narrow them into easily discernable thoughts or ideas. Frames not only provide simplified meaning but also provide insights into whom or what to blame, who is responsible for overcoming the problem, and what outcomes are desired or acceptable.

A frame is perhaps most powerful when it can be expressed in a single word or phrase. Like an arrowhead seeking its target, this frame drills into the schema of its intended audience, taking advantage of that person's education, knowledge, life experiences, memories, and biases to impact understanding and reactions.

This process is clearly exemplified by the two competing words used to frame the civil unrest that exploded on July 23, 1967, at the corner of Clairmount Avenue and 12th Street in Detroit. The "riot" frame evokes images of a mob mentality with participants acting as consenting malefactors, choosing to impose their misdeeds on an unsuspecting and innocent citizenry. The "rebellion" frame evokes images of participants resisting the inherent injustices that arise from a hegemonic power structure.

There exists a level of exculpation within the rebellion frame that is clearly lacking in the riot frame. Under the rebellion frame, societal inequity plays a leading role in the event, and society itself is responsible for overcoming the underlying pressures that led to the uprising. By allowing for a social foundation as a potential cause, the acceptable remedies are greatly expanded. Instead of limiting the remedy to the individuals involved, this frame allows for multiple solutions, including public policy aimed at overcoming inequities.

In 1967, the media frames used to describe the uprising primarily centered on the riot frame. In the first few days, newspapers took advantage of the contextual similarities between the streets of Detroit and the war in Vietnam, invoking images of guerrilla warfare, door-to-door combat, and blood-soaked battlefields.

"Negroes" were often described as the aggressors. Whether they were portrayed as rioters, looters, or snipers, one thing that was presented as fact was that most were black. Whites were often described as the victims of the uprising, with black aggression being focused on white business owners as the main target. One particular group emerged as an opportune scapegoat: the "militant blacks."

After all, Detroit was touted as the last place where an uprising of this magnitude was supposed to happen. While similar unrest was reported in cities throughout the United States in the mid-1960s, Detroit, under the leadership of a progressive mayor, was heralded as a model city in regard to race relations. African Americans held positions of power, including both of Detroit's congressional seats, seats on the Board of Education, and even judgeships. Newspapers noted that Detroit blacks held important jobs in business and industry, as well as in the labor movement.

But if this was the case, what could explain the number of local participants in the uprising, as evidenced by the thousands who were arrested
and charged with riot-related crimes? The short answer is that they were
caught up in the moment, driven there by the powerful rhetoric of the
"militant blacks."

Militant blacks were not blamed for taking part in the uprising per se
but rather for being conspiring agitators who fanned the flames of distrust
and anger. Generally nameless, these individuals were portrayed as outsiders who lacked traditional connections to Detroit society. This group
comprised a small subset of blacks depicted as particularly violent and
threatening to white society as well as to middle-class blacks, penetrating
the city specifically to goad locals into action. Soon, media coverage began
questioning whether the uprising would have happened at all or been as
severe without the influence of these dangerous and organized interlopers.

Generally, a riot frame would indicate that those who took part in the
uprising would ultimately be responsible for its aftermath. By placing
blame on blacks in general, and the militant blacks specifically, the media
were clearly framing the uprising as a riot. Curiously, coverage attempting
to assign responsibility for recovery and healing was not entirely focused
on the participants. Instead, media reports included political leaders who
suggested that the remedy lay with social programs. Vice President Hubert
Humphrey, for example, called for a restoration of efforts to root out the
conditions that had created slums in America and for helping communities take advantage of programs designed to improve the conditions of the
impoverished. Humphrey likened the establishment of safe communities
to that of previous social commitments, such as military defense, exploration of outer space, and rebuilding western Europe after World War II. Others, such as Michigan State Representative David S. Holmes, focused on
the need for educational improvements, including smaller class sizes, additional vocational programs, and enhanced Head Start. Fair-housing laws
and employment opportunities for residents of the riot-torn areas were
also stressed. In essence, it was suggested that social programs enhanced
social values such as equality, a commitment to urban cities, and respect for
law and order.

Poverty, as well as a lack of policies to address it, was a consistent theme
among many editorials and articles. While the media pointed to the gains
that had been made by some blacks, they acknowledged that most blacks
were still denied many opportunities afforded to whites. Modest gains only
served to intensify frustrations. Governor George Romney called for full

integration of public schools, affordable housing, and an end to restrictions on job opportunities for blacks, all of which aimed at relieving the effects of poverty.

Police brutality was one social ill that was reported by many black and white citizens to be a primary cause of the uprising. One unfolding incident, covered extensively by the *Free Press* and the *Detroit News*, became a symbol of brutality by authorities during the uprising. The Algiers Motel incident became the most pronounced instance of institutional inhumanity and ultimately became a symbol of the uprising. The story was initially reported as three black snipers who were killed during a gunfight with authorities. The three had been found dead inside the Manor House annex, a three-story converted house adjacent to the Algiers Motel. Soon, rumors began to surface in black neighborhoods that there was more to the story than what was being reported. Detroit newspapers began to take notice, and the Algiers event became synonymous with overzealous—even barbaric— police activity. The *Detroit Free Press* began an independent investigation of the Algiers Motel incident, and on July 31, 1967, the newspaper reported its conclusions: the three were shot at close range and were likely lying down or kneeling at the time. Witnesses located by the newspaper described in detail an evening of unmistakable brutality at the hands of uniformed men, culminating with the execution-like deaths of the three young men.

– –

Given this deviation from the standard assignation of responsibility, it became clear that the uprising was framed as a riot in 1967 media coverage but that, even then, the frame was unstable and open to reframing. Forty years later, coverage of the uprising—much like the city itself—looked very different. In 2007, local media commemorated the fortieth anniversary of the uprising, but this retrospective coverage, unlike its 1967 counterpart, did not focus on those who took part. There was no mention of the militant blacks or looters caught up in the moment. Instead, the coverage included full-length articles detailing diverse eyewitness accounts of their experiences during the unrest and how it had shaped their lives since.

While not focusing on participants, the Detroit papers did focus on identifying the causes of the uprising as well as its long-term impact. As with the coverage at the time of the uprising, articles pointed to the fact that blacks in 1967 suffered discrimination in housing, employment, and education. Pent-up anger, the result of discrimination, was also cited. Other articles highlighted the role that race played in 1967 and continued to play

An 1967 advertisement used by the *Detroit News* to publicize its coverage of the disturbance. From the Detroit Historical Society Collection.

in 2007, with blacks reporting a different reality than whites did. The white power structure that had existed in Detroit in 1967 was also considered a factor in the uprising, indicating that there were few blacks in positions of leadership. This directly contradicted arguments made in the 1967 coverage that African Americans in Detroit enjoyed positions of power in the city and were more likely to be a part of the power structure than were blacks in other parts of the country.

The 2007 coverage, like its counterpart forty years earlier, tried to identify the causes for the uprising. Coverage of the fortieth anniversary indicated that, for those who saw the event as a rebellion, the cause was often related to the 1960s environment of racial injustice in which many had lived. Disparities in employment, housing, and economic opportunity all led to a growing dissatisfaction among many of Detroit's residents.

One factor that received considerably more attention in 2007 than in 1967 was the treatment of blacks by police leading up to the uprising. Coverage pointed to the fact that the police force in Detroit in the 1960s was predominantly white and included four-man police units assigned to patrol predominantly black neighborhoods. These "Big Four" police units were known to many residents for their particular brutality and harassment of African Americans.

The competition between the riot and rebellion frames is symbolic of the divide that exists in southeastern Michigan today. The region continues to be one of the most racially segregated areas in the country. The so-called Eight Mile Divide separates the majority-white suburbs and the majority-black city both geographically and symbolically. Many people in the region see the Detroit uprising as a major contributor to this schism. Notably, most whites still call the event the "riots." Those who use the term "rebellion" are usually black.

-- --

As time passes, the civil unrest that marked Detroit in 1967 continues to undergo a transformation in how we think about it, whom we blame, and whom we hold responsible for making it right. What can explain this transformation?

First, demographic changes in newsrooms and among positions of power have led to far more diverse voices being represented in every facet of information exchange. In 1967, African Americans were nearly nonexistent in American newsrooms. By 2007, the demographics of the newsroom had changed, and reporters were more representative of the population on which they were reporting. That year, the American Society of News Editors found that nationally, the percentage of journalists in newsrooms who were minorities was 13.62 percent, and they accounted for nearly 11 percent of all newsroom supervisors. The two daily newspapers in Detroit were even more diversified: 30 percent of journalists at the *Detroit Free Press* were minorities (19.8 percent were black), and 27.7 percent of *Detroit News* journalists were minorities (17 percent were black).

Forty years after the uprising, diversity also marked the political class in Detroit. The mayor of Detroit, Kwame Kilpatrick, served as the third consecutive black man to hold the office. The governor of Michigan, Jennifer Granholm, was the first woman to hold this position. In addition, 2007 saw many African Americans holding positions of power throughout southeastern Michigan. Within the city of Detroit, this included members of the City Council, the police chief, and administrative appointees.

As a reflection of these changing demographics, the sources utilized in news articles also changed dramatically from 1967 to 2007. In 1967, journalists relied on official sources, often to the neglect of including those who were most affected by the violence. Since most officials were white, an overreliance on white perspectives was clearly evident. For example, when describing those who took part in the uprising and why they chose to do so, local papers relied heavily on judges and prosecutors for this insight, rather than asking the participants to comment for themselves. This was underscored by the Kerner Commission, which was charged with investigating the causes of civil unrest, when its report indicated that the media portrayed blacks as if they "do not read the newspapers or watch television, give birth, marry, die, go to PTA meetings." In 2007, local coverage relied primarily on individuals to recollect what they experienced during the uprising. Instead of relying extensively on official sources, the coverage included eyewitness accounts and explored how the uprising had impacted individual life choices.

A final explanation may rest in the nature of coverage itself. Framing-effects research suggests that blame assignment may be related to episodic or thematic reporting. Episodic framing, which is often more visually appealing, presents the news as a series of individual stories. Episodic framing often leads to blame being placed on the individuals being depicted and thereby reduces the likelihood of officials being held responsible for finding solutions. Thematic framing, on the other hand, presents the news in a more general fashion and places information in a larger context. A historical perspective allows for greater concentration on cause and effect, which can have a clear impact on how people think about a subject.

The 1967 coverage followed an episodic approach, meaning that it focused on individual events and actors, rather than in-depth analysis. For example, uprising-related deaths were often treated as individual occurrences. In 2007, the coverage followed a thematic approach by including historical references and recollections. Rather than detail a specific event, this coverage included descriptive analysis of historically relevant information, evidenced by the use of graphs, charts, and timelines. By including a more in-depth examination of the topic, thematic-framing effects encourage assigning blame to elected officials or the government, as opposed to individuals. It is not surprising that the fortieth-anniversary coverage included a more thematic focus, as this coverage had the benefit of both hindsight and forty years of data collection. It may be the case that retrospective coverage is naturally inclined toward the thematic and that the coverage would therefore follow this pattern regardless of demographic changes.

History is marked by events that are so memorable that those who lived through such an event remember where they were, what they were doing, and how it felt. Ask people who were in Detroit in 1967 about the uprising and you will hear about their personal experiences with the unrest. But as the years pass and new generations of Detroiters learn about the uprising, media framing becomes increasingly critical to our collective understanding of the civil unrest that dominated the streets of Detroit for days. These frames have the power to either confirm or redefine history, depending on which frame dominates. One thing is clear: the debate is far from over.

Hindsight

It *Can* Happen Here

MODEL CITY ONCE AGAIN?

Desiree Cooper

Most Detroiters would be hard-pressed to recognize—much less describe—the official flag of their beloved city. Yet woven into the prophetic images of fire and resurrection, despair, and hope shines their story. To be a true Detroiter, you have to know how to walk through fire.

On the morning of June 11, 1805, a blaze purportedly started in the barn of a local baker and quickly spread to nearby homes. Soon enough, the little enclave of six hundred people was engulfed in flames. A group of citizens formed a bucket brigade from the Detroit River to the business district, but it was no use. Within a few hours, the entire city was reduced to ashes, leaving only the stone chimneys and one storehouse standing. Miraculously, no one died in the fire—and neither did Detroit's spirit.

The fire engulfed the school built by Father Gabriel Richard, as well as his church, St. Anne's, ancestor of the parish that still ministers to southwestern Detroiters. After he looked over the destruction, he penned the motto that still appears today on the city's seal: *Speramus meliora; resurget cineribus*: "We hope for better things; it will arise from the ashes." That motto is now the centerpiece of the city's flag, which depicts a mournful woman looking back toward burning ruins, arm in arm with a hopeful woman gesturing toward a gleaming utopia.

Since the Great Fire of 1805, Detroit has circled between success and cinders—from the Arsenal of Democracy to the crack epidemic, from the Paris of the Midwest to the pre-Halloween blazes of Devil's Night, from the halcyon days of the "Big 3" to the city's historic bankruptcy. But no matter what the challenge, Detroiters have never stopped hoping for better things.

In the months following the 1967 riots, Detroit-area leaders formed New Detroit Inc., the nation's first urban coalition of corporate CEOs and leaders from the community, nonprofit, education, and faith sectors. The idea was that, if these sectors had been listening to each other in the first place, they would have been able to anticipate and perhaps deflate the racial tensions that exploded in 1967.

It is telling that half a century later, New Detroit is still operating, and the urban ills that it was designed to address are still as present as they were fifty years ago. The anger within Detroit's disenfranchised, marginalized, impoverished black communities has not diminished. In fact, hardly a hot summer has passed since the riots without dire warnings from community activists and social-service providers that the city was on the verge of another uprising. That has not happened—yet. Instead, the explosive zeitgeist of the 1960s has cooled to a steady simmer, earning the city its hard-baked, violent, gritty reputation.

That is not to say that there has not been continued racial provocation since the '60s. On November 5, 1992, Malice Green was a thirty-five-year-old, unemployed African American steel worker when he drove his friend to a dilapidated building on Detroit's west side. The building was abandoned and a known shelter for the homeless and crack addicts.

At about 10:00 p.m., two white plainclothes police officers approached Green's car and asked him for identification. He reached into his glove compartment and put something (some reports say it was drugs) in his hand. When he refused to open his hand, the officers began to beat him with their metal flashlights. Emergency medical services responders at the scene later testified that officers hit Green fourteen times in the head with their metal flashlights. By the time it was over, Malice Green was dead.

Green's death came a little more than a year after white Los Angeles police officers beat the African American cab driver Rodney King in 1991. There, rioters took the streets after an all-white jury acquitted the officers of assault. City leaders feared that riots would erupt in Detroit as well. The tension across the city was palpable: "Not again."

A mural of Green appeared near the place where he was killed. People held vigils and led protests. But no riots ensued. Pundits guessed that the swift action of the government quelled unrest. The day after the incident, Police Chief Stanley Knox suspended without pay seven of the nine officers who were at the scene. Then-mayor Coleman A. Young (the city's first black mayor, whose legacy is still a source of political pride for many Detroiters) publicly condemned the officers, telling NBC News that "a young man who was under arrest was literally murdered by police," a comment reported by the *Free Press* on November 10. And within eleven days of Green's death, Wayne County Prosecutor Kym Worthy charged officers Larry Nevers and Walter Budzyn with second-degree murder.

Perhaps it was the swift action of the criminal justice system that prevented the incident from reigniting a city where the hot cinders of racism had been smoldering since 1967. People realized that the life of a drug-addicted, unemployed Detroiter would be valued by the legal system—if not by the white police. When the officers were convicted of second-degree murder in 1993, Mayor Young declared in the August 24 edition of the *Free Press*, "I believe justice has been done, and I assume that we will have a quiet and orderly reaction in the city." It was quiet then and over the next four years while the officers' convictions were overturned on appeal and while they were retried and convicted of involuntary manslaughter.

Quiet persisted in 2000, when a black man was killed by security personnel in the parking lot of suburban Fairlane Town Center over a shoplifted, $4 bracelet. Quiet still persisted in 2015, when the Inkster police officer William Melendez was caught on his cruiser dash cam pummeling the black motorist Floyd Dent in the head more than sixteen times during a routine traffic stop.

Certainly, the social issues that gave rise to the conflagration in 1967 are still relevant today. The city remains mired in poverty, unemployment, poor race relations, mass incarceration, and a failing education system. Why, then, have the fears of new riots never been realized?

One real difference between Detroit of 1967 and Detroit today is the makeup of its police force. In 1967, Detroit's citizenry was more than a third African American, with a police force that was 95 percent white. Following the riots, the Detroit Police Department created STRESS (Stop the Robberies, Enjoy Safe Streets), an antirobbery squad that had a reputation for harassment and aggressive tactics.

STRESS was disbanded by the newly elected Mayor Young. Young also appointed William Hart as the city's first black police chief. The sense of black political empowerment that Young embodied had a profound effect on police-community relations and even on the general feeling that—while things were not getting appreciably better—at least the city administration had the interests of African Americans at heart.

The civil unrest of 1967 hastened the white flight that had begun in the 1950s. Today, the city is 83 percent African American, and its police force is 61 percent black. Riot training is baked into police training, and there is never a citywide celebration—from sports championships to Christmas-tree lightings and Freedom Festival fireworks—that does not include massive police preparations.

That is not to imply, however, that police killings ended with the integration of the force and the rise of black political power. In fact, according to FBI statistics analyzed by David Ashenfelter and Joe Swickard and published by the *Detroit Free Press* on May 15, 2000, Detroit led the nation in fatal shootings by police, and well-publicized incidents have continued to occur. In 2010, the white officer Joseph Weekley was charged with involuntary manslaughter and reckless endangerment with a gun after he allegedly shot seven-year-old Aiyana Stanley-Jones, an African American girl who was sleeping with her grandmother on the couch at home. Weekley was leading a SWAT team that was pursuing a murder suspect when he burst into the house. In the chaos that ensued, Weekley claimed that his gun went off accidentally, killing the child. Adding controversy to the incident, a documentary film crew was on location during the raid, raising issues of motivation and professionalism.

After two mistrials, Wayne County Prosecutor Worthy dismissed the misdemeanor charge against Weekley and declared that the police officer would not be tried a third time. While the incident was reported nationally, and the prominent civil rights leader Rev. Al Sharpton eulogized the murdered child, there was public outcry, community outrage, and shared grief—but no riots.

It appears that Detroit has maintained a fragile peace while other urban centers have seen a repeat of the '60s after a string of videos have shown white police using lethal force against unarmed blacks. Incidents in Chicago, Ferguson, Baltimore, and Milwaukee, among others, have become rallying events for a reinvigorated civil rights movement, often involving reminiscent violence and looting.

"In Detroit, we've had police-involved shootings by both black and white officers and there's been no outcry," Police Chief James Craig told CNN's Candy Crowley on November 30, 2014. "That's because we have a strong relationship with our citizens."

That relationship has not been so evident in nearby suburbs. In December 2015 and January 2016, Dearborn police were involved in two deadly incidents involving blacks. Each case generated angry protests, shutting down the main street of Dearborn—but no riots. Studies show that black drivers are disproportionately more likely to be pulled over than white drivers are in a number of cities that surround Detroit, a fact not lost on the black community. In a *Detroit News* story on February 25, 2016, referencing the region, the former Detroit mayor Dave Bing cautioned, Detroit is "maybe just one incident away."

— —

If Father Gabriel Richard were to stroll along Cass Avenue in Detroit's Midtown today, he would be amazed at the accuracy of his prophecy more than two hundred years later. Indeed, the revitalization of the area is proof that when Detroiters hope for better things, they can rise from the ashes—even if the ascendency takes decades.

Why has Detroit's "comeback" been so long in the making? It certainly was not the only city that went up in flames in 1967 and 1968. Nationwide, there were nearly four dozen major riots in America's urban centers during those years, including in Cleveland and Newark. In addition, there were more than one hundred smaller cases of civil unrest. But Detroit's 1967 uprising was the bloodiest and most costly. Historically, few cities have paid a higher price for rioting than Detroit has. Beyond white flight, there was a near-complete white economic abandonment. While the city gained black political strength, it lost nearly all economic investment and jobs and, with that, its tax base. Property values never recovered. Schools became segregated, underfunded warehouses for poor children. Tensions mounted between the black city and what Mayor Young once famously called the hostile suburbs. The result has been decades of social, political, and economic retribution against Detroit and an exacerbation of racial tensions. The rise of "ruin porn" in the media has had the tenor of both fascination and comeuppance: here is what happens when "civilization" goes "native."

The mostly black citizens who remained in Detroit (by choice or a lack of it) have learned to live with a complicated twoness: They are some of the poorest, least educated, and desperate people in the United States. And they are also some of the country's most educated barrier breakers in the areas of law, medicine, engineering, business, architecture, and politics. They inhabit communities that are intractably poor. But they have also built solid middle- and upper-middle-class neighborhoods that have been the backbone of the city for decades. Together with their remaining white neighbors, they are nearly singular in their view of a city wronged and abandoned by the power structure. For decades, they have dug in, waiting for Detroit to rise from the ashes.

— —

The Detroit skyline as seen from Windsor. 2016 photograph by Joel Stone, from the Detroit Historical Society Collection.

Perhaps their wait is over. Despite the Great Recession of 2008 (which Detroit experienced as a depression) and the near collapse of the auto industry, the negative narrative about Detroit is now in full remission. The city has become an international media darling, with stories abounding about its entrepreneurial spirit, its burgeoning creative class, its history of urban farming, its expanse of empty land, and its bargain-basement real estate. The media's love affair with pictures of the city's spectacular ruins and stories about gruesome crimes and corrupt politicians has now been replaced by fawning stories about quirky business start-ups, posh restaurants, and upscale retail. As Ben Austen of the *New York Times* said recently, "The city now teems with a post-post-apocalyptic optimism."

It may be more accurate to say that the *nation* is embracing a post-post-apocalyptic optimism about Detroit. For many Detroiters, this new narrative is as suspect as it is welcome. Detroit was never the Wild West of crime and abandonment. But neither is it the Mecca of unbridled opportunity as it is depicted today.

Somewhere in between, real Detroiters are living the real Detroit experience. They are surprised by the bicycle paths that now line their streets and perplexed at a major investment in a rail line that will support only a small fraction of the city's residents, the vast majority of whom depend on inadequate public transportation every day. They welcome new shops and retail in a city that, until recently, had been redlined out of basic conveniences. But they wonder at brands like the outdoor adventure clothing retailer Moosejaw and the handmade watch designer Shinola locating in a city that has only a couple of major retail chains. The question is not whether Detroit is rising from the ashes. The question is . . . for whom is it rising?

The *Detroit News* columnist Nolan Finley raised the issue publicly in December 2014 when he asked the pointed question, "Where are the black people?" when talking about Detroit's promising comeback. The answer is the same as it was in the 1960s. The black people are where they have always been, trying to stake their claim in a city where their basic needs go largely ignored.

If Detroit learned anything from the riots—and the decades of fear, divestment, and racial segregation in the aftermath—it is that when a city goes up in flames, everyone suffers. It is unlikely that Detroit will see another riot anytime soon—the dynamics have changed, the politics have changed, the police have changed, and the economy has changed. Hope is blossoming everywhere. But just because you cannot see flames does not mean that something is not smoldering.

"In a city that has had tons of racial tension, extreme violence and racial oppression, and some would say extreme segregation, leadership has to step forward with a plan," Ken Harris told Kimberly Hayes Taylor of NBC News in late 2015 when asked about gentrification in Detroit. Harris, the president and CEO of the Michigan Black Chamber of Commerce Inc., continued, "People need to talk and hold each other accountable and develop Detroit in the right way as opposed to the evils of the past."

Fifty years after the riots, Detroit is living up to its motto. It is seeing better things. It is rising from the ashes. And if city leaders, residents, and businesses are willing to build a city that works for everyone, they are sure to avoid the fire next time.

Bibliography

Abbreviations

BHC   Burton Historical Collection, Detroit Public Library
BHL   Bentley Historical Library, University of Michigan
LBJ   Lyndon Baines Johnson Library and Museum, or LBJ Presidential Library
WPR   Walter P. Reuther Library, Archives of Labor and Urban Affairs, Wayne State University

Primary Sources

Axtell, Bill. *Seven Days in July, July 23–29, 1967: One Radio Station's Coverage of the Nation's Worst Riot.* Southfield, MI: WXYZ Radio, 1967.

Baker v. Detroit, 483 F. Supp. 930 (E.D. Mich. 1979).

Balkin, Steven. 1967. "A Presentation of Grade School Children's Thoughts about the Detroit Riot, Summer 1967." Unpublished manuscript. Personal collection.

Bingay, Malcolm. *Of Me I Sing.* New York: Bobbs-Merrill, 1949.

Bradley v. Milliken, 338 F. Supp. 582 (E.D. Mich. 1971).

Breakthrough. *Battle-Line.* Newsletter of the Breakthrough organization, January 1968–August 1971. Detroit Historical Society Collection.

Cavanagh, Jerome P. Activity log. Cavanagh Papers, WPR.

———. Statement, July 1, 1965. Box 255, Cavanagh Papers, WPR.

———. Transcript, Oral History Interview I, 3/22/1971, by Joe B. Frantz. LBJ.

Cavanagh, Jerome P., Martin Hayden, Haynes Johnson, William C. Matney, John L. Steele, and Edwin H. Newman. *Meet the Press Sunday, July 30, 1967 with Guest Jerome P. Cavanagh, Mayor of Detroit, Michigan.* St. Paul, MN: 3 MIM, 1972.

Christ, Harding, Daryle M. Feldmeir, I. William Hill, John D. Paulson, and John Strohmeyer. "Report of the Local Investigative Reporting Jury." March 5, 1965. In *Local Reporting 1947–1987: From a County Vote Fraud to a Corrupt City Council*, edited by Heinz-Dietrich Fisher et al., xxxvi. Munich: K. G. Saur, 1989.

Courville District Improvement Association. "Action! Courville." Folder 4, Box 26, Detroit Commission on Community Relations / Human Rights Department Collection, WPR.

De Lisle, Tom. Interview with Timothy Kiska. Detroit, January 2, 2016.

DeRamus, Betty. "Black Power, Black Rebellion." *Negro Digest*, November 1967, 24–28.

Detroit (MI). Appearance of the City of Detroit before the President's National Advisory Commission on Civil Disorders. 1967.

———. Detroit Police Department Photograph Collection. 1967.

———. *Guardians—Detroit Police Association: A Tribute to Black Police Officers.* VHS. 1989.

———. *Statistical Report on the Civil Disorder Occurring in the City of Detroit.* [Detroit]: The Bureau, 1967.

Detroit (MI), and Andrew F. Wilson. Detroit Police Department Additional Papers. 1965–1993.

Detroit Commission on Community Relations. "Race Relations in Housing." 1946. Folder 128, Box 25, Detroit Commission on Community Relations / Human Rights Department Collection, WPR.

Detroit Future City. *Detroit Strategic Framework Plan.* Detroit: Inland, 2012.

"Detroit Is Dynamite." *Life*, August 17, 1942, 15–23.

Detroit Scope. News magazine, 1968–1970. Detroit Historical Society Collection.

Detroit Urban League. "Summary of Known Improvement Association Activities in the Past Two Years: 1955–1957." July 12, 1957. Folder 36, Box 25, Detroit Commission on Community Relations / Human Rights Department Collection, WPR.

Drachler, Norman. *A Report on Immediate Needs of Public Schools in Areas Affected by Civil Disturbances of July 1967.* Detroit: Board of Education of the City of Detroit, 1967.

Exhibit of Petition, Ordinance, and Ballot Proposed by Greater Detroit Homeowners' Council. Folder: Housing—Homeowners' Ordinance—Friendly Statements, Box 10, Part 1, Metropolitan Detroit Council of Churches Collection, WPR.

FBI. Memo to director from SAC Detroit, August 1, 1967. Document ID 59169260. FBI-FOIA.

Federal Housing Commission. *Underwriting Manual.* Washington, DC: Government Printing Office, 1936.

"Federated Property Owners of America, Articles." Folder 35, Box 25, Detroit Commission on Community Relations / Human Rights Department Collection, WPR.

Films Media Group, Films for the Humanities & Sciences (Firm), and National Archives and Records Service. *The Detroit Riots, 1967.* New York: Films Media Group, 2010. https://ezproxy.uu.edu/login?url=http://digital.films .com/PortalPlaylists.aspx?aid=13753&xtid=48844.

Forman, James. "Black Manifesto: The Black National Economic Conference." *New York Review of Books*, July 10, 1969. http://www.nybooks.com/articles/ 1969/07/10/black-manifesto/.

Girardin, J. A. "Slavery in Detroit." In *Report of the Pioneer Society of the State of Michigan*, vol. 1. Lansing, MI: Robert Smith, 1900.

Girardin, Ray, to Gordon Rowe, March 14, 1966. Box 272, Records of President's Commission on Law Enforcement and Administration of Justice, LBJ.

Goltz, Gene. *The Pasadena Story*. Raleigh, NC: Lulu, 2015.

Gregory, Karl. Interview with Tobi Voigt. Recorded oral history for Detroit Historical Society. Detroit, September 1, 2015.

Hamilton, John A. "Tears of Fear and Grief: The Meaning of Detroit's Riot." *Detroit Free Press*, July 24, 1967, 4.

Haney, Don. Interview with Timothy Kiska. Detroit, July 29, 2001.

Harris, Sydney. "Negro Riots Disease of Social Despair." *Detroit Free Press*, October 16, 1967.

Hay, Edward, and Lyle Thayer. "Report to Commander." Homicide File 7182, Algiers Motel File, Detroit Police Department.

Holmes, Susan. "Block Clubs Join to Combat Crime." *Detroit Free Press*, March 14, 1967.

Inner-City Sub-Center. *New Inner City Sub Center*. Promotional brochure, 2009. http://www.slideshare.net/TBArchitect/InnerCitySubCenter85x11.

Johnson, Arthur. *Race and Remembrance: A Memoir*. Detroit: Wayne State University Press, 2008.

"Keeping Negroes Out of the Area Is Basic Aim of CHOA." *East Side Shopper*, December 7, 1950. Folder 25, Box 35, Detroit Commission on Community Relations / Human Rights Department Collection, WPR.

Kerner Commission Report. See National Advisory Commission on Civil Disorders.

Lachman, Sheldon J., and Benjamin Donald Singer. *The Detroit Riot of July 1967: A Psychological, Social and Economic Profile of 500 Arrestees*. Detroit: Behavior Research Institute, 1968.

Lane, Ray. Interview with Timothy Kiska. Detroit, August 2009.

Lee, Owen, William Fyffe, and Ken Thomas. "News Coverage of the Detroit Riots of July, 1967." Detroit: WXYZ-TV, 1967.

Lincoln, James H. *The Anatomy of a Riot: A Detroit Judge's Report*. New York: McGraw-Hill, 1968.

Lovett, William P., to Oswald Garrison Villard, January 20, 1943. Box 40, Correspondence Files, Detroit Citizen League Papers, BHC.

Lowell, Jon. *A Time of Tragedy: A Special Report; Detroit's Riot from 3:30 a.m., July 23, 1967, When It Began, until the Moment It Stopped*. Detroit: Detroit News, 1967.

Luby, Elliot D., and James Hedegard. "A Study of Civil Disorder in Detroit." *William and Mary Law Review* 10 (3) (1969): 586–630. http://scholarship.law .wm.edu/wmlr/vol10/iss3/6.

Luedtke, Kurt. Interview with Danielle McGuire. Detroit, December 22, 2015.

Lukas, Anthony. "Postscript on Detroit." *New York Times Magazine*, August 27, 1967, 142.

McHugh and Hoffman. "Community Assessment among Black Television Viewers in Detroit." McHugh and Hoffman Records, Box 10, BHL.

———. "Television in the Greater Detroit Area: A Study of Viewer Attitudes in Late Winter, 1968." McHugh and Hoffman Records, Box 9, BHL.

McIntyre, Kenneth G. Interview with Danielle McGuire. Detroit, October 22, 2015.

Meyer, Philip. *Return to 12th Street: A Follow-Up Survey of Attitudes of Detroit Negroes.* Detroit: Detroit Free Press, 1968.

Michigan State University. Detroit Riots, 1967: File of Clippings and Miscellanea, 1970.

Milio, Nancy. *9226 Kercheval: The Storefront That Did Not Burn.* Ann Arbor: University of Michigan Press, 1970.

Molette, O. Lee, to John Hannah, June 11, 1963. Folder OGC/FPP Detroit-Incidents, Box 2, Police-Community Relations in Urban Areas, 1954–1966, Records of the Commission on Civil Rights, National Archives and Records Administration, College Park, MD.

Montgomery, Wardell, Jr. *Teenage Widow and Her Friends.* Script. 1971.

National Advisory Commission on Civil Disorders. *Report of the National Advisory Commission on Civil Disorders.* New York: Bantam Books, 1968.

National Archives and Records Administration. *The Detroit Riots, 1968.* College Park, MD: National Archives and Records Administration, 2009.

National Association for the Advancement of Colored People. NAACP Detroit Branch Records, 1943–1970.

New Detroit Committee. *Progress Report.* Detroit, 1969.

Newspaper Guild Local 22. Papers. WPR.

Norris, Harold. "Arrests without Warrant." *Crisis,* October 1958, 481–486.

———. "Recent Detroit Police Policies versus the Rule of Law and Constitutional Law Enforcement." Address, January 16, 1961. Folder 20, Box 1082, American Civil Liberties Union Records (ACLU), Seeley G. Mudd Manuscript Library, Princeton University.

Nye, Phil. Interview with Timothy Kiska. Detroit, May 12, 2003.

"Operating Grant for a Summer In-Service Training Program in Community Relations." May 1965. Folder 17, Box 65, Series VI, Part III, Detroit Commission on Community Relations, WPR.

"Police Brutality Complaints Reported to the Detroit Branch." *Crisis,* October 1958, 487–491.

Police In-Service Training Program in Community Relations. Staff log, August 25, 1965. Folder 18, Box 65, Series VI, Part III, Detroit Commission on Community Relations, WPR.

Randall, Dudley. Letter to Etheridge Knight, n.d. Etheridge Knight Papers, Ward M. Canaday Center, University of Toledo Library, Toledo, Ohio.

———. *More to Remember: Poems of Four Decades.* Chicago: Third World, 1971.

Rashid, Frank. Interview with Noah Levinson. Recorded oral history for Detroit Historical Society. Detroit, September 13, 2015.

Reece, Jason, and Christy Rogers. *Inequity, Linked Fates and Social Justice in Detroit and Michigan.* Columbus, OH: Kirwan Institute for the Study of Race & Ethnicity, 2008. http://www.kirwaninstitute.osu.edu/reports/2008/07_2008_MIRoundtableOppMap_FullReport.pdf.

"Report of the Detroit Bar Association Committee on Civil Liberties on Detroit Police Department Policy of 'Arrests for Investigation.'" N.d. Folder 27, Box 66, Series VI, Part III, Detroit Commission on Community Relations, WPR.

"Report of the Ruritan Park Civic Association Meeting." Folder 101, Box 25, Detroit Commission on Community Relations / Human Rights Department Collection, WPR.

Riley, Dwayne X. Interview with Timothy Kiska. Detroit, May 12, 2003.

Schwaller, Albert. "Synopsis of Sorter, Forsythe, Green, Malloy, Hysell Statements." Homicide File 7182, Algiers Motel File, Detroit Police Department.

Scott, Thelma. *Case Studies in Practical Career Guidance, Number 7: Developmental Career Guidance Project Detroit Public Schools, Detroit, Michigan*. Report AIR-346-6-73-TR-7. Palo Alto, CA: American Institutes for Research in the Behavioral Sciences, 1973. http://files.eric.ed.gov/fulltext/ED078336.pdf.

Scott, William Walter, III. *Hurt, Baby, Hurt*. Ann Arbor, MI: New Ghetto, 1970.

"Sift Ashes for Reasons behind Ghetto Outbreak." *Detroit Free Press*, July 27, 1967.

Sudomier, William V. "More Police Urged by Wadsworth." *Detroit Free Press*, November 24, 1965.

Thrilling Narrative from the Lips of the Sufferers of the Late Detroit Riot, March 6, 1863, A. Detroit, 1863. Electronic edition in "Documenting the American South," Apex Data Services, Academic Affairs Library, University of North Carolina, Chapel Hill, 2001. http://docsouth.unc.edu/neh/detroit/detroit.html.

United Automobile Workers. "Negro Employment in Detroit Area." December 12, 1944. Folder 9-24, Box 9, UAW-RD, WPR.

US Commission on Civil Rights. *Police and the Blacks: U.S. Civil Rights Commission Hearings*. New York: Arno, 1971.

US Department of the Army, Office of the Adjutant General. *Civil Disorders—TF Detroit*. Washington, DC: Department of the Army, Office of the Adjutant General, 1967.

US Department of Labor, Manpower Administration. *The Detroit Riot—a Profile of 500 Prisoners*. Washington, DC: US Department of Labor, Manpower Administration, 1968.

Vance, Cyrus R. *Final Report of Cyrus R. Vance, Special Assistant to the Secretary of Defense concerning the Detroit Riots, July 23 through August 2, 1967*. Washington, DC: Office of Assistant Secretary of Defense (Public Affairs), 1967.

Warren, Donald. "Suburban Isolation and Race Tension: The Detroit Case." *Social Problems* 17 (1970): 324–339.

West Side Home and Property Owners' Protective Association. "Attention West Siders!" Folder 27, Box 13, Detroit Commission on Community Relations / Human Rights Department Collection, WPR.

Williams, Paige. "Drop Dead, Detroit." *New Yorker*, January 27, 2014.

WJBK Reports 1962–1968. McHugh and Hoffman Records, BHL.

Woodward, Augustus. "Subject of Slavery: Opinion" (October 23, 1807). In *Report of the Pioneer Society of the State of Michigan*, vol. 12, 519–522. Lansing, MI: Thorp and Godfrey, 1888.

Secondary Sources

Austen, Ben. "The Post-Post-Apocalyptic Detroit." *New York Times Magazine*, July 11, 2014.

Babson, Steve. *Working Detroit*. New York: Adama Books, 1984.

Bergesen, Albert. 1982. "Race Riots of 1967: An Analysis of Police Violence in Detroit and Newark." *Journal of Black Studies* 12 (3) (1982): 261–274.

Berlatsky, Noah. *The 1967 Detroit Riots*. Detroit: Greenhaven / Gale, Cengage Learning, 2013.

Berlin, Ira. "American Slavery in History and Memory and the Search for Social Justice." *Journal of American History* 90 (4) (2004): 1251–1269.

Black, Harold. "Detroit: A Case Study in Industrial Problems of a Central City." *Land Economics* 34 (3) (1958): 219–226.

Boskin, Joseph. "The Revolt of the Urban Ghettos, 1964–1967." *Annals of the American Academy of Political and Social Science* 382 (1969): 1–14.

Boyle, Kevin. *Arc of Justice: A Saga of Race, Civil Rights, and Murder in the Jazz Age*. New York: Henry Holt, 2004.

Buchanan, Heather, Sharon Stanford, and Teresa Kimble. *Eyes on Fire: Witnesses to the Detroit Riot of 1967*. Detroit: Aquarius, 2007.

Burns, Andrea A. "Waging Cold War in a Model City: The Investigation of 'Subversive' Influences in the 1967 Detroit Riot." *Michigan Historical Review* 30 (1) (2004): 3–30.

Capeci, Dominic J. *Race Relations in Wartime Detroit: The Sojourner Truth Housing Controversy of 1937–1943*. Philadelphia: Temple University Press, 1984.

Carr, Homer Bruce. "Before the Ghetto: A Study of Detroit Negroes in the 1890s." PhD diss., Wayne State University, 1968.

Castellanos, Jorge. "Black Slavery in Detroit." *Detroit in Perspective* 7 (2) (1983): 42–57.

Clive, Alan. *State of War: Michigan in World War II*. Ann Arbor: University of Michigan Press, 1979.

Conot, Robert. *American Odyssey*. New York: William Morrow, 1974.

Cray, Ed. *The Enemy in the Streets: Police Malpractice in America*. Garden City, NY: Anchor Books, 1972.

Darden, Joe T., Richard Child Hill, June Thomas, and Richard Thomas. *Detroit: Race and Uneven Development*. Philadelphia: Temple University Press, 1987.

Darden, Joe T., and Richard W. Thomas. *Detroit: Race Riots, Racial Conflicts, and Efforts to Bridge the Racial Divide*. East Lansing: Michigan State University Press, 2013.

Demers, E. A. S. "John Askin and Indian Slavery at Michilimackinac." In *Indian Slavery in Colonial America*, edited by Alan Gallay, 391–416. Lincoln: University of Nebraska Press, 2009.

Dykes, De Witt S., Jr. "Cornelius Langston Henderson, Sr." In *African American Architects*, edited by Dreck S. Wilson, 199–201. New York: Routledge, 2004.

———. "Frederick Blackburn Pelham." In *African American Architects*, edited by Dreck S. Wilson, 315–316. New York: Routledge, 2004.

———. "Meta Elizabeth Pelham." In *Notable Black American Women*, vol. 3, edited by Jessie Carney Smith, 466–467. Farmington Hills, MI: Thompson Gale, 2003.

Edgar, Julie, and Julie Wiener. "Out of the Ashes." *Detroit Jewish News*, July 25, 1997, 52–59.

Farley, Reynolds, Sheldon Danziger, and Harry J. Holzer. *Detroit Divided*. New York: Russell Sage Foundation, 2000.

Fine, Sidney. *Violence in the Model City: The Cavanagh Administration, Race Relations, and the Detroit Riot of 1967*. Ann Arbor: University of Michigan Press, 1989.

Finley, Nolan. "Where Are the Black People?" *Detroit News*, December 15, 2014.

Fishman, Robert. "Detroit: Linear City." In *Mapping Detroit*, edited by June Manning Thomas and Henco Bekkering, 77–99. Detroit: Wayne State University Press, 2015.

Frost, Karolyn Smardz. *I've Got a Home in Glory Land: A Lost Tale of the Underground Railroad*. New York: Farrar, Straus and Giroux, 2007.

Galster, George. *Driving Detroit: The Quest for Respect in the Motor City*. Philadelphia: University of Pennsylvania Press, 2012.

Gavrilovich, Peter, and Bill McGraw. *The Detroit Almanac: 300 Years of Life in the Motor City*. Detroit: Detroit Free Press, 2000.

Georgakas, Dan, and Marvin Surkin. *Detroit: I Do Mind Dying*. New York: St. Martin's, 1975.

Geschwender, James A. *Class, Race, and Worker Insurgency: The League of Revolutionary Black Workers*. New York: Cambridge University Press, 1977.

Goldberg, Louis C. "Ghetto Riots and Others: The Face of Civil Disorder in 1967." *Journal of Peace Research* 5 (2) (1968): 116–132.

Gordon, Leonard. *A City in Racial Crisis: The Case of Detroit Pre- and Post- the 1967 Riot*. Dubuque, IA: W. C. Brown, 1971.

Green, William, III. "Victims of the 1967 Detroit Riot." Unpublished manuscript, 2016.

Grimsted, David. *American Mobbing, 1828–1861: Toward Civil War*. New York: Oxford University Press, 1998.

Hammer, Peter J. "Letter to Judge Rhodes: Evaluation of the 'Expert Report of Martha E. M. Kopacz Regarding the Feasibility of the City of Detroit Plan of Adjustment.'" *Journal of Law in Society* 17 (1) (2015): 19–47.

Henrickson, Wilma Wood. *Detroit Perspectives: Crossroads and Turning Points*. Detroit: Wayne State University Press, 1991.

Herman, Max Arthur. *Summer of Rage: An Oral History of the 1967 Newark and Detroit Riots*. New York: Peter Lang, 2013.

Hersey, John. *The Algiers Motel Incident*. New York: Knopf, 1968.

Hoult, Thomas F., and Albert J. Mayer. *The Population Revolution in Detroit*. Detroit: Institute for Regional and Urban Studies, Wayne State University, 1963.

Hunter, Kim D. "1967: Detroiters Remember the Rebellion." *Against the Current* 12 (4) (1997): 19–25.

Hurley, Neil. "The Automotive Industry: A Study in Industrial Locations." *Land Economics* 35 (11) (1959): 1–14.

Hyde, Charles K. *Arsenal of Democracy: The American Automobile Industry in World War II*. Detroit: Wayne State University Press, 2013.

———. *Riding the Roller Coaster: A History of the Chrysler Corporation*. Detroit: Wayne State University Press, 2003.

Jargowsky, Paul A. *Architecture of Segregation: Civil Unrest, the Concentration of Poverty, and Public Policy*. Century Foundation, August 7, 2015. https://tcf .org/content/report/architecture-of-segregation/.

Katzman, David. *Before the Ghetto: Black Detroit in the Nineteenth Century*. Urbana: University of Illinois Press, 1973.

Kelly, Cynthia H. "Detroit: Since Last Summer." *American Journal of Nursing* 68 (6) (1968): 1278–1282.

Kenyon, Amy Maria. *Dreaming Suburbia: Detroit and the Production of Postwar Space and Culture*. Detroit: Wayne State University Press, 2004.

———. "Of Rumor and Riot." *Belt*, July 2015. http://beltmag.com/of-rumor -and-riot/.

Kirsbaum, Harry, and Sharon Luckerman. "Remembering the Riots." *Detroit Jewish News*, July 26, 2002, 16–19.

Kiska, Timothy. "Jerry Blocker Was a TV Pioneer." *Detroit News*, November 5, 1997.

Kooker, Arthur. "The Anti-slavery Movement in Michigan, 1796–1840: A Study in Humanitarianism on the American Frontier." Ph.D. diss., University of Michigan, 1941.

Lester, Sondai. *Crossing Generations to Reflect On: The 1967 Detroit Rebellions*. Detroit: Broadside Press, 1999.

Lichtenstein, Nelson. "Life at the Rouge: A Cycle of Workers' Control." In *Life and Labor: Dimensions of American Working-Class History*, edited by Charles Stephenson and Robert Asher, 237–259. Albany: State University of New York Press, 1986.

Lichtenstein, Nelson, and Stephen Meyer. *On the Line: Essays in the History of Auto Work*. Urbana: University of Illinois Press, 1989.

Lincoln, James H. *The Anatomy of a Riot: A Detroit Judge's Report*. New York: McGraw-Hill, 1968.

Lipsitz, George. 2011. *How Racism Takes Place*. Philadelphia: Temple University Press, 2011.

Locke, Hubert G. *The Detroit Riot of 1967*. Detroit: Wayne State University Press, 1969.

Loewen, James. *Sundown Towns: A Hidden Dimension of American Racism*. New York: New Press, 2005.

Loukopoulos, Loukas. *The Detroit Police Department: A Research Report on Previous Studies; Criminal Statistics; and Police Technology, Productivity and Competence*. Detroit: Committee on Public Awareness, 1970.

Lowinger, Paul, and Frida Huige. *The National Guard in the 1967 Detroit Uprising*. Detroit: Department of Psychiatry of Wayne State University School of Medicine and the Lafayette Clinic, 1968.

Luby, Elliot D., and Boyce Rensberger. *City in Crisis: The People and Their Riot: A Social Psychological Study of the Detroit Uprising and Its Aftermath.* Detroit: Lafayette Clinic, 1969.

Mallas, Aris A., Jr., Rea McCain, and Margaret K. Hedden. *Forty Years in Politics: The Story of Ben Pelham.* Detroit: Wayne State University Press, 1957.

McGraw, Bill. *The Quotations of Coleman A. Young.* Detroit: Wayne State University Press, 2005.

Meier, August, and Elliott Rudwick. *Black Detroit and the Rise of the UAW.* New York: Oxford University Press, 1979.

Metzger, Kurt. "Racial and Ethnic Trends in Southeast Michigan." Presentation at Wayne State University Law School, January 25, 2012.

Mirel, Jeffrey. *The Rise and Fall of an Urban School System: Detroit, 1907–81.* Ann Arbor: University of Michigan Press, 1999.

1967 Detroit Riots: A Community Speaks, The. Directed by S. Sawyer, 2003. Small Screen Productions and Carousel Films, 2003. Film.

Post, Argie White. *Rape of Detroit.* Hicksville, NY: Exposition, 1975.

Powell, John A. *Racing to Justice: Transforming Our Conceptions of Self and Other to Build an Inclusive Society.* Bloomington: Indiana University Press, 2012.

Rahman, Ahmad A. "Marching Blind: The Rise and Fall of the Black Panther Party in Detroit." In *Liberated Territory: Untold Local Perspectives on the Black Panther Party,* edited by Yohuru Williams and Jama Lazerow, 181–231. Durham, NC: Duke University Press, 2008.

Raleigh, Erica. "Data Driven Detroit: Detroit by the Numbers." Presentation to Detroit Revitalization Fellows, August 2015.

Raskin, A. H. "Detroit: Focus of the Basic Duel." *New York Times,* May 4, 1958.

———. "Negroes 'Being Trained for Unemployment.'" *New York Times,* December 10, 1967.

Reece, Jason, and Christy Rogers. *Opportunity for All: Inequity, Linked Fate and Social Justice in Detroit and Southeast Michigan.* Columbus: Kirwan Institute for the Study of Race and Ethnicity at the Ohio State University, 2008.

Rist, Ray C. *The Quest for Autonomy: A Socio-Historical Study of Black Revolt in Detroit.* Los Angeles: Center for Afro-American Studies, University of California, 1972.

Rushforth, Brett. *Bonds of Alliance: Indigenous and Atlantic Slaveries in New France.* Chapel Hill: University of North Carolina Press, 2012.

Rusk, David. *Cities without Suburbs: A Census 2010 Perspective.* 4th ed. Baltimore: Woodrow Wilson Center Press with Johns Hopkins University Press, 2013.

Sands, Gary, and Mark Skidmore. *Detroit and the Property Tax: Strategies to Improve Revenue and Enhance Equity.* Cambridge, MA: Lincoln Institute of Land Policy, 2015.

Satrun, Nicole. "British Métis in Eighteenth-Century Detroit." In *Revolutionary Detroit: Portraits in Political and Cultural Change, 1760–1805,* edited by Denver Brunsman and Joel Stone, 42–48. Detroit: Detroit Historical Society, 2009.

Sauter, Van Gordon, and Burleigh Hines. *Nightmare in Detroit: A Rebellion and Its Victims.* Chicago: Henry Regnery, 1968.

Singer, Benjamin D., Richard W. Osborn, and James A. Geschwender. *Black Rioters: A Study of Social Factors and Communication in the Detroit Riot.* Lexington, MA: Heath Lexington Books, 1970.

Stephenson, Charles, and Robert Asher. *Life and Labor: Dimensions of American Working-Class History.* Albany: State University of New York Press, 1986.

Sugrue, Thomas J. "From Motor City to Motor Metropolis: How the Automobile Industry Reshaped Urban America." *Automobile in American Life and Society,* 2014. http://www.autolife.umd.umich.edu/Race/R_Overview/R_Overview.htm.

Sugrue, Thomas J. *The Origins of the Urban Crisis: Race and Inequality in Postwar Detroit.* Princeton, NJ: Princeton University Press, 1996.

———. "Report of Thomas Sugrue." Document 133. Filed June 27, 2014. Case 1:12-cv-07667-VEC-GWG. US District Court, Southern District of New York. https://www.nclc.org/images/pdf/.../sugrue-expert-adkins-stanley.pdf.

Sumner, Gregory. *Detroit in World War II.* Charleston, SC: History Press, 2015.

Taylor, Kimberly Hayes. "Gentrification of Detroit Leaves Black-Owned Businesses Behind." NBC News, December 1, 2015. http://www.nbcnews.com/news/nbcblk/gentrification-detroit-leaves-black-residents-behind-n412476.

Taylor, Paul. *"Old Slow Town": Detroit during the Civil War.* Detroit: Wayne State University Press, 2013.

Thomas, June Manning. *Redevelopment and Race: Planning a Finer City in Postwar Detroit.* Detroit: Wayne State University Press, 2013.

Thomas, June Manning, and Henco Bekkering. *Mapping Detroit: Land, Community, and Shaping a City.* Detroit: Wayne State University Press, 2015.

Thomas, Richard W. "The Black Community Building Process in Post–Urban Disorder Detroit, 1967–1997." In *African American Urban Experience: Perspectives from the Colonial Period to the Present,* edited by Joe W. Trotter, with Earl Lewis and Tera W. Hunter, 209–240. New York: Palgrave Macmillan, 2004.

———. *Life for Us Is What We Make It: Building Black Community in Detroit, 1915–1945.* Bloomington: Indiana University Press, 1992.

Thompson, Heather Ann. *Whose Detroit? Politics, Labor, and Race in a Modern American City.* Ithaca, NY: Cornell University Press, 2001.

Trotter, Joe W., with Earl Lewis and Tera W. Hunter, eds. *African American Urban Experience: Perspectives from the Colonial Period to the Present.* New York: Palgrave Macmillan, 2004.

Trudel, Marcel. *Canada's Forgotten Slaves: Two Hundred Years of Bondage.* Translated by George Tombs. Montreal: Vehicule, 2013.

Ulbrich, Casandra E. "Riot or Rebellion: Media Framing and the 1967 Detroit Uprising." PhD diss., Wayne State University, 2011. http://digitalcommons.wayne.edu/oa_dissertations/338.

Warren, Donald I. "Neighborhood Status Modality and Riot Behavior: An Analysis of the Detroit Disorders of 1967." *Sociology Quarterly* 12 (3) (1971): 350–368.

Weber, Peter. "The Rise and Fall of Detroit: A Timeline." *The Week,* July 19, 2013. http://theweek.com/articles/461968/rise-fall-detroit-timeline.

Welch, Susan. *Race and Place: Race Relations in an American City.* Cambridge: Cambridge University Press, 2001.

Widick, B. J. *Detroit: City of Race and Class Violence.* Detroit: Wayne State University Press, 1989.

Williams, Paige. "Drop Dead, Detroit! The Suburban Kingpin Who Is Thriving off the City's Decline." *New Yorker,* January 27, 2014.

Contributors

Rev. Daniel W. Aldridge Jr. has been one of Detroit's most respected activists since his arrival in the city in 1965. Drawn to the call for self-reliance in the black community, he was involved in Black Nationalist organizations both locally and nationally, including the Student Nonviolent Coordinating Committee. After the uprising, Aldridge, at the behest of H. Rap Brown and attorney Milton Henry, worked with Rev. Lonnie Peek to organize a People's Tribunal to address the tragic police shootings at the Algiers Motel.

Steven Balkin is a professor emeritus of economics at Roosevelt University in Chicago and researches urban economic development and the economics of criminal justice. He is the author of *Self-Employment for Low-Income People* (1989).

Kevin Boyle teaches modern American history at Northwestern University. His book *Arc of Justice: A Saga of Race, Civil Rights, and Murder in the Jazz Age* (2004) received the National Book Award for nonfiction. It was also selected for the Detroit area's "Everyone Reads" program and the statewide "Great Michigan Read."

Ken Coleman is a Detroit-based author and historian. He has served as senior editor at the *Michigan Chronicle* and as press secretary for US Representatives Gary Peters and Brenda Lawrence of Michigan. He has published three books about African American history in the city of Detroit, including *Soul on Air: Blacks Who Helped Define Radio in Detroit* (2015).

Desiree Cooper is a former lawyer, Pulitzer Prize–nominated journalist, and Detroit community activist whose fiction delves deeply into racism and sexism. Her first collection of flash fiction, *Know the Mother*, was published by Wayne State University Press in March 2016. Cooper was a founding board member of Cave Canem, a national residency for emerging black poets.

Betty DeRamus is an award-winning journalist who has written for the *Michigan Chronicle, Detroit Free Press*, and *Detroit News*, as well as *Essence, Time-Life*, and *Black World*. A Pulitzer Prize finalist in 1993, she was inducted into the Michigan Journalism Hall of Fame in 2015. She is the author of *Freedom by Any Means* and *Forbidden Fruit: Love Stories from the Underground Railroad*, the latter of which is being adapted into an NBC television mini-series. The *Negro Digest* article reprinted here was DeRamus's first published freelance piece.

De Witt S. Dykes Jr. is an associate professor of history at Oakland University and has done extensive research and writing on African American history, the history of urban America, family history, and biography.

Alex Elkins is writing a dissertation in history at Temple University on street policing, get-tough politics, and the sixties rebellions. His research interests include African American history, urban history, and the history of riots and police. He currently teaches at the University of Michigan.

Berl Falbaum was born in Nazi Germany. His family escaped to Shanghai, China, before coming to the United States when he was ten years old. Prior to his graduation from Wayne State University, Falbaum was hired as a reporter by the *Detroit News* and eventually ran the paper's City Hall bureau, covering Mayor Jerome Cavanagh's office during the summer of July 1967. He later became an administrative aide to Michigan Lieutenant Governor James Brickley during the Milliken administration.

Roy E. Finkenbine is a professor of history and director of the Black Abolitionist Archive at the University of Detroit Mercy. He frequently consults on museum exhibits and films on the Underground Railroad and is vice chair of the Michigan Freedom Trail Commission. He contributed a chapter to *A Fluid Frontier: Slavery, Resistance, and the Underground Railroad in the Detroit River Borderland* (2016).

Mike Hamlin was born in Mississippi in 1935 and came to Detroit twelve years later. Following the uprising of July 1967, Hamlin was instrumental in founding several left-wing collectives, including the Dodge Revolutionary Union Movement, Inner-City Voice, League of Revolutionary Black Workers, Motor City Labor League, and Conflict, Control, Change.

Contributors

Peter J. Hammer is a professor at Wayne State University Law School and director of the Damon J. Keith Center for Civil Rights. Hammer was instrumental in editing and compiling Judge Damon J. Keith's biography, *Crusader for Justice: Federal Judge Damon J. Keith* (2013). Hammer has become a leading voice on the economic and social issues impacting the city of Detroit and is a recipient of an Investigator Award in Health Policy Research from the Robert Wood Johnson Foundation.

Jeffrey Horner is a senior lecturer in the Department of Urban Studies and Planning at Wayne State University in Detroit and serves as director of the urban studies program. In addition to professional planning and consulting experience, Horner's research includes the Detroit Empowerment Zone Field Group Assessment and a series of assessment papers pertaining to the formation and progress of Detroit's Empowerment Zone Strategic Plan.

Charles K. Hyde is a retired professor of history at Wayne State University and the author of several books on the automotive industry. His most recent publications for Wayne State University Press are two volumes exploring the Arsenal of Democracy.

Tommie M. Johnson is a retired educator and former assistant provost at Wayne State University. She grew up in Detroit, Michigan, and worked for the city of Detroit before becoming a teacher. Johnson has had a lifelong dedication to the civil rights movement and marched with Dr. Martin Luther King Jr. on Woodward Avenue in 1963.

Timothy Kiska began as a copyboy at the *Detroit Free Press* in 1970, producing a regular column through 2002. Since then, he has been an assistant professor of history at the University of Michigan–Dearborn. His books include *A Newscast for the Masses: The History of Detroit Television Journalism* (2009).

Thomas A. Klug is the assistant provost, an associate professor of history, and director of the Institute for Detroit Studies at Marygrove College in Detroit. He has written numerous articles and papers about Detroit industry, immigration, and urban development from the post-antebellum period through today.

Kathleen Kurta grew up in the northwest section of Detroit, Michigan, where she lived in 1967. She served as both a teacher and a school principal before becoming a hospice social worker at Sparrow Hospice House of Mid-Michigan in Lansing, Michigan.

A freeborn native of New Jersey, William Lambert arrived in Detroit prior to 1840 and became an ardent activist for African American causes. Trained as a haberdasher, his talents as an orator and writer served a number of organizations on both sides of the Detroit River. As a founder of Detroit's Colored Vigilant Committee, he was intimately involved in the Underground Railroad.

Hubert G. Locke is a retired professor and dean emeritus of the Daniel J. Evans School of Public Affairs at the University of Washington. He also taught public policy and urban studies at the University of Nebraska–Omaha and Wayne State University in Detroit. After serving the Detroit Police Department as administrative assistant to the commissioner of police in 1966–67, he published *The Detroit Riot of 1967* (1969).

Bill McGraw, a Detroit native, has been exploring the city's history, old and new, for decades. He spent thirty-two years at the *Detroit Free Press* as a city-desk reporter, sports writer, Canada correspondent, editor, and columnist. Along with Peter Gavrilovich, he edited *The Detroit Almanac* (2001). His writing has appeared in the *New York Times, Washington Post, Newsweek, Toronto Globe and Mail, Fifth Estate,* and *Bridge* magazine.

Danielle L. McGuire is an award-winning author and associate professor in the Department of History at Wayne State University. She is a distinguished lecturer for the Organization of American Historians, and her essays have appeared in the *Journal of American History* and on the *Huffington Post, TheGrio.com,* and *TheRoot.com.* McGuire's most recent book explores the Algiers Motel incident in detail.

Marsha Music is a longtime Detroit–Highland Park writer, poet, and cultural activist and recipient of a 2012 Kresge Literary Arts Fellowship. Her stories are published in *Untold Tales, Unsung Heroes: An Oral History of Detroit's African American Community, 1918–1967* (1993) and *A Detroit Anthology* (2014), among others. She has contributed to films and an HBO documentary and has received accolades for her one-woman show, *Live on Hastings Street!*

Joel Stone is the senior curator with the Detroit Historical Society and editor of *Detroit 1967*. He has previously coedited books about Detroit during the American Revolution and the War of 1812. His most recent work is *Floating Palaces of the Great Lakes: A History of Passenger Steamships on the Inland Seas* (2015).

Thomas J. Sugrue is a professor of social and cultural analysis and history and the director of the Program in American Studies at New York University. He is a native Detroiter and author of *The Origins of the Urban Crisis: Race and Inequality in Postwar Detroit* (1996), winner of the Bancroft Prize in History, and several other books, including *Sweet Land of Liberty: The Forgotten Struggle for Civil Rights in the North* (2006).

Gregory Sumner has been a professor of history at the University of Detroit Mercy since 1993. He holds a doctorate from Indiana University and a Juris Doctor from the University of Michigan. His latest book is *Detroit in World War II* (2015).

Casandra E. Ulbrich serves as the vice president for college advancement and community relations at Macomb Community College. She holds advanced degrees in communication and was previously employed as director of corporate and foundation relations at Wayne State University. Ulbrich was elected to a second term on the Michigan Board of Education in 2014.

William Winkel is a researcher with the Detroit Historical Society and comanager of the *Detroit '67* oral history project. He has conducted extensive fact-finding on this subject and performed dozens of interviews in this regard. Winkel is a graduate of Wayne State University.

Index

Page numbers in italics refer to tables, photographs, and figures.

Holmes, Susan, 192

Holzer, Harry J., 88

homeowners associations, 97, 97; Cobo supporting, 101; Communist Party of Michigan and, 100; DUL monitoring, 103–4; Greater Detroit Homeowners' Association, 101; modern Detroit and, 95; nonaligned whites and, 103; propaganda for white, 98, 98; segregation and, 5, 94–95; Seven Mile–Fenelon Improvement Association as, 96; threats of, 99; top-down structures of, 100–101; treasury of, 101–2; umbrella, 102; white flight and, 105

Homeowners' Rights Ordinance, 104, 105

home-rule laws, 275

Hood, Nick, 153–54

Hooker, John Lee, 78

Hoover, Ellen, 27

Horton, William Wattison, 82, 93

House Un-American Activities Committee, 58; Young, C., defying, 90

housing, 270, 281; activism and, 242; Brewster-Douglass housing project, 58–59; Cleage and, 242; Collier's magazine on, 87; discrimination and, 86–87, 94, 97; Great Depression and, 87; homelessness and, 281; homeownership and, 98–99; housing market, 276, 280; landlords and segregation of, 43–44; new units for, 94; 1943 race riot and, 79; The Origins of the Urban Crisis and, 86–87; Paradise Valley and, 55, 82, 94; police protection and, 99–100; property taxes and, 280; "Race Relations in Housing" report on, 99; real-estate bubble and, 271–72, 280; restrictive covenants and minorities, 95, 96–97; Sojourner Truth Homes as public, 52, 55, 95–96; spatial racism and, 274–76; World War II and, 52, 53, 95. See also Black Bottom neighborhood; homeowners associations; open-housing laws; segregation

Howison, Arthur, 142, 143

Hubbard, Orville, 276

Huber Foundry, 72–73

Hudnell, Ezekiel, 24

Hudson, Joseph, 268

Humphrey, Hubert, 285

Hunter, Kim, 166, 167

Hurley, Neil, 66

Hurt, Baby, Hurt (Scott, W.), 137, 148

ICPC (Inner City Parents Council), 241

Iggy Pop, 90

immigrants, European, 3, 4

infant mortality rate, 44

Inner City Business Improvement Forum, 241

Inner City Parents Council (ICPC), 241

Inner-City Sub-Center, 211, 242

Inner-City Voice, 248; DRUM and, 247, 257; start of, 257

In re Richard Pattinson, 21

Institute of Urban Dynamics, 92

integration, 157, 254; activist organizations and, 236; Cobo opposing, 90; Detroit Fire Department and, 36; Detroit Police Department and, 107, 109, 139; education and, 34, 103, 241, 269, 276, 285–86; local media and, 184, 192–93; University of Michigan 1956 study on, 103; University of Michigan residence hall, 38; Wallace and, 224. See also housing

Interfaith Action Council, 243

Interreligious Foundation of Community Organizations, 243

Interstate Highway Act, 82

investigative arrests, 107

Jamerson, James, 78–79

Jazz Age, 39

Jefferson, Thomas, 16

Jeffries, Edward, 54, 58

Jim Crow, 54; Plessy v. Ferguson and, 87–88

Joe's Record Shop: blues and, 76, 77, 78; Franklin, and, 77; urban renewal and, 78

John J. Pershing High School, 138

Johnson, Arthur: as head of NAACP, 154; Race and Remembrance by, 100

Johnson, Lyndon, 127; Kerner Commission and, 84, 117, 118; national address by, 130

Johnson, Tommie M.: family of, 60–61; 1943 race riot and, 61; at Pittsburgh Courier, 62

Josaitis, Eleanor, 267

Joyce, Frank, 231

Kennedy, John F., 64

Kercheval uprising, 92, 113–14; DPD and, 153